In *Interreligious Dialogue*, Christoffer Grundmann has assembled a truly extraordinary collection of writings on interreligious dialogue by some of its most important and respected thinkers and practitioners. The introduction speaks of these as "remarkable essays." This is an understatement. What a wonderful text for college students and theology students, as well!

—Stephen Bevans, SVD
Catholic Theological Union, Chicago

Editor's Acknowledgment

The editor wants to acknowledge with heartfelt gratitude and thanks the untiring support he received from Jerry Ruff, editorial and acquisitions director of Anselm Academic, Winona, MN. Without Jerry's constant encouragement and the support received by his colleagues at Anselm, the project would not have materialized the way it finally did.

Publisher's Acknowledgments

Thank you to the following individuals who reviewed this work in progress:

Aaron Gross, *University of San Diego*

Rabbi Abie Ingber, *Xavier University, Cincinnati*

Elochukwu Uzukwu, *Duquesne University, Pittsburgh*

Interreligious
Dialogue

An Anthology of Voices
Bridging Cultural and Religious Divides

Christoffer H. Grundmann

ANSELM
A C A D E M I C

To the younger generations
to which
Katharina-Chitra-Kirubai,
Gabriele-Shakti-Shantini
and
Friederike-Cornelia
with their children belong

Created by the publishing team of Anselm Academic.

Printed in the United States of America

7067

ISBN 978-1-59982-676-9

Contents

PART II / 92

INTERRELIGIOUS DIALOGUE:
THE VIEW OF DIFFERENT TRADITIONS

PART III / 146

INTERRELIGIOUS DIALOGUE:
SOME PRACTICAL SAMPLES

Editor's Preface

Christoffer H. Grundmann, editor

Compiling an anthology requires a conscious decision of what to include and what to leave out based on a critical rationale. The rationale behind the selection of texts in this volume is to present accessible, seminal original contributions on the topic of interreligious dialogue for individual reading as well as for in-depth study in classes and elsewhere. No anthology is either fully representative or without shortcomings.

Absent from this text are voices about interreligious dialogue from people of indigenous religions, as noted by some of our peer reviewers. Yet, to the editor's knowledge, such voices—if they are recorded at all—are not well documented and available in English. What we have are descriptions of indigenous religions by cultural anthropologists and scholars of comparative religions. Likewise this anthology lacks texts addressing the need for interreligious dialogue addressed to youth from within the Muslim, the Hindu, and the Buddhist traditions of faith. No doubt there are other lacunae in this text as well, like the absence of explicitly female voices. To realize these limitations points to the need for further inquiry, research, and documentation, as well as to supplement use of this text with other resources, other voices, to fill the inevitable gaps and also to raise the profile of all those involved in contributing to this critical conversation.

Although the editor, who is Christian, has taken pains to include as many diverse contributions to interreligious dialogue as possible, readers will notice a disproportionate number of chapters written by Christians, as well as the absence of documentation about "failed" dialogues. This is owed to the fact that (a) to date, most of the written documentation on interreligious dialogue is done by Christians, and (b) failed dialogue is no longer dialogue and thus no longer serves the aim of this text, which is to provide exemplars of successful dialogue and principles of dialogue. It is true that individuals and groups may cease or even shun dialogue, but to do so means to refuse human communication and foster a potentially dangerous situation because people, then, are bereft of the opportunity to converse, including about their conflicts.

On a final note I would like to mention that all contributions have been reprinted with proper permission and with utmost faithfulness to the content and style of the respective authors. In some few instances, this may go against more contemporary sensibilities and conventions, such as to use inclusive language with respect to gender. Finally, explanation is sometimes provided for important technical terms that may be unfamiliar to the nonexpert. In such cases, the added information is enclosed in square brackets [ ] or in a footnote, if it is a longer one.

The human future of the earth depends not only upon political, economic, or ecological decisions. In an age marked by global migration and networking, the peaceful living togetherness of people also depends critically on mutual understanding of differences rooted in distinct religious identities, an understanding that interreligious dialogue attempts to facilitate.

Introduction

Interreligious Dialogue and Peace in the Age of Globalization

Christoffer H. Grundmann

Globalization and Interreligious Dialogue

We live in a globalized world. To say this is to express awareness of the fact that we live in a highly interdependent environment of global dimensions presenting unique challenges. These challenges not only affect economies and ecology, they also affect politics, culture, and religion alike. Living in a country that is heavily reliant in its functioning and well-being on the give-and-take with other nations with distinct cultures, religions, and mores[1] necessitates competence in inter-cultural and interreligious understanding so as to avoid the dreaded "clash of civilizations."[2] While many just enjoy the obvious advantages of globalization—lower prices, more choices, broader variety, greater freedom of movement and contacts—others fear the idiosyncrasies of civilizations not their own. Whereas globe trekkers seek the exotic of foreign cultures—the strange languages spoken, the taste and smell of unaccustomed food, the indigenous ways of dress and attire—those less curious tend to be scared by and suspicious of anything unfamiliar that they do not understand. Such fear and suspicion, at its most extreme, can lead to shocking violence, as occurred in the Sept. 11, 2001 attacks when Islamist terrorists declared "war" on Western society, the United States in particular.[3]

Investigating the 9/11 attacks and advising on how best to prevent such assaults in the future, the official report concluded that "there is no common

---

1. *Culture* here refers to the general perception of lived distinctiveness and identity; *religion* references spiritual and philosophical-theological beliefs and practices, and *mores* refers to ethical standards.

2. See Samuel P. Huntington, *The Clash of Civilizations and the Remaking of World Order* (New York: Simon & Schuster, 1996).

3. See Osama Bin Laden, *Declaration of War Against the Americans Occupying the Land of the Two Holy Places* at *www.terrorismfiles.org/individuals/declaration_of_jihad1.html.*

ground—not even respect for life—on which to begin a dialogue" with the ideology driving such terrorists; for this reason, according to the report, "it can only be destroyed or utterly isolated."[4] As understandable as such reaction is in light of the atrocities committed, the consequences drawn and the recommendations given are anything but helpful in furthering mutual understanding of differences in order to prevent such violence in the future. The suggestions made just perpetuate the vicious circle of hate and revenge—they don't break it. In today's globalized world, retaliation and noncommunication with those determined to inflict harm pose serious problems that threaten to destroy the fragile equilibrium of power that warrants the functioning of globalization in the first place.

Efficiently stopping terrorist activities is not enough; a robust culture of mutual understanding and trust across cultural and religious divides must be fostered as well. Religious diversity particularly must be addressed, as religion is at the very core of culture and civilization. Therefore, promotion of dialogue at all levels of society among people of different faith traditions and cultures is of prime importance for keeping peace. However, to say so requires some clarification of the meaning attached to the principal terms used in this argument: *religion* and *dialogue*.

What Is Religion?

A U.S. Religious Landscape Survey conducted in 2008 concluded that "Americans love to shop, even for religion. More than 40 percent of U.S. adults have changed their faith since childhood. . . . For America's faithful, it's a buyer's market."[5]

While religious diversity has existed from the beginnings of human culture, the market perspective on religion—not only in the United States, but in Western society in general—is a comparatively new phenomenon, the emergence of which is an expression of a drastic change in the understanding of religion itself. People in the Western world tend to perceive religion as an exclusively private affair and as a matter of choice, only thereby turning a blind eye to the fact that religion, actually, is at the core of culture.

Take food, for instance. While people today delight in the breadth of international cuisine available nearly everywhere—Indian, Chinese, Thai, Middle Eastern, Ethiopian, Mexican, Indonesian, Japanese—few realize that the fare typical of each is often determined by religious dietary regulations. These regulations concern not only the style and manner of preparing food (*kosher* in Judaism; *halal* in Islam; *Shiva*—undefiled by outcasts—in Indian religions) but also

---

4. *The 9/11 Commission Report: Final Report of the National Commission on Terrorist Attacks Upon the United States*, authorized ed. (New York: Norton, 2004), 362.

5. Jackson Dykman, "The Marketplace of Faith," *Time*, Feb. 29, 2008, 41. The URL for the survey is *www.pewforum.org/2008/02/01/u-s-religious-landscape-survey-religious-affiliation/*.

the diet itself. One will not find meats of "unclean animals" on the menu of Jewish and Muslim restaurants, which in practical terms means pork. For orthodox Hindus, abstinence from beef (and for Hindus of the highest castes who disavow meat consumption in principle, strict vegetarianism, called "Shiva food") is obligatory. Likewise, orthodox Islam and Buddhism decree abstinence from fermented drink, as do the Sikhs, who also relinquish any use of drugs or narcotics, including cigarettes. In "shamanistic" religions, in contrast, intoxicating drink is essential to the proper celebration of religious rites, as in the Mesoamerican Peyote cult or the classic Vedic *Soma* sacrifice.[6]

Alongside differences in food, religious directions often rule the dress code. For instance, most Muslim women are advised to wear the *hijab*, a headscarf or veil, while some are expected to disguise their entire body with a *burka*.[7] A male Sikh must cover his head with a turban; Hindus and Muslims also wear turbans, as do Arabs and other desert-dwellers. The color of the gowns of Buddhist monks is a religious statement, too; its reddish yellow or dark red symbolizes the setting sun as an indication of forsaking the world.[8]

Likewise, ways of hallowing time and celebrating festivals reflect the exclusivity and distinctiveness of cultures. No two calendars are alike—secular or religious. In the United States, citizens annually commemorate the Fourth of July and Thanksgiving, recalling events central to the freedom and opportunity for which the United States is known around the world. Religious calendars,

---

6. Vol. 63.3 (1995) of *The Journal of the American Academy of Religion* is a thematic issue on the topic of food and religion; see also Daniel Sack, *Whitebread Protestants: Food and Religion in American Culture* (New York: St. Martin's Press, 2000) and Carolyn Walker Bynum, *Holy Feast and Holy Fast: The Religious Significance of Food to Medieval Women* (Berkeley: University of California Press, 1987). For the Shamanistic religions see Åke Hultkrantz, *Shamanistic Healing and Ritual Drama* (New York: Crossroad Publishing, 1997), esp. pp. 142–146, and R. Gordon Wasson, *Soma: Divine Mushroom of Immortality* (New York: Harcourt Brace Jovanovich, 1971). For the Hindu *Soma* sacrifice see the voluminous study by Frits Stall, *Agni: The Vedic Ritual of the Fire Altar*, 2 vols. (Berkeley: Asian Humanities Press, 1983).

7. The word *hijab* comes from the Arabic for "veil" and is used to describe the headscarves worn by Muslim women. These scarves, regarded by many Muslims as a symbol of both religion and womanhood, come in a myriad of styles and colors. The *niqab* is a veil for the face that leaves the area around the eyes clear. However, it may be worn with a separate eye veil. It is worn with an accompanying headscarf. The *burka* is the most concealing of all Islamic veils. It covers the entire face and body, leaving just a mesh screen to see through. The *al-amira* is a two-piece veil. It consists of a close-fitting cap, usually made from cotton or polyester, and an accompanying tube-like scarf. The *shayla* is a long, rectangular scarf popular in the Gulf region. It is wrapped around the head and tucked or pinned in place at the shoulders. The *khimar* is a long, cape-like veil that hangs down to just above the waist. It covers the hair, neck, and shoulders completely, but leaves the face clear. The *chador*, worn by many Iranian women when outside the house, is a full-body cloak. It is often accompanied by a smaller headscarf underneath. The type most commonly worn in the West is a square scarf that covers the head and neck but leaves the face clear. There have been attempts to ban both the *niqab* and *burka* in some European countries, notably France.

8. On the issue of religious dress codes see Mary M. Crain, "Dress and the Body," *American Ethnologist* 27, no. 3 (2000): 790–791.

however, go back much further in time and revolve around quite different events. Jews who live by a calendar based on the lunar cycle count the years from the very beginning of time, which in practical terms means that the year 2015 CE, according to Jewish counting, is year 5775/76 since the creation of the world. The distinctive mark for Christians is the Resurrection of the crucified Christ at Easter. It is from Easter that all the other festivals and liturgical days are set. Not only that, the actual beginning of the new time, according to Christian belief, sets in with God's Incarnation in the birth of Jesus Christ, according to which I am composing this introduction in the year 2015 AD (*Anno Domini*, the 2015th "Year of the Lord," with AD being the preferred terminology before CE or Common Era gained preference in most quarters). For Muslims the most decisive event is the foundation of the Islamic community, the *Umma*, which happened when Mohammed and his first followers left Mecca to take refuge in Medina (Hijra) in 622 CE; counting 622 CE as the beginning of a new time for Muslims (who, like Jews, observe a lunar calendar), 2015 will be 1436/37. It is from events like these that each religion determines its particular rhythm of time, hallowing certain periods as festive while declaring others as times of public mourning and fasting, and setting the days for worship and prayer.

Further, religious perceptions also shape pivotal events in the lives of individuals, families, and communities. Consider the Shabbat celebration of Jews, Sunday worship by Christians, and Friday prayers for Muslims, or consider Christmas in Christian celebration, the *Chanukah* and *Purim* festivals in Jewish observance, or the *Eid al-Adha'* (the Feast of Sacrifice) in Islam. Religious directions come most powerfully to the fore in critical life events such as giving birth, celebrating a wedding, or handling dying, death, and burial through ritual observance. Yet, these rituals differ distinctively from culture to culture, a feature that becomes most obvious in funerals. While Muslims never cremate their dead, Hindus do, and the Parsi (the Indian branch of Zoroastrianism) place the cadavers in so-called "Towers of Silence" for vultures to feed on, a powerful reminder not just of their nomadic past, but also of the circle of life.

The most obvious element in which religions differ is the language of their Holy Scriptures, at least as far as the so-called world religions are concerned. Even though most people—save the trained experts—are unable to read the scriptures of their own religious tradition in the language of their original composition, these texts, nonetheless, bring about a perceivable unity and cultural identity in that they are regularly used in ritual formulas and prayers as parts of all significant religious ceremonies. In many religious traditions, readers recite passages of Holy Scriptures as appointed readings in worship or on occasion of private ceremonies. By their constant repetition at critical junctures in life, these texts create an impression and identity from the earliest days of childhood. Equally important, these texts contribute to the formation of a collective memory.

Rabbi Simon Philip de Vries (1870–1944) once described this all-inclusive aspect of religion with regard to Judaism:

> Judaism can be recognized outwardly by its peculiar features, unfamiliar and conspicuous to a non-Jew. It stands out by its Sabbath, its festivals, its worship, its dietary regulations, its ritual and ceremonies. Naturally . . . above all, there is its concept of God and its core religious thought, the most important of which is contained in the word, in the concept of monotheism. . . . As a people of worship . . . it [Judaism] has, like every other religion, its worldview, and a valid order of life for its adherents. To be sure, in actuality it doesn't *have* a worldview—because it *is* a worldview. In it everything is contained as a unity. It comprehends creation and life as a *unit*, and indeed, in the absolute and widest sense. This worldview is a culture of its own, in which everything belonging to life, as touching and pertaining to life, has its greater or smaller share . . . in this unity. From this point of view everything is judged and considered. Its object is humanity and the human person. It is exactly as with the state and its members as it is with society in general and the life of individuals in interpersonal, social relationships. Therefore the political order is not excluded. There is also room here for criminal justice and civil jurisdiction. Likewise the home, the synagogue, and ritual belong to this unity.[9]

Indeed, religion is at the core of culture. At the heart of the diverse aspects comprising a culture is a distinct, noninterchangeable worldview communicated by well-established, holy tradition and enacted again and again in ceremonies and rituals.

Religion as Lived Relationship Toward an Ultimate

Religion and interreligious dialogue deal with worldviews and their impact on communal as well as individual life. In secularized Western culture, no longer does this necessarily indicate *established* religion, but rather a more general attitude toward life that focuses on personal satisfaction. This is particularly true of more affluent, individualistic societies.

People may deny belief in anything "religious," but they cannot deny the witness of their lifestyle and life choices. A profoundly secular lifestyle bears witness to the core values of the individual practicing it. Deny it or not, the way

---

9. S. Ph. de Vries, *Joodsche riten en symbolen*, 8th ed. (Amsterdam: De Arbeiderspers, 1996). The quoted text is rendered from the German edition *Jüdische Riten und Symbole* (Wiesbaden: Fourier Verlag, 1982), 314f; original emphasis.

one lives—as atheist, nonspiritual pragmatist, consciously religious, observant and pious, and so on—witnesses what one holds dear and where one's treasure lies. In other words, how we live tells the religious dimension of our lives, provided "religion" is understood as lived relationship toward an Ultimate—whatever that Ultimate may be. That people lost sight of this religious dimension of life and of religion's comprehensive impact on the shaping of a common culture is—at least in part—the result of an extended discourse on "religion" in Western intellectual history that established "religion" as a subject matter.[10]

In general, philosophers conceding "religion" to have immense practical value for social cohesion and political order for the good or the bad distorted religion by assuming that there does exist something like a "natural religion" with an "idea of God" or a "higher being" at its core. Yet, "religion" is not just a mental construct of abstract concepts. Concepts do not do justice to the vibrant vitality of religions actually lived. Concepts are void of colorful detail. They single out certain aspects of "religions" only, distill these to the taste of intellectual clarity and declare what is left to be the essence of "religion." However, "religion" never exists in the singular. "Religion" exists—and always did exist—in a colorful plurality of different lived "religions." These vary to such a degree that one wonders if the single, general term *religion*, under which to subsume these manifold cultural phenomena, is appropriate at all.

For instance, the concept of God or of gods, respectively, plays a significant role only for a particular group of religions, the so-called theistic religions such as the religion of ancient Egypt, Greece, and Rome, or today's Shivaism and Vishnuism in India. Monotheistic religions like Judaism, Christianity, and Islam represent a subgroup of this type of religions. But there are also nontheistic religions like Buddhism, Daoism, and Confucianism, besides innumerable religious practices in Shamanism and divination, not tied to the worship of deities at all.

What complicates matters further is that until the eighteenth century, with the beginning of the Enlightenment, an articulated concept of religion as such did not exist and was not a matter of concern. Even today, many traditions do not self-describe using the term "religion." The Romans used "religion" (*religio*) as just one term among several others—*lex, pietas, fides, cultus, secta*—to designate particular acts of worship, devotion, and religious practice. The Indian religions commonly subsumed under the term "Hinduism" such as Shivaism, Vishnuism, and Shaktism, for instance, speak of *dhārma* instead, a Sanskrit noun which above all means "order" as "cosmic law." *Dhārma* understood as

---

10. For a qualified survey on the topic see E. Feil "The Problem of Defining and Demarcating *Religion*," in *On the Concept of Religion*, eds. E. Feil, B. McNeil (Atlanta, GA: Scholar Press, 1999), 1–35, and especially Feil's monumental four-volume study *Religio: Die Geschichte eines neuzeitlichen Grundbegriffs* [Religion: History of Modern Concept] (Göttingen: Vandenhoeck & Ruprecht, 1986–2007).

"cosmic order" or "cosmic law" is, evidently, "eternal law," or as Hindus would say *sanātana dhārma*. But the term *dhārma* also oscillates among many other meanings like "duty," "caste duty," "legal system," "offering," "justice," "essence," and "virtue."[11] In Buddhism, on the other hand, the same concept, *dhārma*, which in Pali (the language of Buddhist holy texts) is *dhamma*, signifies the teaching of the Buddha. Interestingly though, Buddhism not only lacks a concept of religion, it actually shows no interest in one. Buddhism is mainly concerned with the perception and realization of the true essence of world and life as revealed in the *dhamma* of the Buddha. However, since the Buddha likened his teaching to a vehicle and specifically a raft (translated from the Sanskrit *yana*), "vehicle" or "raft" may be considered to function as the Buddhist equivalent to the idiom "religion." But even this meaning covers only a fraction of what lived religion actually implies, specifically the concrete, empirical, experiential aspects of the lived relationship toward an Ultimate. Just what, then, does one actually converse and communicate about in interreligious dialogue with Buddhists?

In Islam there is no synonym for "religion" either. The two Arabic terms used by Muslims to signify the entirety of religious expressions of life are *milla* and *din*. These terms, however, pose problems in various respects, because both are loanwords from other languages. While *milla* stems from Aramaic (a Semitic language) and, as a rule, signifies the actual "religious community" in a certain place, the more frequently used *din* is of Persian origin, the etymology of which cannot be established beyond doubt. The issue is whether *din* derives from *dayn* (meaning "guilt" or "credit") or from *dana li* (meaning "to submit"). Thus *din* can take on entirely different overtones, such as "custom," "directive," "reprisal," "judgment," "obedience," "submission," or "tradition." In theological discourse among the *Ulama* (the Muslim theologians), *din*, as a rule, signifies the divine institution that hands down the faith and doctrines while at the same time points the faithful to good works. Thus, closely observing *din* leads to salvation in this world and the next. Therefore, *din* might denote religion in its broadest sense.[12]

For Judaism the term *berith*, which means "covenant" or "contract," serves as the central concept, one most likely considered the equivalent of religion. But the etymology of this term is also not clear. Quite specifically, *berith* means, "the making of a covenant sealed by an offering," like the one on Mount Sinai, through which, by the power of God's election, Israel became the "people of the covenant," the "people of God." But in a broader sense *berith* signifies a somewhat generic "covenant" as well, a "regulation," an "agreement," a "solemn

---

11. See Monier-Williams, *Sanskrit-English Dictionary* (1899; repr., New Delhi: Motilal Banarsidass Publishers, 1971), 510–511, s.v. "*dhārma*."

12. See *The Encyclopaedia of Islam*, new edition, vol. 5 (Leiden: Brill, 1981), 431ff.

pledge," denoting, more specifically, the "right leading" of people by means of the commandments and the "law."[13]

Therefore, when speaking of interreligious dialogue one must remain conscious of the intellectual—even ideological—construct this term presents. More than that, one has to acknowledge that the idiom "religion" not only fails to correspond to lived reality but actually distorts it. Practically speaking, Muslims, Hindus, or Buddhists, to name just a few, might be suspicious if asked to participate in a substantive conversation about "religion," because this is a concept rooted in a culture not theirs. Yet, to recognize this does not imply that pursuing interreligious dialogue is in vain and doomed to fail; this recognition, rather, points to some of the more demanding implicit challenges in the venture. The papers and articles presented in this anthology amply document those challenges and how they can be met and overcome successfully.

What Is Dialogue?

The distinctive means by which human beings communicate with each other is by words, and especially spoken words. People speak to one another to share feelings, information, and thoughts. They converse to socialize, to learn, to gain understanding, and to argue. As long as people are in conversation with one another there is a real chance of avoiding violence. What a hopeful sign, when news breaks that two sides to a bitter conflict have returned to the negotiating table, like Protestants and Catholics in Northern Ireland, Hindus and Muslims in Kashmir, and Israelis and Palestinians in the Near East. As long as those who are suspicious of and hostile to one another still talk, there is hope for maintaining peace, which is so essential for life to thrive. In the words of Jewish philosopher, translator, and journalist Martin Buber (1878–1965):

> In a genuine dialogue each of the partners, even when he stands in opposition to the other, heeds, affirms, and confirms his opponent as an existing other. Only so can conflict certainly not be eliminated from the world, but be humanely arbitrated and led towards its overcoming.[14]

Recognizing this, however, should not lead to an attitude that styles dialogue as a means to look for the least common denominator among people holding conflicting worldviews. Those who peddle their worldview in an

---

13. See G. Quell, "The OT term ברית," in *Theological Dictionary of the New Testament*, transl. and ed. G. W. Bromiley, vol. 2 (Grand Rapids, MI: Eerdmans, 1964), 106–124; A. J. Avery-Peck, "Covenant," in *The Encyclopedia of Judaism*, ed. J. Neusner, A. J. Averey-Peck, W. S. Green, vol. 1 (New York: Continuum, 1999), 136–151.

14. Martin Buber, "Genuine Dialogue and the Possibilities of Peace," in Martin Buber, *Pointing the Way—Collected Essays*, transl. and ed. by M. Friedman (New York: Harper & Brothers, 1957), 238.

exhibitionist manner, even at the cost of selling their own cultural-religious tradition at bargain prices, cut themselves off from their roots and lose their grounding. However sensitive and original the gestures toward commitment to an ideologically styled religious pluralism under these circumstances, such gestures are hardly other than systematic enticements to forfeit any orientation grounded in a binding tradition. This attitude will gain little if any appreciation from those who are seriously concerned about dialogue and who don't seek consensus but understanding.

It is necessary, therefore, to distinguish dialogue from other ways in which people are in conversation with one another. Dialogue is more than just exchanging information on issues or problems. Of course, exchange of information is always part of what it means to be in dialogue, but that certainly is not distinctive of dialogue. Even less is dialogue equivalent to a negotiation in which opposing parties try to reconcile their conflicting interests in an attempt to reach a compromise acceptable on all sides. As mandated representatives of disagreeing parties, negotiating partners have to be concerned with the preservation of interests—an attitude that would be quite deadly for any dialogue, especially if it were interreligious. Dialogue as genuine conversation among humans is not concerned about domination and power. Dialogue, rather, has everything to do with gaining insights and growing in understanding while being in conversation, insights which cannot be gained and do not come about otherwise, neither by debate nor by discussion. In terms of function, dialogue resembles roundtable talks, a well-established means of conflict resolution since the beginning of the twentieth century. The aim is to resolve problems not through confrontation— that is why one sits at a round table—but in agreement. Still, dialogue does not exhaust itself in mere problem solving.

According to the Greek root of the term, dialogue means "to be in conversation." Thus, dialogue is a predominantly language-based interpersonal interaction that recognizes the counterpart not as an impersonal object but as an autonomous individual other. Dialogue may entail honest conversation about contentious questions, in the process bringing about a better understanding of existing tensions and differences. This is the prime goal of dialoguing—not solving problems, even though problems may well get solved once existing differences are properly understood. Hence, to refuse dialogue is a signal of isolation and growing estrangement from one another which, at its extreme, may lead to violence, such as the attacks of 9/11/2001. Dialogue, interreligious dialogue in particular, is indeed vital for human survival.

As interpersonal conversation, dialogue is not immune from abuse, of course. Speaking and talking back, asking questions and giving answers are essentially successions of speech-acts. Since dialogue is essentially a speech-event, its success depends directly on the way individuals use language, as well as on the speakers' intentions and authenticity. Thus participants in dialogue ought to be mindful of factual adequacy—the adequacy of what they articulate in relation to perceived reality, as well as congruence between what they are saying and what they are, in fact, thinking or intending. Success depends on whether their speaking is truthful and sincere. One can speak eloquently, all the while aiming to disguise actual intentions, in order to leave conversation partners in the dark, or to render them compliant by subtle manipulation. For speaking is not everything there is to dialogue. Merely speaking with others is by no means in and of itself pursuing dialogue; actually, it may be just a staging of monologues intended to accomplish something quite different from the goal of dialoguing. Any such kind of inauthentic speech is a subtle form of despotism since its intention is to manipulate others, not to communicate in order to come to true understanding. Such exploitation of language becomes especially dangerous when used for ideological ends such as political propaganda or ideological brainwashing.

Abuse of language threatens to be fatal for every community because it destroys authentic human communication. Plato (428/427–347 BCE) branded the eloquent, intelligent Sophists as the most evil and most corrupt twisters of wisdom and truth. It is not without good reason that "right speech," meaning speaking authentically and faithfully, is counted as one among the basic steps of the Noble Eightfold Path in Buddhism leading to salvation.[15] Very much along the same line is the call to guarding the tongue in Judaism[16] and, in Christianity, Jesus' exhortation, "Let your word be 'Yes, yes' or 'No, no'; anything more than this comes from the evil one" (Matthew 5:37).

In 1953 Martin Buber, speaking about "Genuine Dialogue and the Possibilities of Peace," diagnosed the crisis of his time—the Cold War marked by escalating confrontations between East and West—as caused primarily by the loss of the ability to dialogue:

> The man in crisis will no longer entrust his cause to conversation because its presupposition—trust—is lacking. This is the reason why the cold war which today goes by the name of peace has been able to overcome mankind. In every earlier period of peace the living word has passed between man and man, time after time drawing the poison from the antagonism of interests and convictions so that these antagonisms have not degenerated into the absurdity of "no-further," into the madness of "must-wage-war." The living word of human dialogue that from time to time makes its flights until the madness smothers it, now seems to have become lifeless in the midst of the non-war.[17]

15. See Conze, Edward, *Buddhism: Its Essence and Development* (Birmingham, UK: Windhorse, 2001).

16. See Pliskin, Zelig, *Guard Your Tongue: A Practical Guide to the Laws of Loshon Hora Based on Chofetz* (New York: Weissman, 1975).

17. Buber, "Genuine Dialogue," 236–237.

Recognizing the indisputable importance of dialogue, to engage in it is not only arduous but also risky. It requires trust one will not be deceived by the others, and the preparedness to break away from cherished suppositions if it turns out that these are no longer plausible. To dialogue means travelling down unknown roads with unfamiliar companions, who take a like risk. What is common to all is the existential quest to arrive at an authentically renewed plausibility of the meaning of life and world. There is no excuse—and herein lies the chief evil and pitfall of refusal to dialogue—for exempting *any* content from dialogue, even the most treasured. To withhold the core of one's belief spoils dialogue, because however ready for dialogue one may be in terms of attitude, no authentic communication can take place. The most that might be achieved by withholding one's heart will be a lukewarm, unconvincing, and fraternizing gesture, keeping dialogue partners at arm's length and not taking them seriously. The price of this kind of mock-dialogue is high, for it will prove incapable of controlling anxieties about loss and fears of potential or seemingly imminent threats, attitudes which tend to aggravate proportionally the less prevailing differences are understood. Since reservations cannot dispel suspicion or dismantle mistrust, mock- or sham-dialogues subliminally cultivate anxieties and fears, and actually undermine peaceful coexistence in multicultural, multireligious environments.

In contrast, genuinely religious people will always acknowledge the worldview they have been raised in as well as the specific insights and perceptions of world and life with its accompanying system of values and mores handed down to them by hallowed tradition. They will enter into dialogue with an attitude shaped by values, norms, and convictions from their particular religious background. They cannot do otherwise, because truly religious people will not fear losing their identity in dialogue, since they know that they can retain their own identity only when they bring it into conversation with the challenges posed by significant others. Thus, neither fundamentalism nor conservatism, neither pluralism nor willed-ignorance nor isolationism is a viable option for them. They are aware and know it in their heart that without authentically re-owning their belief in dialogical confrontation with contemporaries and the challenges of the times, their cultural-religious identity will become shallow and dulled, doomed to lose its plausibility. Once cultural-religious norms and directives lose their plausibility they sooner or later will be abandoned, perhaps with a certain sense of relief from their "repressive" claims. Therefore, the only option to reaffirm cherished values and convictions that remains viable is engaging in unconditional, open dialogue.

A dialogical attitude of the kind just outlined requires a fundamental, mature, and daring openness, an openness willing to take risks, which cannot be expected everywhere of everyone at all times, because it renders one vulnerable. This is because such an attitude has nothing in its hands to combat the abuse of language and the exploitation of the situation except its own sincerity, its authenticity in speaking, and its continual, concerted effort to that end. Still less is such an attitude able to call a halt to the ravages of raw and brute power by resorting to a corresponding counterforce. Trust in the power of the right and proper word is all that remains, the word that not only unmasks dubious intentions, but also brings about renewed trust, reconciled communication, and better understanding. Such trust in the power of words has to be cultivated, of course, for the success of the entire venture. The contributions selected for this compilation reflect such an attitude.

Interreligious Dialogue Lived and Practiced

This book has been compiled to make remarkable articles on interreligious dialogue accessible to a broader, more general audience, especially to college students. The intent is to alert people at an early and decisive stage in life to the pressing need for competent interreligious dialogue and to give firsthand accounts of how this might be done and what it looks like. Instead of repeating what already has been said well and published elsewhere, we decided to select a few seminal articles on the topic of interreligious dialogue from the pen of Jews, Christians, Muslims, Hindus, and Buddhists. All authors—some of whom write from within a monastic tradition, some as religious scholars, some as members of a hierarchy—recognize the urgent need for interreligious dialogue and contribute to it by sharing the insights gained from their lived practice in Asia, America, and Europe.

Each of these articles stands on its own and deserves to be studied in depth. The authors do not all share a singular, common view on the topic. Rather, readers will notice a remarkable diversity of approaches and understandings and ways of addressing interreligious dialogue. What is common to all, however, is the seriousness and disarming honesty with which every writer attends to the issue. As such, this anthology powerfully bears witness to what has been explained in this introduction regarding dialogue and religion. There is no idle talk *about* interreligious dialogue. These chapters document *involvement in* interreligious dialogue. They must be studied with this reality in mind, as a sharing of insightful lived reality. Every other approach will miss the point.

As may be expected, the style of these presentations varies considerably. Some pieces are more theoretical and reflective while others are descriptive, narrative, or very personal in character. Given this diversity of backgrounds, contexts, and styles, each article is presented with a short paragraph introducing the author, the original context in which the piece was published, and peculiarities of style and argument. The chapters are arranged in three subsections, beginning with more general reflections about concepts and principles of interreligious dialogue, followed by chapters addressing dialogue from within specific religious or spiritual traditions, and concluding with reports about contemporary interreligious projects from around the world. An epilogue summarizes some of the basic insights of the various contributions documented here and highlights pertinent features of interreligious dialogue. An appendix provides additional information about several pertinent websites and some other material for supplementary study of the topic.

All this is meant to further the cause of interreligious dialogue and encourage its pursuit—on college campuses, at home, and in society at large.

I

PART

INTERRELIGIOUS DIALOGUE

Why does it matter?

مؤتمر الدو
التـاسع لحـ
الأديا

٢٤ ـ ٢٦ أكـتوبـر١

Rabbi Henry Sobel

Not only Western societies are concerned with interreligious dialogue, as demonstrated in this photo taken in 2011 at a formally staged event—the ninth of its kind—in Dohar, capital of the Emirate of Qatar. Note also the distinguishing dress of the religious traditions represented by these members of the three Abrahamic traditions: Judaism, Christianity, and Islam.

1

CHAPTER

Interreligious Dialogue

What? Why? How?[1]

Paul F. Knitter

EDITOR'S NOTE

Contemporary Roman Catholic theologian Paul F. Knitter, an American, is one of the most articulate advocates for a pluralistic conception of religion. Actively engaged in interreligious dialogue himself, Knitter reflects here about the what, the why, and the how of such pursuits. He safeguards the now almost fashionable call for interreligious dialogue—the "dialogical imperative"—from turning into a trivial truism by highlighting the challenges, difficulties, and gains of any such endeavor. Knitter does not brush aside the claims to ultimate validity of each religion or faith tradition; rather, he honors these. Instead of focusing on the least common denominator of different religions, however, he focuses on what he describes as the shared imperative among religions to announce "a liberating message to . . . the world." The article unpacks in detail this liberation-centered (or "soteriocentric") model for interreligious dialogue. Knitter challenges his readers, especially his Christian audience, to reconsider well-established concepts of God, Jesus, and Christ. "If in our interreligious dialogue we can agree that our first concern is not the primacy of our names or the accuracy of our doctrines but, rather, the healing of cripples [i.e., that something gets effectively changed for the better], we will grow in the ability to understand and to call on each others' names." Knitter's learned contribution is a personally authenticated voice for the cause by a deeply religious Christian intellectual raised in Western culture, a voice deserving an attentive hearing.

---

1. Paul F. Knitter, "Interreligious Dialogue: What? Why? How?," in *Death or Dialogue? From the Age of Monologue to the Age of Dialogue*, by Leonard Swidler, John B. Cobb Jr., Paul F. Knitter, Monika K. Hellwig (Philadelphia, PA: Trinity Press, 1990). Copyright © 1990 Leonard Swidler, John B. Cobb Jr., Paul F. Knitter, Monika K. Hellwig. A portion of the original chapter is reprinted in this book with permission from Bloomsbury Publishing Inc.

From my own experience—gained in conference rooms, libraries, and meditation halls—I would describe interreligious dialogue as the confrontation with utter, bewildering, often threatening *differences* and at the same time, the *trust* that such differences are, for the most part, friendly rather than hostile, fruitful rather than barren. In dialogue one faces the utterly other and trusts that one can speak to, learn from, even work with that other. Within the heart of dialogue, therefore, beats a deep act of faith and trust.

Unpacking this description, I find four pivotal elements in dialogue: (1) the experience of *difference*; (2) the *trust* that such differences are unitive rather than separative; and flowing from these two experiences, (3) the resolve to *witness*, that is, to make known to one's dialogical partner one's own religious experiences and convictions; and (4) the resolve to *listen and learn* from the experiences and convictions of one's partner. As part of my efforts to state what for me constitutes the nature and goals of dialogue, I will try to explore the meaning and demands of these four ingredients. Then I'd like to state why I think that the present state of our suffering and liberation-needy world is providing all religious believers with a newly felt *imperative* and *opportunity* to mix those ingredients and pursue interreligious dialogue. Responding to this new imperative and opportunity, I would then like to suggest a liberation-centered (or "soteriocentric") model for interreligious dialogue which, I think, will both make for a more effective encounter of religions and will enable Christians to remove one of their main stumbling blocks to dialogue—their traditional understanding of the exclusivity or superiority of Christ and Christianity. All this makes for the what, the why, and the how of dialogue.

Dialogue: What Is It?

Differences

Anyone who begins an interreligious conversation with the announcement of how much we have in common or that we are really saying "the same thing in different words" has done just that—only begun the conversation. Such announcements, though they may have their element of truth, can be maintained only on the surface of dialogue; they begin to fade away as one goes deeper into the experience, the beliefs and practices, and the historical development of the different religious traditions. Like a newly married couple growing out of the first stages of infatuation into real living together, partners in religious sharing, as they get to know each other, soon arrive at the existential realization of how bewilderingly different they are. What had been initially experienced as similarities now become differing, even opposing, faces. The Tao and God, Zen meditation and Christian prayer, Jesus and Buddha, *avidya* [Sanskrit: ignorance, delusion] and original sin—become as different as they once were similar. One gradually becomes aware of the naiveté and the downright danger of proclaiming a "common essence" or a "common core" within all the religions of the world. Yes, one might still believe that Ultimate Reality or God is one and that ultimately differences will be swallowed in oneness; but right now, in the dust and dirt of the real world, we have to deal with the manyness, the differences, among the religions before we can ever contemplate, much less realize, their possible unity or oneness.

In reflecting on this experience of difference, I find myself in basic agreement with the so-called "antifoundationalists." Today, philosophers such as Richard Rorty and Richard Bernstein, together with theologians such as George Lindbeck, Francis Schüssler Fiorenza, David Tracy, and Raimundo Panikkar chide religious dialoguers who are looking for a common "religious Esperanto" or are proposing a "universal theology of religions"[2] or a "world theology,"[3] that they may be searching for a chimera or imposing an ideological system.[4] As far as we can tell, in this finite world of many cultures and religions and histories, there is no universal foundation outside the fray of history and diversity on which we can make universal judgments and assess the diversity. Plurality is it! It will not yield an Archimedean point by which we can lift ourselves beyond the plurality to a final unity. Or so it seems.

We are, in a sense, caught in our own cultural-religious perspectives—or at least inescapably influenced by them. If there is no such thing as "pure experience"; if all experience is "interpreted," then we are always looking at the world through our inherited cultural-religious spectacles.[5] As Lindbeck convincingly points out, we don't first have an experience of God or of ultimacy and then turn to our religion to "interpret" or "represent" it; rather, our religion's interpretation or language has a determinative influence on what kind of religious experience we have.[6] If the interpretations are markedly different ("Emptiness" [referring to the core Buddhist concept of *shunyata/sunyata*] vs. "God" [implying personal presence and substance]), then the experiences will be equally different.

---

2. Leonard Swidler, ed., *Toward a Universal Theology of Religion* (Maryknoll: Orbis Books, 1987).

3. Wilfred Cantwell Smith, *Toward a World Theology* (Philadelphia: Westminster Press and London: Macmillan, 1981).

4. Raimundo Panikkar, "The Invisible Harmony: A Universal Theory of Religion or a Cosmic Confidence in Reality?" in *Toward a Universal Theology of Religion,* ed. Leonard Swidler (Maryknoll: Orbis, 1987), 118–53; Raimundo Panikkar, "The Jordan, the Tiber, and the Ganges: Three Kairological Moments in Christic Self-Consciousness," in *The Myth of Christian Uniqueness: Toward a Pluralistic Theology of Religions,* eds. John Hick and Paul F. Knitter (Maryknoll: Orbis Books and London: SCM Press, 1987), 89–116.

5. Steven T. Katz, "Language, Epistemology, and Mysticism," in *Mysticism and Philosophical Analysis,* ed. Steven T. Katz (NY: Oxford University Press, 1978), 26.

6. George Lindbeck, *The Nature of Doctrine: Religion and Theology in a Postliberal Age* (Philadelphia: Westminster Press, 1984), 40, 49.

Between the religions of the world, therefore, there yawn "incommensurability gaps"—even between their mystics![7] We can look at and speak to one another, we can form some "picture" of who the other is, but we cannot really understand one another sufficiently to pass judgments on the truth or falsity, the goodness or harmfulness, of one another's religious beliefs and practices. That would require moving beyond our own historico-cultural perspectives or limitations and taking on, thoroughly, that of the others. But that is extremely difficult, if not impossible. Since there seems to be no universal "foundation" beyond our particular "standpoints," every time we judge another's religion we are doing so from our own "standpoint," not theirs. We are doing so from outside their religion. And that's not fair.

Given my own experience of dialogue and thanks to the chidings of my antifoundationalist friends, I have realized over the past years that I, like many proponents of religious pluralism, have too hastily hoisted the banner of "pluralism," before sufficiently recognizing the reality of "plurality." We pluralists have been too quick to propose an "ism" or a system on the vast, buzzing array of plurality; and in so *proposing* we have *imposed*. David Tracy's admonition, arising out of his own experience of religious otherness, rings true:

> . . . the official pluralist too often finds ways to reduce real otherness and genuine differences to some homogenized sense of what we (who is this "we"?) already know . . . some pluralists, the vaunted defenders of difference, can become the great reductionists—reducing differences to mere similarity, reducing otherness to the same, and reducing plurality to my community of right-thinking competent critics. In this light, there is truth in Simone de Beauvoir's[8] bitter charge that "pluralism is the perfect ideology for the bourgeois mind."[9]

Trust

And yet, though we stare at each other's religious traditions across these incommensurability gaps, though we well realize the difficulty of understanding, and the danger of judging, another person's religious beliefs and practices, we find ourselves borne or grasped by a suspicion, a hope, a resolve that we *can* speak to each other across our religious barriers; that it is worthwhile, even necessary, to do so. This is, indeed, an act of faith. It is a deep-seated feeling which seems to be given to us or to take hold of us; we find ourselves believing in something

---

7. Steven T. Katz, ed., *Mysticism and Religious Traditions* (NY: Oxford University Press, 1982).

8. Simone de Beauvoir (1908-1986), French existentialist philosopher.

9. David Tracy, "Christianity in the Wider Context: Demands and Transformations," *Religion and Intellectual Life* 4, no. 4 (1987): 12.

which, though rooted in experiential evidence, goes beyond that evidence. It is similar to Luther's "*trotzdem*," his "despite all that": despite the stark differences between religions, we believe that the sheer actuality of *plurality* can lead to the inter-relatedness of *pluralism*. There is *life* in the differences. In speaking to one another across our gaps, we can come closer.

In fact, it seems that this coming closer, this conversation with those who are genuinely different, is an indispensable condition for growing in the understanding of reality, in the pursuit of truth. If there is no absolute criterion of truth given to us from above, if there is no foundation outside the waves of history for evaluating the many forced opinions that face our world, then we must plunge into the conversation, listen to each other's differences, and in this engagement fashion, step by difficult step, our understanding of reality. In order to "grow in wisdom and truth before God and our fellow human beings," we must talk to each other. In order to enrich and save our world we must embrace pluralism. "Pluralism is a responsible and fruitful option because it allows for (indeed demands) that we develop better ways as selves, as communities of inquirers, as societies, as cultures, as an inchoately global culture to allow for more possibilities to enrich our personal and communal lives."[10]

In the ebb and flow of conversing, with all its complexity and dangers, we can create, not foundations, but "shaky common ground." Not with prepackaged methods or systems but by genuinely trying to "pass over" to the otherness of the other, by stretching our own visions and paradigms, we can establish new, shared ground on which we *can* truly understand another culture or religion, and they us. The gap of incommensurability *can* be bridged—but the bridge will never be set in cement; it will, rather, sway in the wind and have to be frequently reconstructed or torn down to be rebuilt at a better crossing. Just how these bridges are built and how this common shaky ground is discovered cannot be stated in advance of the conversation. It can be discovered, created, maintained only in the act and process of dialogue.

Witnessing

In interreligious dialogue we confront otherness as something we want not only to embrace but also to address. Ideally, we come to the conversation from a position of richness, not impoverishment—that is, we speak to each other out of our own religious experience. We speak because we have discovered something of value—the pearl of great price. As Raimundo Panikkar has continuously insisted, in order to have religious encounter, we must speak from religious experience— or at least from religious quest. Such "subjective" contents and perspectives are not to be cut out and packed in some kind of deep-freeze "epoché" [detached

---

10. Ibid., 9.

reflection] but, rather, are to be poured, warm and bubbling, into the conversation.[11] The "object" of dialogue is approached through a meeting of "subjects."

And because we speak out of our different religious experiences and convictions, we will seek not only to explain but to *persuade*. If genuinely experienced, religious truth, like all truth, can never be only "for me." If it is, it is somehow diluted or not yet fully grown. A quality of "universal relevance" is ingredient to every encounter with or revelation of the Ultimate; what one has seen, felt, been transformed by—can also so affect others. All interreligious dialogue, therefore, is animated by a certain missionary élan. We want our partners to see what we have seen; we want their lives to be touched and transformed as ours have been. Yes, let me use the offensive word: we want to *convert* our partners.

But the conversion that is sought is not one of "winning over" but of sharing. This is a big difference—between saving from damnation and sharing the light. This distinction is based on the difference between religious truth experienced as "universally relevant" and as "one and only." Authentic religious experience naturally includes the former quality, not the latter. When experienced, truth is always felt to be *universal*; it is not necessarily felt to be *singular* or *final*. In Christian terms, the God who has spoken for *all peoples* in Jesus Christ has not necessarily spoken *only* in Jesus Christ. Therefore, what animates me in the dialogue is not the conviction that you are lost without my understanding of truth, but that there *is* something missing in your life until you have seen what I have seen. You can be different, richer, if I can pass on to you what has been passed on to me.

All this paints a rather idealistic picture of the element of witnessing in dialogue. Witnessing can take in other forms, and be present in different degrees. We might enter the dialogue not from a position of strength but from one of weakness; or better, a position of searching rather than of discovery; perhaps it is a position of dissatisfaction with one's own tradition. While genuine conversation can arise from such states of dissatisfaction or insecurity, I would not spotlight them as the ideal, as does Peter Berger when he urges that the most profitable kind of religious dialogue is that "between people who are very unsure of their position rather than people who are firmly committed to their traditions."[12] Also, in holding that we give witness in order to "enrich" not to "save," I don't want to rule out the demands of situations in which we confront what we feel is genuine *evil* in the other's attitude or practices; then the conversion we seek is much more a matter of *metanoia* [Greek: repentance], of trying to "turn around" our partners, rather than of clarifying or enhancing what they already know. Or, as the liberation theologians would put it, announcing often requires denouncing.

---

11. Raimundo Panikkar, *The Intrareligious Dialogue* (NY: Paulist Press, 1978).

12. Peter Berger, "The Pluralistic Situation and the Coming Dialogue between the World Religions," *Buddhist-Christian Studies* 1 (1981): 36.

Learning

But the dialectical pendulum swings back, and just as much as we desire to witness and convert, we feel the need to be witnessed to and, yes, converted by our partners. Witnessing will go astray unless it is accompanied by listening and learning. This need to learn from others is rooted in the same "trust," described above, that the "other" has words of life to speak to us. But it is also rooted in and demanded by our own religious experience. In Christian terms, to experience the living God is not only to experience a truth and a power that is "universally relevant," to be proclaimed to all the nations; it is also to fall into the embrace of a Mystery that will always and enticingly be more than what we have experienced. To experience this Mystery of God authentically is to know for sure that we are experiencing it only *partially*. All religious traditions seem to bear witness to this aspect of religious experience—that God, Allah, Brahman [the basic principle in Hinduism], Sunyata [i.e., emptiness], the Tao—can never be known *in toto* but only *in parte*. And if only partially, then we must be open to discovering "other parts"; we must look through other windows out on to the universe of Truth and Mystery. As wonderful as is the view from our window, it impels us to look through others. Max Müller's worn dictum holds true: "Those who know one, know none."

The need to learn from others is also fostered by what cultural historians have called our age of "post-modernity." As post-moderns, we have lost much of the innocence or bright-eyed optimism that was bequeathed to us by the Enlightenment. Still hopeful about the future, we are also suspicious of all grandiose or sure-fire visions of the future. Thanks to the progenitors of the "hermeneutics of suspicion" such as Nietzsche, Freud, Marx, we have come to realize the limits and the corruptions of reason and the human heart; in our noblest and most reasoned efforts to know the truth and fashion our world, in every effort to interpret the revelation given us by God, there is the worm of *ideology*—the ever lurking propensity to use our "truth" as a means of assuring our own advantage or control over that of others. Ideology stalks our noblest ideals and projects. As Walter Benjamin has said, "Every work of civilization [we could add, every work of religion] is at the same time a work of barbarism."[13]

Such ideological abuse of religion is not just an "error" that can be pointed out and neatly removed. It is, rather, a "systemic distortion."[14] We cannot defend ourselves against such distortions by ourselves. We need others—the insights and perspectives of others who look at the world differently than we do, who can look at our visions of truth from a critical standpoint outside our circle, who perhaps can tell us how our "truth" has excluded or victimized them. We must,

---

13. Benjamin in David Tracy, *Plurality and Ambiguity: Hermeneutics, Religion, Hope* (NY: Harper & Row and London: SCM Press, 1987), 69.

14. Ibid., 73.

again, *learn* from others, so they can point out our distortions, our self-centered abuse of the truth that has been given us. Combining the insights of Max Müller and Walter Benjamin, we can say, "Those who know one, turn that one into a work of barbarism."

But our heightened awareness of the *need* to learn from others does not diminish our realization of the *difficulty* of doing so. As stated above, every interreligious encounter reveals how utterly different we really are and how much our understanding of the other is limited and clouded by our own perspectives; we are always looking into, rather than from out of, the other religion. If we somehow trust that we can look from within and genuinely understand, how might we act on this trust?

One way of answering that hermeneutical question lies along the lines of David Tracy's *analogical imagination*. Tracy states succinctly what this means for interreligious dialogue:

> The phrase can remind conversation partners that difference and otherness once interpreted *as* other and *as* different are thereby acknowledged as in some way possible and, in the end, analogous. . . . Authentic analogical language is a rare achievement since it attempts the nearly impossible: an articulation of real differences as genuinely different but also similar to what we already know.[15]

Tracy is inviting us to let our imaginations have free play as we attempt to "pass over" to the differences in the other religions; entering into these differences we may well discover that the very strangeness and difference becomes for us an unthought-of *possibility*. What was foreign, perhaps threatening, now becomes an invitation. The "other" in its otherness becomes a *disclosure* of new possibility, new truth. The other becomes analogical: both dissimilar and similar at the same time. In Tracy's words:

> In the to-and-fro movement of the game of conversation where the question or subject matter is allowed to "take over," we learn to abjure our constant temptation to control all reality by reducing all difference to the "same" (viz., what "we" already believe). In that same to-and-fro movement of conversation, we learn to allow the other, the different, to become other *for us*—i.e., as a genuinely *possible* mode-of-being-in-the-world, *as* other, *as* different, *as* possible, thus as a similarity-in-difference, an analogy.[16]

Tracy's advice helps, but we feel the need for more concrete direction. How to put this analogical imagination into practice? Where do we start? Answers to

---

15. Ibid., 93.

16. Tracy, "Christianity in the Wider Context," 18.

such practical questions can be found, I suggest, in the new context for interreligious dialogue that is presented by our contemporary world.

A New Context and *kairos*[17] for Dialogue

The title of a recently published book by David Lochhead captures what mainline Christian churches are growing aware of: a "dialogical imperative."[18] No doubt, this imperative is fed by the more philosophical considerations we have already mentioned: given the "lack of foundations," dialogue is the only show in town for an authentic pursuit of truth, and given the post-modern awareness of ideology, we have to talk with others to keep ourselves from turning "truth" into tools of oppression. There are also more expressly religious and theological reasons why the Second Vatican Council[19] and recent statements of the World Council of Churches[20] have pointed to interreligious dialogue as an imperative for all Christians.

Two pivotal Christian beliefs convince Christians that dialogue is no longer a frill that can be pursued on Sunday afternoon when the rest of the chores are done, but something that pertains to the essence of Christian life. (1) The God of Abraham and of Jesus is a God whose love and revealing activity are universal and not to be confined to any one period or people; this means that there is most likely revelatory "gold in the hills" of other religions. (2) Also, if the entire law and the prophets are indeed summarized in the law of love of neighbor, then respecting and listening to our non-Christian neighbors has a clear priority over subjecting them to doctrinal claims about the finality of Christ and the inadequacy of extra-biblical religion. The ethics of love takes precedence over the doctrine of uniqueness.

Recognizing the validity of these reasons for the dialogical imperative, I want to suggest that our present-day world confronts us with an even greater and more urgent need for interreligious cooperation and conversation. It is a need that not only places dialogue in the center stage of every religion's concern but, in doing so, provides new opportunities for an even richer, more fruitful interreligious encounter. I am talking about the need for *liberation*.

---

17. Greek for "opportune time."

18. David Lochhead, *The Dialogical Imperative* (Maryknoll: Orbis Books and London: SCM Press, 1988).

19. See the Vatican II document *Nostra Aetate* (Declaration of the Church to Non-Christian Religions), promulgated by Pope Paul VI on October 28, 1965.

20. The World Council of Churches (WCC) is the global communion of Protestant churches organized in 1948 and headquartered at Geneva, Switzerland. In 1979 they produced *Guidelines for Dialogue with People of Living Faiths and Ideologies* (Geneva: WCC, 1979).

Liberation: Demanding and Facilitating Dialogue

Somewhat audaciously I am taking up the battered question of a "common core" within all religions. Today, most authorities have long dismissed this question as either impossible (we can never tell) or dangerous (the common core is defined by *me* for *you*). Certainly I do not want to resurrect the quest for a neatly defined "common essence" within all religions that can be found if we just scratch away the differing cultural accretions.[21] And yet, with others, I believe that although the religions of the world are apples and oranges and are more different than they are alike, still there is a quality of "fruit-fulness" that characterizes them all and out of which a "common ground" for shared conversation can be established.

What this commonality is, is hard to find or define. Some still look for it in the depths (or heights) of mystical experience.[22] Others find it in the shared concern of all religions to move their followers from ego-centeredness to Reality-centeredness.[23] Vatican II's *Nostra Aetate* holds to the more traditional and cautious assertion that all religions deal with common questions and concerns that have weighed on humankind since its birth. Revisionist theologians would seem to concur when they claim that there is a "common human experience" that serves as the sounding-board and criterion for the truth-claims of all religions.[24]

I suggest that our contemporary world enables us, not so happily, to lend precision to this quest for what might be common to our varied religious pursuits. Today there are particular, concrete questions, dangers, problems that, willy-nilly, are confronting all religions and demanding responses from them. They are questions that transcend cultural and religious differences, and if they do not require the religions to look at each other, they certainly require them all to look in the same direction. They touch *all* religions because they are the kind of questions that not only demand immediate attention but cannot be answered, so it seems, without some kind of transformation of the human species, without some kind of new vision or new way of understanding who we are as humans and how we are to live on this dizzying, threatened planet. In calling for a radically different way of viewing our world and acting in it, in confronting the

---

21. Arnold Toynbee, "The Task of Disengaging the Essence from the Non-essentials in Mankind's Religious Heritage," in *An Historian's Approach to Religion* (London and NY: Oxford University Press, 1956), 261–83.

22. Thomas Merton, *The Asian Journal of Thomas Merton*, eds. Naomi Burton, et al. (NY: New Directions Books and London: Sheldon Press, 1968), 311, 315; David Steindl-Rast, "Who is Jesus Christ for Us Today?" in *The Christ and the Bodhisattva*, eds. Donald S. Lopez Jr. and Steven C. Rockefeller (Albany: State University of New York Press, 1987), 99–116.

23. John Hick, "On Grading Religions," *Religious Studies* 17, no. 4 (1981): 464–7; Tracy, *Plurality and Ambiguity*, 84, 89–90.

24. Schubert Ogden, "What is Theology?" *The Journal of Religion*, 52, no. 1 (1972): 22–40; David Tracy, *Blessed Rage for Order: The New Pluralism in Theology* (NY: Seabury, 1975), 43–63.

limits of the human condition as we know it, they are *religious* questions—questions that every religion either has tried to answer, or will want to answer, or will be required to answer.

What is common to these cross-cultural, cross-religious questions is that all of them, in different ways, are calling for some form of this-worldly, earthly (as opposed to purely spiritual) *liberation*. Our contemporary world is a world aware, as never before so it seems, of oppression—oppression in an array of horrible forms. It is, in other words, a world painfully aware of the need for liberation, for breaking bonds, for preserving, restoring, fostering life. I am suggesting, therefore, that *liberation*—what it is and how to achieve it—constitutes a new arena for the encounter of religions. Briefly, I will list (more is not possible or necessary at the moment) the forms of oppression and needed liberation that can gather all religions into a new community of concern and conversation.

A World in Need of Liberation

1. *Liberation from physical suffering.* Certainly most of us are familiar with—to the point, perhaps, of immunity—the appalling statistics about the vast numbers of people who suffer chronically from some form or forms of physical suffering because they are deprived of the most fundamental human necessities. They—and most painfully, their children—suffer because they do not have enough to eat, or do not have a balanced diet, or do not have a reliable or clean water supply, or must live in disease-infested conditions, or do not have access to needed medical care or supplies. We are told that the majority of our earth's population lives in some such conditions.

For more and more people, such realities scream to heaven and to religious sensitivities. Whatever their tradition, religious believers are coming to feel that their religion must confront such basic physical needs and sufferings and that whatever salvation or enlightenment or *moksha*[25] may mean, such beliefs have to say something about this kind of suffering. Granted that we have to bear with the effects of karma,[26] granted that we will never realize the fullness of the kingdom, granted that *dukkha*[27] adheres to the human condition, granted that there will be another life here or elsewhere—still, Hindus, Christians, Jews, Muslims, Buddhists are recognizing that if any of these traditional beliefs become the reason or occasion for ignoring or condoning such human suffering, then such beliefs lose their credibility. Even the most traditionally "other-worldly" religions are showing concern and trying to formulate some kind of response to our world's growing awareness of human suffering. Tables bare of bread and water can become the tables around which the religions of the world gather to talk and act.

---

25. Sanskrit for "salvific liberation, release," important in Hinduism.

26. Sankskrit for "'action' impacting fate," a basic concept in Indian religions.

27. Pali for "suffering," a basic concept in Buddhism.

2. *Liberation from socio-economic oppression.* The world of widespread physical suffering impinges all the more on our religious sensitivities when we face up to the further reality that most of these sufferings are not natural—that they are caused by the way human beings treat other human beings or use others for their own self-serving purposes. Oppression and injustice are chains that crisscross our globe, nationally and multi-nationally, and have become almost an "unavoidable" part of socio-economic and political structures. Forged as they often are in the kilns of racism and sexism, these chains keep vast portions of our national or global population in bondage, denying them a voice in the decisions of power and in determining their own lives. There is a vast "underbelly" of history—people who, in their victimization, produce the labor, the raw materials, the armies that have sustained the course of history.

Yet this "silent majority" of oppressed is, today, no longer silent. Centuries of injustice are erupting in the consciousness of Third World peoples and flowing into the conscience of the First and Second Worlds. As the final conference of the Ecumenical Association of Third World Theologians (EATWOT) in New Delhi, 1981, announced:

> Over against this dramatic picture of poverty, oppression, and the threat of total destruction, a new consciousness has arisen among the downtrodden. This growing consciousness of the tragic reality of the Third World has caused the irruption of exploited classes, marginalized cultures, and humiliated races. They are burst from the underside of history into the world long dominated by the West. It is an irruption expressed in revolutionary struggles, political uprisings, and liberation movements. It is an irruption of religious and ethnic groups looking for affirmation of their authentic identity, of women demanding recognition and equality, of youth protesting dominant systems and values. It is an irruption of all those who struggle for full humanity and for their rightful place in history.[28]

As the EATWOT theologians stated, this eruption is a challenge not only for Christianity but for all religions—a challenge that does seem to be transforming the consciousness of members of all religions as they realize that unless they can speak a word of protest against socio-political oppression and announce a message of liberation, their religious words will grow more and more feeble. The hope that Hans Küng has drawn from his experience of interreligious dialogue is shared by many: "Numerous conversations in the Far and Near East have convinced me that in the future all the great religions will foster a vital awareness of the guarantee of human rights, the emancipation of women, the

---

28. Sergio Torres and Virginia Fabella, eds., *The Irruption of the Third World: A Challenge to Theology* (Maryknoll: Orbis Books, 1983), 195.

realization of social justice, and the immorality of war."[29] Thus the need for socio-economic justice is calling all religions to a forum in which they all need to and want to speak.

3. *Liberation from nuclear oppression/holocaust.* There is another form of oppression even more pervasive than that of socio-economic injustice; it grips First, Second, and Third Worlds equally. The realization that the entire population of the planet could be snuffed out by the pressing of a few buttons by a few political figures—whose political and psychological judgment and saneness we often have good cause to question—terrorizes us all. For the first time in its history, the human race is capable of something never before possible: humanocide. Humanity is able to commit communal suicide. "We thought to go to the moon, to divine the bottom of the ocean, to become God, but never did we think to wipe out humanity as such."[30]

Liberation from nuclear oppression, some would say, is the hour's most pressing and most communal issue; it touches and terrorizes all of us. Gordon Kaufman is right: "The possibility of nuclear holocaust is the premier issue which our generation must face . . . [it is among] the central and defining features of our lives as human beings in the so-called civilized world in the late twentieth century."[31] If then, as Einstein said, after the dropping of the first atom bomb, everything is different, it is also different for the religions of the world. As evinced in worldwide religious peace movements such as the World Conference of Religions for Peace,[32] religious believers are recognizing that they cannot continue with their religious "as usuals" but must draw on the riches of their traditions to address the oppressive menace of war and nuclear conflict. Peace, understood as the overcoming of this nuclear oppression, is becoming a *universal religious symbol* that challenges and calls together all religions.

4. *Liberation from ecological disaster.* Some would argue that there is an even more menacing oppression that threatens our lives and especially the lives of our children. Today, not only is the human species unjustly exploiting and killing off its own, not only is it maddeningly on the brink of humanocide, but it is also strangling the source of all life—mother earth and the eco-system. The industrial revolution, which has brought such advantages to our species, has also created an altar of consumerism and profiteering on which daily the lifeblood of mother earth is poured. Thomas Berry, one of the most forceful of earth-prophets, does not exaggerate: "Our industrial economy is closing down the planet in the

29. Hans Küng, "What is True Religion? Toward an Ecumenical Criteriology," in *Toward a Universal Theology of Religion,* ed. Leonard Swidler (Maryknoll: Orbis Books, 1987), 241.

30. R. Rapp, "Cultural Disarmament," *Interculture* 18, no. 4 (1985): 16.

31. Gordon D. Kaufman, *Theology for a Nuclear Age* (Philadelphia: Westminster, 1985), 14, 12.

32. The World Conference of Religions for Peace is a multireligious congress that first convened in Kyoto, Japan, in 1970. Religions for Peace invites world religious leaders to take part in congresses to share their goals and contribute to world peace in the spirit of interreligious cooperation.

most basic modes of its functioning. The air, the water, the soil are already in a degraded condition. Forests are dying on every continent. The seas are endangered. Aquatic life forms in lakes and streams and in the seas are contaminated. The rain is acid."[33] For Berry, such ecological oppression should precede every other issue on the international and interreligious agenda:

> For the first time we are determining the destinies of the earth in a comprehensive and irreversible manner. The immediate danger is not *possible* nuclear war but *actual* industrial plundering.[34]
>
> The issue of inter-human tensions is secondary to earth-human tensions. If humans will not become functional members of the earth community, how can humans establish functional relationships among themselves?[35]

However we might rank the need for ecological liberation, it clearly is another issue that stares all religions in the face and demands answers and actions and new visions.

> Concern for the wellbeing of the planet is the one concern that hopefully will bring the nations [and religions] of the world into an inter-nation [and interreligious] community.[36]

If the need for socio-economic, nuclear, ecological liberation is *the* "common human experience" painfully present to all religions, if in light of this experience representatives of the different religious traditions are looking into their individual soteriologies [the salvific concepts they hold dear] and realizing that they have a liberating message to announce to the world, then we can indeed claim that the religions today are standing on a common ground on which they can construct a more fruitful dialogue. And if we consider that this liberation cannot be realized piecemeal, in this or that culture or nation, but must be a worldwide, interconnected effort, then it becomes clear that a new dialogue among religions is not only possible, it is absolutely *necessary*. Worldwide liberation calls for a worldwide religious dialogue. The religions must talk to each other not only, as John Cobb has announced, to undergo "mutual transformation" but to foster world-transformation.

Which brings us to our third interrogative—if we face this newly felt imperative for dialogue, *how* can we best respond to it?

---

33. Thomas Berry, "Economics as a Religious Issue," in *Riverdale Papers X* (Riverdale, NY: Riverdale Center for Religious Research, 1985), 4.

34. Ibid., 3.

35. Thomas Berry, "The Cosmology of Peace," in *Riverdale Papers X* (Riverdale, NY: Riverdale Center for Religious Research, 1985), 3–4.

36. Ibid., 3.

How to Dialogue?

Much useful advice has been given on the "rules for dialogue."[37] Perhaps one of the simplest and most useable sets of guidelines can be found in Bernard Lonergan's "transcendental precepts" for human knowing and deciding:[38]

1. *Be attentive.* We must be open and able genuinely to listen to what the dialogue partner is saying, no matter how foreign or strange or false it might seem. This requires our being able to step outside of our own world and our own interests and convictions—not to give them up, but to see beyond them. One of the best "techniques" for attempting this is described by John Dunne as "passing over"; using our feelings and imagination, we try to follow the symbols and stories and world-views of another culture or religion in order to enter and walk in its world. We allow, as it were, the other tradition to study us as much as we it.[39]

2. *Be intelligent.* We must make the sincere effort to understand what we have experienced and heard. This, of course, is even more difficult and will call for even more stretching. Here something like David Tracy's "analogical imagination," as described above, can serve us well.

3. *Be reasonable.* This is the step many of the rules for dialogue leave out or water down. We must try to evaluate the truth or falsity, the rightness or wrongness, of what we have understood. Without such effort to judge, dialogue becomes a purely academic pastime or innocuous chit-chat—aimed perhaps at understanding the world but providing no energy to change it. And yet, in the interreligious conversation, this transcendental principle is as dangerous as it is necessary; we noted above how easily and unconsciously we can impose our criteria of right or wrong on another. We need some kind of *shared* criteria or common ground, which, however, cannot be an ontological, unchangeable *foundation*, but must be created or discovered as shared "shaky ground" within the dialogue itself. Yet as we asked earlier, how to go about this creation or discovery?

4. *Be responsible and change if you must.* What we have understood and judged to be true and good lays claim on us. If dialogue is to be honest and fruitful, we must respond to these claims. Having come to new insights, having identified the good where we did not expect it, we must live those insights and do that good. This may well mean changing certain previous beliefs,

---

37. Swidler, *Toward a Universal Theology of Religion,* 13–16.

38. Bernard Lonergan, *Method in Theology* (NY: Herder & Herder and London: Darton Longman and Todd, 1972), 3–25; cf. Vernon Gregson, *Lonergan, Spirituality, and the Meaning of Religion* (Lanham, MD: University Press of America, 1985).

39. John Dunne, *The Way of All the Earth* (Notre Dame: University of Notre Dame Press and London: SPCK, 1972), ix, 53.

attitudes, practices. It may mean, in Cobb's terms, transformation, even the kind we didn't plan on.[40] Dialogue without this possibility of conversion is like a sleek aircraft that can take us anywhere but is not allowed to land.

Conditions for the Possibility of Fruitful Interreligious Dialogue

Clearly, the obstacles to living out these transcendental principles for dialogue are many. Overcoming the obstacles is a matter of experience, perseverance, and increasing skill. I would like to suggest two conditions which, if fulfilled, will facilitate the "art of dialogue" and will help remove the roadblocks. In fact, I am tempted to state that unless these conditions are met, dialogue is bound to bog down in entrenched or imposed positions.

First of all, religious believers cannot approach the table of dialogue with claims (on or below the table!) of having "the final word," or the "definitive revelation," or the "absolute truth," or the "absolute savior." Such claims stymie each of the transcendental principles: (1) How can we be genuinely *attentive* to what is different when our final norm has judged what is different to be inferior? (2) How can we freely and with abandon apply an analogical imagination to *understand* new possibilities when our final and unsurpassable revelation has excluded any worthwhile possibilities better than our own? (3) In trying to make interreligious *evaluations* of truth and value, doesn't a definitive revelation meant to fulfill all others oblige us "in God's name" to impose our criteria on all others? (4) Finally, how can we *change* and endorse the differing visions of other religious figures if ours is the absolute savior, before whom every other religious knee must bend?[41] It would seem, therefore, that the revision of traditional understandings of "the uniqueness of Christ and Christianity" (together with similar understandings of the uniqueness of the Qur'an or of Krishna [one of the main deities in Hinduism] or of Buddha) is a condition for the possibility of fruitful dialogue.

Such a statement rankles many. Let me clarify what is intended. In questioning absolute or final truth claims, I am not at all questioning the necessity of entering the dialogue with firm convictions, with personal commitments to what one holds to be true and sacred, and with a universal message. Such clear, strong positions are the stuff of dialogue. But I am suggesting that in order for our commitment to be full and our claims to be clear and universal, they need not be final, superior, unsurpassable. For something to be *really* true, it need not be the *only* truth; conversely, to allow for *many* truths does not automatically

---

40. John Cobb Jr., *Beyond Dialogue: Toward a Mutual Transformation of Christianity and Buddhism* (Philadelphia: Fortress Press, 1982).

41. This is a reference to Philippians 2:10.

permit *any*. What I am trying to say is more clearly lived than explained. Langdon Gilkey describes it as the paradox of practice that is required of any believer in our world of religious pluralism: we must be *absolutely* committed to positions that we know are *relative*. How to combine such absolute personal commitment with a recognition of the relativity of all religious forms and figures is one of the central challenges and responsibilities of religious believers today.[42]

I venture to propose another condition for the possibility of authentic dialogue that is, on the other end of the spectrum, even more controversial than the first, for it carries the appearance of a veiled foundationalism. Picking up another pivotal element in Lonergan's analysis of the dynamics of cognitional structure, but moving in a direction different from Lonergan, I would suggest that for dialogue to really work it should, ideally, be "founded" (dangerous word!) on a conversion shared by all participants. Lonergan speaks about conversion as the foundation for applying his transcendental principles to theology: an *intellectual conversion*, by which we realize that knowing is not a matter of hearing or taking a look but of appropriating the process of experiencing, understanding and judging; a *moral conversion*, by which we attempt to *do* and live up to the truth we affirm; and especially, *religious conversion*, by which we "fall in love unrestrictedly" with the Mystery of the true and the good and so become empowered to know it and live it.[43] With his religious conversion, which sublates intellectual and moral conversion, Lonergan ends up with a form of mystical experience as the foundation of religious dialogue. This is where I want to shift directions.

Rather than calling for a common religious or mystical conversion as the starting point of dialogue, I would suggest, in light of our present *kairos* of "liberation" that presses on all religions, that religious believers begin their conversations with a common moral conversion by which they commit themselves to addressing and removing the sufferings of our race and of our planet. A shared commitment and a shared praxis toward promoting justice and socio-economic, nuclear, and ecological liberation would be the starting point (not the absolute foundation) that would enable religious believers to be attentive to, understand, and judge each other and so transform each other and the world. Let me explain how such a *liberation-centered* (or soteriocentric) model for dialogue might work.

A liberation-centered model for interreligious dialogue

I am well aware (or, I think I am) that what I am proposing as a *center* may sound like, or easily develop into, *a foundation*; and that opens the door to the danger of imperialism, for it is usually the people with the power who

---

42. Langdon Gilkey, "Plurality and Its Theological Implications," in *The Myth of Christian Uniqueness: Toward a Pluralistic Theology of Religions,* eds. John Hick and Paul F. Knitter (Maryknoll: Orbis Books and London: SCM Press, 1987), 44 50.

43. Lonergan, *Method in Theology,* 101–24, 267–93.

determine the foundation. So I want to stress that when I hold up conversion to the suffering and commitment to liberation as the starting point for dialogue, I am *proposing* not *imposing*. It is a proposal which I believe representatives from all religious traditions have accepted or will accept. The awareness of oppression and of the need for liberation is permeating and challenging religious consciousness throughout the world. The issues, as I argued above, are *religious*, for their solutions call for the energy and hope of religious values and visions; Hindus, Buddhists, Christians are realizing with increasing clarity that unless they respond to the "cries of the oppressed," they will be judged by the world as narcissistic pastimes or as opium.[44]

Furthermore, as believers allow the plight of the poor and the call for liberation to illumine their scriptures and traditions, as they review their soteriologies in the light of our world's oppressions, they realize that they *do* have a liberative word to speak, a message for the suffering planet. I have tried to argue elsewhere that all religions can endorse a soteriocentric model for liberation because all of them, in different ways and degrees, contain a "soteriocentric core," a concern and vision for the welfare of humanity in this world. The models for human welfare and liberation admittedly differ, often drastically—and here we have the stuff of dialogue—but there is a shared concern that human beings be changed and saved, in this world.[45] Whether this is indeed the case, whether there is a soteriocentric core or concern within all religions that would enable a liberation-centered dialogue, can be known, of course, only within the dialogue itself.

Granting that significant numbers of representatives from various traditions can endorse a liberation-centered dialogue, how would it function? I suggest that it might profitably follow the turns of Juan Luis Segundo's hermeneutical circle, which he proposed as a liberation-centered model for revisioning Christian theology.[46]

According to Segundo, the preliminary "warm-up exercise" for the dialogue would call on all participants to train themselves in a wary attitude of hermeneutical suspicion. Before approaching each other, they would try to train and tune themselves to detect where it is in their own beliefs and practices and scriptural interpretations they have turned belief into ideology. They need to prepare themselves for what dialogue will most likely reveal to them—instances where they have used their religion or sold out their original vision to "adjust" to the *status quo*, to curry the favor of the mighty, to hold the reins of dominance over others. That ideology inevitably creeps into all religious consciousness and practice is not the greatest of evils; far more dangerous is it to be unaware or to deny

---

44. This refers to the critique of religion by philosopher Karl Marx, who in 1844 likened religion to "opium," sedating people so they would not challenge unjust and discriminating conditions.

45. Panikkar, "The Jordan, the Tiber, and the Ganges."

46. Juan Luis Segundo, *Liberation of Theology* (Maryknoll: Orbis Books, 1975), 7–9.

that this is the plight of all religions, including one's own. With a healthy dose of hermeneutical suspicion, then, we are warmed up for dialogue.

But we are still not ready for the actual conversation with other religious believers. What the liberation theologians say of Christian theology applies to interreligious dialogue—*dialogue is always a second step*.[47] Here is the hinge-pin of the soteriocentric model for dialogue: we begin not with conversations about doctrine or ritual, nor even with prayer or meditation (though all these elements are essential to the effort to pass over to each other's traditions); rather, we begin with some form of *liberative praxis*. We engage in efforts to liberate ourselves or others or our planet from whatever form of oppression we agree to be pressing in our immediate context—and we do so, not separately in our different religious camps, but *together*.

This will require that as Hindus or Buddhists or Jews we work together in trying to identify and understand the cause of the oppression or suffering we are facing; we attempt some kind of shared socio-economic analysis of the problem and what might be the solution; admittedly the solutions we discuss will be inspired by our different religious convictions. Then we roll up our sleeves together to act—to do whatever we think needs to be done. This will, of course, require that we work with and especially *learn from* those who are the oppressed and suffering. *Liberative praxis means identifying with and learning from the struggling poor*; it recognizes what has been called the "hermeneutical privilege" or the "epistemological priority" of the struggling poor—that unless we are listening to the voice of their experience, our efforts to understand our world and our religious traditions will be vitally maimed.

With the oppressed, then, and as members of different religious communities, we work for justice or for peace or for ecological sustainability. Such acting will gather our differing communities into a common community of shared courage, frustration, anger, anguish; it will bring us together in the common experience of fear, of danger, perhaps of imprisonment and even martyrdom. It will also join us in shared success and victory in changing the structures of oppression into communities of justice, cooperation, unity.

Such liberative praxis, with its peaks and its pits, will be the matrix of—and imperative for—our dialogical *reflection*. Under the momentum of praxis, the hermeneutical circle moves to reflection, discussion, study, prayer, meditation. But in a liberation-centered method of dialogue, such pursuits will not be done only in our separated religious camps but together. Having acted together, Buddhists and Christians and Muslims now reflect and talk together about their religious convictions and motivations. Here is where the partners in dialogue

---

47. Leonardo Boff and Clodovis Boff, *Introducing Liberation Theology* (Maryknoll: Orbis Books and London: Burns and Oates, 1987), 23; Gustavo Gutiérrez, *A Theology of Liberation* (Maryknoll: Orbis Books and London: SCM Press, 1973), II.

can enter into their scriptures and doctrines and explain not only to themselves but to others what it is that animates and guides and sustains them in their liberative praxis.

What has been the experience of Christian theology of liberation might well be realized in interreligious dialogue—that when we reflect on our religious heritage on the basis of a praxis of commitment to the poor and oppressed, we find ourselves "bringing forth new treasures" from old treasures; we see and hear and understand our scriptures and our doctrines with new eyes and a new heart. In a soteriocentric dialogue, this can happen interreligiously—we can understand each other's scriptures and beliefs anew. Having heard and seen, for instance, how the Four Noble Truths[48] or the nirvanic experience[49] of *pratitya-samutpada*[50] are enabling and directing Buddhist partners in the transformation of village life in Sri Lanka, Christians can come to appreciate and appropriate such beliefs/experiences in genuinely new and fruitful ways. And Buddhists will better grasp the Kingdom of God or resurrection-faith of Christians having experienced how it sustains their efforts for justice or their readiness to risk.

This is how we might provide concrete substance for Tracy's analogical imagination. Focusing our imaginations on how we can better cooperate in working for liberation and how we do so as different religious believers, we can better awaken to new *possibilities* in the amazingly different ways each of us is inspired and directed in our commitment to justice and life. As a Christian who shared Gandhi's[51] commitment to socio-political transformation, I can "imagine" more readily the new possibilities for *my* religious practice in the Gita's[52] challenge to "act without seeking the fruits of my actions."

The base Christian communities of Latin America can serve as a practical model for carrying out a soteriocentric interreligious dialogue. In these small grass-roots gatherings, Christians have met to re-read their scriptures and their beliefs in light of their oppression and their efforts to overcome it—and in the process what had been a church of the *status quo* is experiencing new life and vision. In the interreligious encounter, what we can envision and what is already taking place in Asia are *base human communities*—communities which gather people not of one religious tradition but people of different religious beliefs who share *one commitment* to overcoming injustice and working with the oppressed.

---

48. The basic Buddhist teaching essential for achieving ultimate liberation.

49. The experience of the fading away of the Ego.

50. Sanskrit for "dependent origination, dependent arising," a basic concept in Buddhism teaching that all things arise in dependence upon multiple causes and conditions.

51. Mahatma Gandhi (1869–1948), preeminent leader of the nonviolent Indian independence movement in British-ruled India that succeeded in 1947 with the establishment of the Republic of India. He inspired civil rights and freedom movements across the world.

52. The Gita refers to the Bhagavad Gita, the most popular Hindu scripture.

In these communities, the same dynamic as that of the base Christian communities can and is taking place—scriptures are coming alive, doctrine makes sense, religious experience is deepened—between Buddhists and Christians and Hindus. Here is hope for a new form of interreligious dialogue, based on a *common conversion* to the poor and suffering.

And if the blood of martyrs is the seed of hope, we can expect ever greater life from these base human communities, for in Sri Lanka they have had their first martyr. In November 1987, Fr. Michael Rodrigo OMI, one of the most committed and successful promoters of base human communities of Christians and Buddhists, was murdered after celebrating mass with Sri Lankan villagers. His liberation-centered efforts and successes in promoting dialogue and peace between Buddhists, Hindus, and Christians stood in the way of those who preferred military solutions to Sri Lanka's divisions. His commitment to dialogue and justice remains an inspiration and a "dangerous memory."[53] . . .

---

53. Michael Rodrigo, "Buddhism and Christianity: Toward a Human Future—An Example of Village Dialogue of Life," paper presented at the Buddhist-Christian Conference, Berkeley, CA, August 1987.

The Dignity of Difference
Avoiding the Clash of Civilizations[1]

Jonathan Sacks

EDITOR'S NOTE

Jonathan Sacks (also known by his Jewish name, Yaakov Zvi) is one of the most articulate and iconic personalities of contemporary Orthodox Judaism in the United Kingdom. Until 2013 he was Chief Rabbi of the United Hebrew Congregation of the British Commonwealth, the largest, but not the sole Jewish association of synagogues—and thus of Jewish religious authority—in Britain. In recognition of his outstanding contributions to bridging the cultural and religious divides in modern British society by engaging in public dialogue on matters of religion, Sacks was knighted in 2005 and named a member of the House of Lords in 2009.

The article selected for this anthology is based on his Templeton Lecture on Religion and World Affairs, delivered May 21, 2002. In it Sacks eloquently argues against thinking in alternatives of particularistic identities, or "tribalism," and disembodied universalisms, which he traces to Platonism. While the former leads to clashes and wars, the latter, he holds, is "inadequate to our human condition" marked by particularity and diversity. Taking recourse to the Bible as "the great counter Platonic narrative in Western civilization," Sacks pleads for the "dignity of difference," by which he means that "God is to be found in someone who is different from us." According to Sacks, "the real miracle of monotheism" is "not that there is one God and therefore one truth." Instead, it is that "the unity above creates diversity on earth," which must be appreciated as such in order to realize the fullness of life. Sacks is convinced that "God is greater than religion" and, therefore, "only partially comprehended by any one faith."

---

1. "The Dignity of Difference: Avoiding the Clash of Civilizations," by Rabbi Professor Jonathan Sacks (2009), *The Review of Faith & International Affairs*, 7:2, 37–42, copyright © Institute for Global Engagement, is reprinted by permission of Taylor & Francis Ltd., *www.tandfonline.com*, on behalf of Institute for Global Engagement.

Religion has become a decisive force in the contemporary world, and it is crucial that it be a force for good—for conflict resolution, not conflict creation. If religion is not part of the solution, then it will surely be part of the problem. I would like therefore to put forward a simple but radical idea. I want to offer a new reading, or, more precisely, a new listening, to some very ancient texts. I do so because our situation in the twenty-first century, post-September 11, is new, in three ways.

First, religion has returned, counter-intuitively, against all expectation, in many parts of the world, as a powerful, even shaping, force.

Second, the presence of religion has been particularly acute in conflict zones such as Bosnia, Kosovo, Chechnya, Kashmir and the rest of India and Pakistan, Northern Ireland, the Middle East, sub-Saharan Africa, and parts of Asia.

Third, religion is often at the heart of conflict. It has been said that in the Balkans, among Catholic Croats, Orthodox Serbs, and Muslims, all three speak the same language and share the same race; the only thing that divides them is religion.

Religion is often the fault line along which the sides divide. The reason for this is simple. Whereas the twentieth century was dominated by the politics of ideology, the twenty-first century will be dominated by the politics of identity. The three great Western institutions of modernity—science, economics, and politics—are more procedural than substantive, answering questions of "What?" and "How?" but not "Who?" and "Why?" Therefore when politics turns from ideology to identity, people inevitably turn to religion, the great repository of human wisdom on the questions "Who am I?" and "Of what narrative am I a part?"

When any system gives precedence to identity, it does so by defining an "us" and in contradistinction to a "them." Identity divides, whether Catholics and Protestants in Northern Ireland, Jews and Muslims in the Middle East, or Muslims and Hindus in India. In the past, this was a less acute issue, because for most of history, most people lived in fairly constant proximity to people with whom they shared an identity, a faith, a way of life. Today, whether through travel, television, the Internet, or the sheer diversity of our multi-ethnic and multi-faith societies, we live in the conscious presence of difference. Societies that have lived with this difference for a long time have learned to cope with it, but for societies for whom this is new, it presents great difficulty.

This would not necessarily be problematic. After the great wars of religion that came in the wake of the Reformation, this was resolved in Europe in the seventeenth century by the fact that diverse religious populations were subject to overarching state governments with the power to contain conflict. It was then that nation-states arose, along with the somewhat different approaches of Britain and America: John Locke and the doctrine of toleration, and Thomas Jefferson and the separation of church and state. The British and American ways of resolving conflict were different but both effective at permitting a plurality of religious groups to live together within a state of civil peace.

What has changed today is the sheer capacity of relatively small, subnational groups—through global communications, porous national borders, and the power of weapons of mass destruction—to create havoc and disruption on a large scale. In the twenty-first century we obviously need physical defense against terror, but also a new religious paradigm equal to the challenge of living in the conscious presence of difference. What might that paradigm be?

In the dawn of civilization, the first human response to difference was tribalism: my tribe against yours, my nation against yours, my god against yours. In this premonotheistic world, gods were local. They belonged to a particular place and had "local jurisdiction," watching over the destinies of particular people. So the Mesopotamians had Marduk and the Moabites Chamosh, the Egyptians their pantheon and the ancient Greeks theirs. The tribal, polytheistic world was a world of conflict and war. In some respects that world lasted in Europe until 1914, under the name of nationalism. In 1914 young men—Rupert Brooke[2] and First World War poets throughout Europe—were actually eager to go to war, restless for it, before they saw carnage on a massive scale. It took two world wars and 100 million deaths to cure us of that temptation.

However, for almost 2,500 years, in Western civilization, there was an alternative to tribalism, offered by one of the great philosophers of all time: Plato. I am going to call this universalism. My thesis will be that universalism is also inadequate to our human condition. What Plato argued in *The Republic* is that this world of the senses, of things we can see and hear and feel, the world of particular things, isn't the source of knowledge or truth or reality. How is one to understand what a tree is, if trees are always changing from day to day and there are so many different kinds of them? How can one define a table if tables come in all shapes and sizes—big, small, old, new, wood, other materials? How does one understand reality in this world of messy particulars? Plato said that all these particulars are just shadows on a wall. What is real is the world of forms and ideas: the idea of a table, the form of a tree. Those are the things that are universal. Truth is the move from particularity to universality. Truth is the same for everyone, everywhere, at all times. Whatever is local, particular, and unique is insubstantial, even illusory.

This is a dangerous idea, because it suggests that all differences lead to tribalism and then to war, and that the best alternative therefore is to eliminate differences and impose on the world a single, universal truth. If this is true, then when you and I disagree, if I am right, you are wrong. If I care about truth, I must convert you from your error. If I can't convert you, maybe I can conquer you. And if I can't conquer you, then maybe I have to kill you, in the name of that truth. From this flows the blood of human sacrifice through the ages.

---

2. Rupert Chawner (Chaucer) Brooke, 1887-1915, was an English poet known for his idealistic war sonnets written during the First World War, among which "The Soldier" became the most famous.

September 11 happened when two universal civilizations—global capitalism and medieval Islam—met and clashed. When universal civilizations meet and clash, the world shakes and lives are lost. Is there an alternative, not only to tribalism, which we all know is a danger, but also to universalism?

Let us read the Bible again and hear in it a message that is both simple and profound, and, I believe, an important one for our time. We will start with what the Bible is about: one man, Abraham, and one woman, Sarah, who have children and become a family and then in turn a tribe, a collection of tribes, a nation, a particular people, and a people of the covenant.

What is striking is that the Bible doesn't begin with that story. For the first eleven chapters, it tells the universal story of humanity: Adam and Eve, Cain and Abel, Noah and the flood, Babel and the builders, universal archetypes living in a global culture. In the opening words of Genesis 11, "The whole world was of one language and shared speech." Then in Genesis 12, God's call to Abraham, the Bible moves to the particular. This exactly inverts Plato's order. Plato begins with the particular and then aspires to the universal. The Bible begins with the universal and then aspires to the particular. That is the opposite direction. It makes the Bible the great counter-Platonic narrative in Western civilization.

The Bible begins with two universal, fundamental statements. First, in Genesis 1, "Let us make man in our image, in our likeness." In the ancient world it was not unknown for human beings to be in the image of God: that's what Mesopotamian kings and the Egyptian pharaoh were. The Bible was revolutionary for saying that every human being is in the image of God.

The second epic statement is in Genesis 9, the covenant with Noah, the first covenant with all mankind, the first statement that God asks all humanity to construct societies based on the rule of law, the sovereignty of justice, and the nonnegotiable dignity of human life.

It is surely those two passages that inspire the words, "We hold these truths to be self-evident, that all men are created equal, that they are endowed by their Creator with certain unalienable Rights . . ." The irony is that these truths are anything but self-evident. Plato or Aristotle wouldn't know what the words meant. Plato believed profoundly that human beings are created unequal, and Aristotle believed that some people are born to be free, others to be slaves.

These words are self-evident only in a culture saturated in the universal vision of the Bible. However, that vision is only the foundation. From then on, starting with Babel and the confusion of languages and God's call to Abraham, the Bible moves from the universal to the particular, from all mankind to one family. The Hebrew Bible is the first document in civilization to proclaim monotheism, that God is not only the God of this people and that place but also of all people and every place. Why then does the Bible deliver an anti-Platonic, particularistic message from Genesis 12 onwards? The paradox is that the God of Abraham is the God of all mankind, but the faith of Abraham is not the faith of all mankind.

In the Bible you don't have to be Jewish to be a man or woman of God. Melchizedek, Abraham's contemporary, was not a member of the covenantal family, but the Bible calls him "a priest of God Most High."[3] Moses' father-in-law, Jethro, a Midianite, gives Israel its first system of governance.[4] And one of the most courageous heroines of the Exodus—the one who gives Moses his name and rescues him—is an Egyptian princess.[5] We call her Batya or Bithiah, the Daughter of God.

Melchizedek, Jethro, and Pharaoh's daughter are not part of the Abrahamic covenant, yet God is with them and they are with God. As the rabbis put it two thousand years ago, "The righteous of every faith, of every nation, have a share in the world to come." Why, if God is the God of all humanity, is there not one faith, one truth, one way for all humanity?

My reading is this: that after the collapse of Babel, the first global project,[6] God calls on one person, Abraham, one woman, Sarah, and says, "Be different." In fact, the word "holy" in the Hebrew Bible, *kadosh*, actually means "different, distinctive, set apart." Why did God tell Abraham and Sarah to be different? To teach all of us the dignity of difference. That God is to be found in someone who is different from us. As the great rabbis observed some 1,800 years ago, when a human being makes many coins in the same mint, they all come out the same. God makes every human being in the same mint, in the same image, his own, and yet we all come out differently. The religious challenge is to find God's image in someone who is not in our image, in someone whose color is different, whose culture is different, who speaks a different language, tells a different story, and worships God in a different way.

This is a paradigm shift in understanding monotheism. And we are in a position to hear this message in a way that perhaps previous generations were not. Because we have now acquired a general understanding of the world that is significantly different from our ancestors'. I will give just two instances of this among many: one from the world of natural science and one from economics.

The first is from biology. There was a time in the European Enlightenment when it was thought that all of nature was one giant machine with many interlocking parts, all harmonized in the service of mankind. We now know that nature is quite different, that its real miracle is its diversity. Nature is a complex ecology in which every animal, plant, bird, every single species has its own part to play, and the whole has its own independent integrity.

We know even more than this thanks to the discovery of DNA and our decoding of the genome. Science writer Matt Ridley points out that the

---

3. So in Genesis 14:18.

4. See Exodus 18:1-20:23.

5. See Exodus 2:5-10.

6. Reference is made to the story of the collapse of the tower of Babel according to Genesis 11.

three-letter words of the genetic code are the same in every creature. "CGA means arginine, GCG means alanine, in bats, in beetles, in bacteria. Wherever you go in the world, whatever animal, plant, bug, or blob you look at, if it is alive, it will use the same dictionary and know the same code. All life is one." The genetic code, bar a few tiny local aberrations, is the same in every creature. We all use exactly the same language. This means that there was only one creation, one single event when life was born. This is what the Bible is hinting at. The real miracle of this created world is not the Platonic form of the leaf, it's the 250,000 different kinds of leaf there are. It's not the idea of a bird, but the 9,000 species that exist. It is not a universal language, it is the 6,000 languages actually spoken. The miracle is that unity creates diversity, that unity up there creates diversity down here.

One can look at the same phenomenon from the perspective of economics. We are all different, and each of us has certain skills and lacks others. What I lack, you have, and what you lack, I have. Because we are all different we specialize, we trade, and we all gain. The economist David Ricardo[7] put forward a fascinating proposition, the Law of Comparative Advantage, in the early nineteenth century. This says that if you are better at making axe heads than fishing, and I am better at fishing than making axe heads, we gain by trade even if you're better than me at both fishing and making axe heads. You can be better than me at everything, and yet we still benefit if you specialize at what you're best at and I specialize at what I'm best at. The law of comparative advantage tells us that every one of us has something unique to contribute, and by contributing we benefit not only ourselves but other people as well.

In the market economy throughout all of history, differences between cultures and nations have led to one of two possible consequences. When different nations meet, they either make war or they trade. The difference is that from war at the very least one side loses, and in the long run, both sides lose. From trade, both sides gain. When we value difference the way the market values difference, we create a non-zero sum scenario of human interaction. We turn the narrative of tragedy, of war, into a script of hope.

So whether we look at biology or economics, difference is the precondition of the complex ecology in which we live. And by turning to the Bible we arrive at a new paradigm, one that is neither universalism nor tribalism, but a third option, which I call the dignity of difference. This option values our shared humanity as the image of God, and creates that shared humanity in terms like the American Declaration of Independence or the UN Universal Declaration of Human Rights.[8] But it also values our differences, just as loving parents love all their children not for what makes them the same but for what makes each of them unique. That is what the Bible means when it calls God a parent.

---

7. David Ricardo (1772–1823), a British political economist.

8. Adopted in 1948.

This religious paradigm can be mapped onto the political map of the twenty-first century. With the end of the Cold War, there were two famous scenarios about where the world would go: Francis Fukuyama's *End of History* (1989) and Samuel Huntington's *Clash of Civilizations and the Remaking of World Order* (1996).

Fukuyama envisaged an eventual, gradual spread first of global capitalism, then of liberal democracy, with the result being a new universalism, a single culture that would embrace the world.

Huntington saw something quite different. He saw that modernization did not mean Westernization, that the spread of global capitalism would run up against countermovements, the resurgence of older and deeper loyalties, a clash of cultures, or what he called civilizations—in short, a new tribalism.

And to a considerable extent, that is where we are. Even as the global economy binds us ever more closely together, spreading a universal culture across the world—what Benjamin Barber calls "McWorld"[9]—civilizations and religious differences are forcing us ever more angrily and dangerously apart. That is what you get when the only two scenarios you have are tribalism and universalism.

There is no instant solution, but there is a responsibility that rests with us all, particularly with religious leaders, to envision a different and more gracious future. As noted earlier, faced with intense religious conflict and persecution, John Locke and Thomas Jefferson devised their particular versions of how different religious groups might live together peaceably. These two leaps of the imagination provided, each in its own way, bridges over the abyss of confrontation across which future generations could walk to a better world.

I have gone rather further than Locke's doctrine of toleration or the American doctrine of separation of church and state because these no longer suffice for a situation of global conflict without global governance. I have made my case on secular grounds, but note that the secular terms of today—pluralism, liberalism—will never persuade a deeply passionate, indeed fanatically passionate religious believer to subscribe to them, because they are secular ideas. I have therefore given a religious idea, based on the story of Abraham, from which all three great monotheisms—Judaism, Christianity, and Islam—descend. A message of the dignity of difference can be found that is religious and profoundly healing. That is the real miracle of monotheism: not that there is one God and therefore one truth, one faith, one way, but that unity above creates diversity here on earth.

Nothing has proved harder in civilization than seeing God or good or dignity in those unlike ourselves. There are surely many ways of arriving at that generosity of spirit, and each faith may need to find its own way. I propose that the truth at the heart of monotheism is that God is greater than religion, that

---

9. See B. Barber, *Jihad vs. McWorld: How the Planet Is Both Falling Apart and Coming Together and What This Means for Democracy* (New York: Ballantine Books, 1995).

he is only partially comprehended by any one faith. He is my God, but he is also your God. That is not to say that there are many gods: that is polytheism. And it is not to say that God endorses every act done in his name: a God of yours and mine must be a God of justice standing above both of us, teaching us to make space for one another, to hear one another's claims, and to resolve them equitably. Only such a God would be truly transcendent. Only such a God could teach mankind to make peace other than by conquest or conversion and as something nobler than practical necessity.

What would such a faith be like? It would be like being secure in my own home and yet moved by the beauty of a foreign place, knowing that while it is not my home, it is still part of the glory of the world that is ours. It would be knowing that we are sentences in the story of our people but that there are other stories, each written by God out of the letters of lives bound together in community. Those who are confident of their faith are not threatened but enlarged by the different faiths of others. In the midst of our multiple insecurities, we need now the confidence to recognize the irreducible, glorious dignity of difference.

Doing Dialogue Interreligiously[1]

Swami Tyagananda

EDITOR'S NOTE

Indian-born Swami Tyagananda is a Hindu monk of the Ramakrishna Order. He has been the head of the Ramakrishna Vedanta Society in Boston since 2002 and has written extensively about aspects of Indian religions (Hinduism) and Neo-Hinduism (Vivekananda and Ramakrishna). He serves currently as the Hindu chaplain to students, faculty, and staff at Harvard University and the Massachusetts Institute of Technology.

In the article *Doing Dialogue Interreligiously*, Swami Tyagananda reflects on practical experiences in interreligious dialogue and shares valuable insights into what attitude is most appropriate for dialogue and how to go about the task of dialogue. Persons engaged in dialogue, he maintains, must do more than simply share experiences. Rather, they must keep the religious dimension alive to prevent interreligious dialogue from becoming talk *about* religion instead of an authentic sharing among genuinely religious people. "Just because a dialogue is interreligious does not guarantee that it is done interreligiously," the Swami cautions. Rather, interreligious dialogue becomes an interreligious activity only when those in dialogue truly engage "the other" by mutually accepting and cherishing that person's differences. The goal of any such dialogue is not to achieve religious uniformity, but to enable everyone participating "to lead richer, more fulfilling religious lives."

Dialogue in Daily Life

Religious diversity has been around for a long time, but it began impacting society only when people of different religious persuasions began coming in close contact with one another. With the ease of travel and increase in trade, this

---

1. Swami Tyagananda's "Doing Dialogue Interreligiously," originally published in *Dialog: A Journal of Theology*, 50:3 (2011): 227–230, is used by permission of the author.

impact has continued to increase. At least in major cities of the world, it is now virtually impossible in the course of a day not to cross paths with someone from another religion. When people of different persuasions—whether different religiously, socially, politically, or sexually—come together, it is natural for them to talk about and share their interests, outlooks, and beliefs with others. That is how dialogue in its most basic form occurs in daily life. When the exchange focuses predominantly on ideas and information related to religion, it becomes religious dialogue, and when the people involved belong to different religions, the dialogue becomes interreligious.

Dialogue occurs not only through personal conversations and encounters but also via the written word: through letters and emails, for instance. Dialogue also can occur through essays and books, followed by responses and counter-responses. That is how dialogue can occur both in real time and also spread over days, years, even centuries. It is the exchange of ideas that is central to a dialogue, not when or how that exchange occurs.

Just because a dialogue is interreligious does not guarantee that it is done interreligiously. It can be a purely secular activity when done by people who are not particularly religious. It also can be a religious activity when done by those who take religion seriously. When does an interreligious dialogue become an interreligious activity? In order to answer this question, it is necessary to examine the various motives for dialogue, the conditions for a meaningful dialogue, and the benefits of a good dialogue.

Motives for Dialogue

Dialogue is a two-way process involving at least two individuals, two groups, two ideologies, or two whatever. It is a way of engaging "the other." The engagement can occur either on an equal or an unequal footing. The purpose of an interreligious dialogue and the goal that is sought depend on how the persons concerned view religion—their own and others'. Many approaches to religious diversity are possible, but the following four models are perhaps most common: replacement, fulfillment, mutuality, and acceptance.[2]

The replacement model is sponsored by those with an exclusivist approach to religion. In this way of thinking, there is only one true religion and all others are false. The goal of all engagement, voluntary or not, is to replace the false religions with the one true religion. Those who hold this view, it may be needless to point out, hold that it is their religion that is true. The implicit idea is that not only is the truth one, but it can be expressed in only one way.

The fulfillment model fits a mindset of those with an inclusivist approach, who believe that other religions have at least some truth and hence serve a

---

2. For a more expanded explanation of these models see Paul Knitter, *Introducing Theologies of Religions* (Maryknoll, NY: Orbis Books, 2002).

preparatory purpose. The hope is that the followers of those religions will eventually be converted to the one true faith ("my faith") and receive the complete truth in all its power and glory. Those who fail to do so are believed to be permanently deprived of the eternal blessing. Real and lasting fulfillment can come only through the one true religion. The inclusivists practice toleration, so it is possible to view the fulfillment model as a toned-down version of the replacement model.

The mutuality model is based on the recognition that religions of the world are equal partners and there may be much to gain by sharing with one another and listening to one another. This model encourages the dialogic approach and it comes in many shades. In every shade the equality of religions may not necessarily be full and unquestioned. Some may see other religions as equal and worthy of engagement on the social or intellectual level but not necessarily on the religious level.

The acceptance model goes beyond mere tolerance of other religions. Here, all religions are viewed as equally true and authentic, and hence dialogue-worthy at every level. Every religion is given the freedom to express itself and grow in its own way. This kind of harmonious approach toward other religions has the strength to affirm spiritual unity without diminishing the value of religious diversity. It sees diversity not as a problem to be overcome, but as a reality to be celebrated and an opportunity to expand one's horizon.

The motive for dialogue is determined by which of these models is active in an engagement. In the replacement model, the decision already has been made. The other religions are wrong and must be brought to light. The intensity of the missionary zeal to proselytize is fed primarily by an exclusivist approach to religion. The dialogue in such a case is really a monologue. If the other must be heard, it is only to know how much work is needed to bring them on the right path. The focus is on telling them what is wrong with their way of life and why they should change it. The goal is to make "them" more like "us." In the fulfillment model, the basic motive remains the same, but the rhetoric is less aggressive and the tone somewhat generous, even if patronizing.

It is the mutuality model that provides an ideal environment for dialogue; and, if the dialogue partners are sufficiently open-minded, there is a real possibility of at least some of them embracing the acceptance model sooner or later. Even people who are not particularly religious may see the utility of interreligious dialogue on a purely secular level. Such social pragmatists reason that, since we have to live as fellow citizens anyway, it is better that we get to know one another well so we can live harmoniously, or at least tolerate one another's presence without too much suspicion, misunderstanding, and distrust.

The dialogue in the acceptance model occurs not in response to a society's need for peace and harmony but out of a natural desire to learn, to expand, and to enrich one's religious consciousness. It is fed by a kind of religious hunger to experience the presence and glory of God in as many ways as possible.

Conditions for a Meaningful Dialogue

Not every interreligious dialogue is successful, as anyone who has participated in them knows. What are the conditions necessary to have a dialogue that can be considered worth the time and energy that are expended on it? At least four conditions come to mind right away.

The first condition is that the dialogue partners accept the possibility that they may have something new to learn from the encounter. If the goal is merely to teach or to inform or to "give," with no interest in or expectation of learning or "receiving" something useful, then the dialogue becomes a series of monologues. People end up talking past one another, with no one learning anything useful. The biases, prejudices, and wrong notions remain intact. Everyone may be civil with one another, the smiles and the handshakes may be warm and genuine, but little is gained from such interreligious encounters. Everyone returns home feeling good, but it is a feeling that evaporates quickly.

On the other hand, if the desire is to share, not only to give but also to receive, then the second condition becomes almost predictable: that the dialogue partners listen to one another with respect, care, and understanding. Unless we respect the other, we won't be able to give him or her our undivided attention. When we listen to our dialogue partners with respect and attention, we demonstrate visibly that we care and are eager to understand them. The respect, if it is genuine, helps minimize the impact of one's inherited biases and prejudices, and the desire to understand may remove at least some of them.

The third condition for a meaningful dialogue is to refrain from making any assumptions. It requires that we come to the table without a predetermined agenda or goal. Nothing should be taken for granted and nothing should be considered nonnegotiable. A dialogue does not necessarily mean agreement at all levels. On the contrary, a dialogue is meant to reveal where we agree and where we do not. Ideally, this should at some stage lead to reflection on the relative value of our mutual agreements and disagreements, and which of these matter more.

Hence the fourth and final condition is that the dialogue partners speak frankly and openly not just about what is shared in common but also about where they differ. The things we share in common help bring us together. Our differences may keep us apart and even raise questions. One obvious question is, since we do (or say or believe) differently, who among us is right? A not-so-obvious question might be, is it necessary that in every form of disagreement, there is only one right answer? Instead of thinking in terms of right or wrong, it may be possible to think in terms of "different." Maybe we are all just different, with no one among us possessing a monopoly on truth. Maybe it is the same truth that we all seek and it feels different when we clothe it in ideas, symbols, words, and ritual.

Speaking in Boston in 1896, Hindu monk and teacher Swami Vivekananda[3] said, "Truth may be expressed in a thousand ways, and each one yet be true. We must learn that the same thing can be viewed from a hundred different standpoints, and yet be the same thing."[4] If photographs of a building are taken from ten different angles, no two of those pictures will look identical, and yet they are pictures of the same building. Perhaps the different word-pictures or conceptual frameworks we have about God may be of the one and the same Being? In a dialogue done interreligiously, such questions acquire importance. Everyone should be free to ask any question, to themselves or to others, and everyone should have the freedom to choose the answer that resonates with his or her head and heart.

Benefits of a Successful Dialogue

When a dialogue is successful, it brings several benefits. One obvious benefit is that it improves our understanding of the other. It is not unusual to discover that some of our deep-seated biases and prejudices were not in fact rooted in reality. That realization helps remove needless distrust and misunderstanding, and in extreme cases, even hatred. A dialogue brings people together and, when they get to know one another as fellow human beings, it breaks the ice and creates warmth. It is difficult to hate a religion when you personally know that warm, intelligent, and considerate people practice it. In a larger context, it helps promote social harmony and peace.

Another benefit is on the religious level. We may discover that every religion has something unique to contribute to the world. If survival of the fittest is the norm, then there is a reason why so many religions are still not only surviving, but also thriving. They have something precious and useful that the world needs. An interreligious engagement through dialogue thus helps us enrich our own religious consciousness. It can be endlessly inspiring to observe the multifarious ways in which the power of God operates in the world.

Odd as it may sound, interreligious dialogue often gives us a better understanding of our own religion. Some idea or some concept from another religion that we hear about in the course of a dialogue may awaken in our minds the memory of an idea or a concept from our own tradition. When we put the two ideas or concepts alongside each other and study them employing not only faith but also reason, there is an opportunity to have a deeper understanding of both. Such comparative study is immensely enriching and fulfilling.

---

3. Swami Vivekananda (1863–1902), the founder of the Ramakrishna Mission movement, was an Indian Hindu monk who represented India at the 1893 Parliament of the World Religions at Chicago, thereby making Hinduism known to the West in the late nineteenth century. See also *www.youtube.com/watch?v=Cm3hT_Zt6CU*.

4. As reported in the *Boston Evening Transcript*, March 30, 1896.

While every religion is complete in itself to bring its followers the highest fulfillment, this does not preclude us from finding through interreligious dialogue additional tools that can be integrated in the understanding and practice of our own spiritual lives. For instance, prayer as an act of communing with God is common to most religions: the love of God that draws a person to prayer is universal, although the method, the language, and the accompanying ritual vary among religions. It is not unusual to see differences even within a religious tradition. No religion is a monolithic group. Seeing how love for God manifests in others, in those from one's own religion, and also from other religions, may provide both education and inspiration to a person who takes religion seriously.

Being Interreligious

Only the mutuality and acceptance models provide a framework for doing interreligious dialogue interreligiously. Science and technology have brought us all closer to one another, sometimes uncomfortably so. In a world of shrinking distances and expanding trade and travel, our lives have become more interdependent than ever before. Any major occurrence in any part of the world now has repercussions upon us all. Being religious is no longer enough in today's world. In order to lead richer, more fulfilling religious lives, each of us must learn to be interreligious, a state of being that travels the pathless path to the truth that is beyond all religious labels.

Christians and People of Other Faiths[1]

Marcus Braybrooke

EDITOR'S NOTE

The Rev. Marcus Braybrooke is a retired Anglican parish priest involved in interreligious dialogue for more than four decades. Besides being Patron of the International Interfaith Centre at Oxford (1993) and co-founder of the Three Faiths Forum (1997), he is presently president of the World Congress of Faith (WCF), a British-based interreligious organization founded in London in 1936. The WCF is committed to fostering respect for people of different faiths by organizing conferences, gatherings, retreats, and visits, in addition to publishing the journal *Interreligious Insight*.

   The article reprinted here focuses on Christian responses to religious diversity by critically evaluating these against pivotal biblical texts and church teachings. Interspersing his theological and philosophical reflections with pointed quotes from Christian authorities past and present, Braybrooke consciously refers to "people of other faiths" rather than to "people of other religions" thus emphasizing that interreligious dialogue always happens as an interpersonal encounter. He pleads to perceive such encounters as a journey with "fellow pilgrims"—from whom to learn and by whom to be enriched—in mutual sharing of the precious gift of faith in its variety.

Introduction

Recent events have highlighted the importance of interfaith dialogue. We have to get to know each other and learn to respect one another's beliefs and religious practices if we are to live together in one society and as a world community.

---

1. "Christians and People of Other Faiths," by Marcus Braybrooke, is from *Islam and Global Dialogue: Religious Pluralism and the Pursuit of Peace*, edited by Roger Boase (London: Ashgate Publishing Limited, 2005). Copyright © 2005 by Roger Boase. Used by permission of the publisher.

On 11 September 2001—that fateful day—a young Muslim from Pakistan was evacuated from the World Trade Center where he worked. He saw a dark cloud coming toward him. Trying to escape, he fell. A Hasidic Jew held out his hand, saying, "Brother, there's a cloud of glass coming at us, grab my hand, let's get the heck out of here."

People of all faiths have held hands to support and comfort each other and to join together in prayer. We need to continue to hold hands as we shape a more just and peaceful society.

I do not, however, want to concentrate on the practical contribution that interfaith dialogue and cooperation can make to peace and social justice, which I have discussed elsewhere,[2] but to suggest that we also need to move beyond tolerance and understanding to a recognition that each faith has a precious gift to share with the world. We not only need to understand other people's beliefs and practices; we can also, while remaining true to our own faith commitment, learn from others. We should see religious diversity as an enrichment, not a problem.

Some time ago, Rabbi Dr. Shaye J. D. Cohen, speaking to Christians and Jews, said, "It is not enough simply to believe in tolerance, not enough simply to allow the other's existence. What we need is a theology on each side to validate the other's existence."[3] In recent years a growing number of Christians have come to recognize the spiritual riches of other faiths and to abandon old exclusive attitudes. This is very much a process in operation, so there are few agreed conclusions and much variety of emphasis among Christians of different churches and traditions.

This rethinking has involved looking again at what the Bible says and taking a fresh look at some Christian doctrines. Inevitably, the rethinking is conditioned by what has gone before, so it is necessary first to consider the assumptions of the majority of Catholic and Protestant Christians in Western Europe in the late nineteenth and early twentieth century—many of whom hoped that the world would be won for Christ in a generation. These assumptions, which the influential Methodist thinker Kenneth Cracknell calls the "inherited entail," were so pervasive that it is necessary to acknowledge them and then to see why they are unsatisfactory before trying to develop a new perspective.

The Inherited Entail

First, Cracknell mentions the *theological exclusiveness* of the Church, which has a long history. Some would trace it back to the New Testament and sayings, such as "No one comes to the Father but through me" (John 14:6), or:

2. Marcus Braybrooke, *Pilgrimage of Hope: One Hundred Years of Global Interfaith Dialogue* (London: SCM Press, 1992); Braybrooke, *Faith and Interfaith in a Global Age* (Grand Rapids, MI: CoNexus Press and Oxford: Braybrooke Press, 1998).

3. Shaye J. D. Cohen, "The Unfinished Agenda of Jewish-Christian Dialogue," *Journal of Ecumenical Studies* 34, no. 3 (Summer 1997): 326.

This Jesus is the stone rejected by the builders, which has become the keystone—and you are the builders. There is no salvation in anyone else at all, for there is no other name under heaven granted to men by which we may receive salvation. (Acts 4:11–12, New English Bible)

This exclusiveness is also enshrined in Church statements. From a decree of the Council of Florence (1438–45):

The Holy Roman Church firmly believes, professes and proclaims that none of those who are outside the Catholic Church—not only pagans, but Jews also, heretics, and schismatics—can have part in eternal life, but will go into eternal fire, "which was prepared for the devil and his angels," unless they are gathered into that Church before the end of life.[4]

More recently, it was said at the Congress on World Mission, held in Chicago in 1960, that "in the years since the war, more than one billion souls have passed into eternity and more than half of these went to the torment of hell fire without even hearing of Jesus Christ, who he was, or why he died on the cross of Calvary."[5]

Second, Cracknell recalls the *missionary background*. He quotes from the *Form of Agreement*, drawn up by the Serampore missionaries Carey, Marshman, and Ward, on October 5, 1805:[6]

But while we mourn over their miserable condition [that is, of the "poor idolaters" among whom they were working], we should not be discouraged as though their recovery were impossible. He who raised the Scottish and brutalised Britons to sit in heavenly places in Christ Jesus, can raise these slaves of superstition, purify their hearts by faith, and make them worshippers of the one God in spirit and in truth. The promises are fully sufficient to remove our doubts, and to make us anticipate that not very distant period when he will famish all the gods of India, and cause those very idolaters to cast their idols to the moles and bats, and renounce for ever the work of their own hands.[7]

As Cracknell says, and has himself shown in his fine study *Justice, Courtesy and Love: Theologians and Missionaries Encountering World Religions, 1846–1914*, some missionaries took a more sympathetic attitude to the religions which they encountered. We should also beware of judging previous generations by our own standards,

---

4. Quoted in Kenneth Cracknell, *Towards a New Relationship: Christians and People of Other Faith* (London: Epworth Press, 1986), 9.

5. Quoted in John Hick, *God and the Universe of Faiths* (London: Macmillan, 1973), 121.

6. "Serampore missionaries" refers to these British missionaries stationed in Serampore, Calcutta metropolitan area, and West Bengal, India.

7. Cracknell, *Towards a New Relationship*, 18–19.

nor overlook the heroism of many missionaries and the contribution that many of them made to Asian and African societies. Cracknell's point, however, is that the missionaries and their many supporters were "programmed to see the darkest and basest side of the religions and cultures among which they ministered."[8]

Third, Cracknell draws attention to the *cultural assumptions of imperialism.* Hardly anyone in Europe or North America had any doubt about the cultural superiority of Western civilization. As Thomas Babington Macaulay, who was the Law member of the Governor General of India's Executive Council, wrote in what is known as "Macaulay's Minute," "A single shelf of a good European library was worth the whole native literature of India and Arabia."[9] Western civilization was also perceived as "Christian" civilization. In 1828, for example, William Huskisson told the House of Commons: "In every quarter of the globe we have planted the seeds of freedom, civilization, and Christianity." The converse of this arrogance was "the belittling of everything that was strange as alien and exotic, childish, and laughable, belonging to the infancy of the human race."[10]

Christians today may not be brought up with this "entail"! But it has colored the debate in recent years because many of the thinkers who have struggled for a new relationship have had to free themselves from this inheritance.

Questioning Traditional Teaching

In the twentieth century a growing number of Christians questioned the dominant view that only those who believe in Jesus, or are members of the Church, can be "saved and go to heaven." They did so for a variety of reasons:

1) The biblical material is ambiguous. Commonly quoted verses, such as John 14:6, or Acts 4:12, to which we will return, need to be read in context and balanced by other passages of Scripture. The Hebrew prophet Malachi (1:11) said: "From furthest East to furthest West my name is great among the nations. Everywhere fragrant sacrifice and pure gifts are offered in my name." Jesus is reported as saying that Gentiles will share in the kingdom of God, and in the parable of the sheep and the goats, people are judged by how they behave (Matthew 25:31).

2) The Christian tradition is not monochrome. The second-century Christian apologist Justin Martyr hoped to meet Plato in heaven. On the walls of some Orthodox monasteries one can see paintings of Plato and Aristotle alongside Isaiah and Jeremiah. In the Middle Ages, Nicholas of Cusa, who was a mathematician and an influential philosopher as well as a cardinal,

---

8. Kenneth Cracknell, *Justice, Courtesy and Love: Theologians and Missionaries Encountering World Religions, 1846–1914* (London: Epworth Press, 1995), 20.

9. Ibid., 22.

10. Ibid., 23.

suggested that behind all religious differences, there was one universal religion—even if it did not include belief in the Trinity and the Mass!

In the seventeenth century, Robert de Nobili, an Italian Jesuit of a good family, who settled in Madurai in South India, started to wear the orange robe of a *sannyasi* [a Hindu holy man]. When he taught the Christian faith in South India, he said, "The law which I preach is the law of the true God, which from ancient times was by his command proclaimed in these countries by *sannyasis* and saints."[11]

3) The belief that millions who have never heard the gospel are condemned to eternal damnation is to many Christians incompatible with a belief in a God of Love. John Hick has written, "Can we then accept the conclusion that the God of love who seeks to save all people has nevertheless ordained that men and women must be saved in such a way that only a small minority can in fact receive this salvation?"[12]

4) Personal contact with people of other faiths has led Christians to acknowledge the goodness and holiness of many people who are not Christian. Sir Francis Younghusband, who founded the World Congress of Faiths, said in a radio talk:

> I have come into the most intimate contact with adherents of all the great religions, Hindus, Muslims, Buddhists and Confucians. I have been dependent upon them for my life. I have had deep converse with them on their religions. . . . It has forced me down to the essentials of my own Christianity and made me see a beauty there I had not known till then. It also forced me to see a beauty in the depths of their religion.[13]

5) Some Christians have found beauty and inspiration in the scriptures of other religions, and there are many anthologies that bring together readings and prayers from the great faiths.[14] Indeed, some Christians in India include readings from the Buddhist and Hindu scriptures in their own worship.

6) Critical scholarship has questioned whether all the sayings of Jesus, especially in John's Gospel, are the actual words of Jesus. Traditional understanding of the Christological claims of the New Testament and of the church have also been questioned by some contemporary theologians.[15]

---

11. Quoted by Stephen Neil, *A History of Christian Missions* (Harmondsworth: Penguin Books, 1964), 185.

12. Hick, *God and the Universe of Faiths*, 122.

13. Marcus Braybrooke, *A Wider Vision* (Oxford: Oneworld, 1996), 19.

14. See, for example, Andrew Wilson, ed., *World Scripture* (St. Paul, MN: Paragon House, 1991); Bede Griffiths, ed., *Universal Wisdom* (San Francisco: CA: HarperCollins, 1994); Marcus Braybrooke, ed., *Bridge of Stars* (London: Duncan Baird, 2001).

15. I discuss these issues more fully in my *Time to Meet* (London: SCM Press, 1990), 84–90.

7) The practical need to combat racism and prejudice, and to create more harmonious societies and a more peaceful world, has also been an important incentive for seeking cooperation with people of other faiths. Paul Knitter has written that "concern for the widespread suffering that grips humanity and threatens the planet can and must be the 'common cause' for all religions."[16]

For these and other reasons, there is now a vigorous debate in the Churches, about the appropriate attitude that Christians should adopt toward people of other faiths.

Different Christian Attitudes to Other Faiths

The views of Christians on the relation of Christianity to other faiths are, following Alan Race, sometimes categorized as "exclusive," "inclusive," and "pluralist." It is recognized that these are very broad terms and that it is hard to pigeonhole particular scholars. Even so, the terms are quite useful and reference is often made to them.[17]

The *exclusive* view is that the Gospel is the only source of authentic knowledge of God. Jesus is the only Savior. The uniqueness of Jesus Christ is affirmed and salvation is only available through his atoning death. Karl Barth and Emil Brunner are well-known exponents of this position as well as the influential missionary theologian Hendrik Kraemer who wrote: "If we are ever to know what true and divinely willed religion is, we can do this only through God's revelation in Jesus Christ and nothing else."[18]

Inclusivism is the view that there is some knowledge of God outside the Christian church, although God's "supreme" or "final" revelation is in Jesus Christ. There is also the hope that good people who are not Christian will be "saved" by God, despite their lack of Christian faith. The second-century apologist Justin Martyr, whom we have already mentioned, wrote:

> It is our belief that those men who strive to do the good which is enjoined on us have a share in God; according to our traditional belief they will by God's grace share his dwelling. And it is our conviction that this holds good in principle for all men. . . . Christ is the divine Word in whom the whole human race shares, and those who live according to

---

16. Paul Knitter, *One Earth Many Religions: Multifaith Dialogue and Global Responsibility* (Maryknoll, NY: Orbis, 1995), 21; see also the writings of Hans Küng.

17. Alan Race, *Christians and Religious Pluralism: Patterns in the Christian Theology of Religions* (Maryknoll, NY: Orbis, 1983; rev. ed., 1993); Race, *Interfaith Encounter: The Twin Tracks of Theology and Dialogue*, (London: SCM Press, 2001).

18. Race, *Christians and Religious Pluralism*, 23.

the light of their knowledge are Christians, even if they are considered as being godless.[19]

A rather similar position is adopted by many Christians today, as, for example, by the contemporary Jesuit scholar Fr. Jacques Dupuis, who says, "Salvation is at work everywhere, but in the concrete figure of the crucified Christ the work of salvation is seen to be accomplished."[20]

Pluralism is the view that no one religion can claim a monopoly on divine revelation. All religions point to the Divine mystery, who or which is the source of all religious life. For example, the historian Arnold Toynbee wrote:

> I think that it is possible for us, while holding that our own convictions are true and right, to recognize that, in some measure, all the higher religions are also revelations of what is true and right. They also come from God, and each presents some facet of God's truth.[21]

Alan Race includes in this group William Hocking, an American philosopher, Ernest Troeltsch, a German theologian, and John Hick, a British philosopher and theologian, whose writings have been especially influential. Hick, in his *God and the Universe of Faiths*, called for a Copernican revolution in theology, involving a shift from the "dogma that Christianity is at the center to the realization that it is *God* who is at the center, and that all religions of mankind, including our own, serve and revolve around him."[22] Hick's views are partly based on the mystical awareness that the Ultimate exceeds all our thoughts and speculation. Religions point beyond themselves to the Divine Mystery. He also produces philosophical arguments suggesting that the varying personal and nonpersonal forms in which God is known are "all alike divine phenomena formed by the impact of God upon the plurality of human consciousness."[23]

Interpretation of Scripture

These varying approaches are reflected in the way Scripture is interpreted, and it is worth giving more attention to some of the verses already mentioned to show that the "exclusive" attitude is not necessarily that of Scripture.

The Prologue to St. John's Gospel, which affirms the incarnation of the Word in Jesus Christ, may also be understood to link the incarnation to the

---

19. Justin Martyr, *Apology* 46, 1–4.

20. Jacques Dupuis, *Towards a Christian Theology of Religious Pluralism* (Maryknoll, NY: Orbis Books, 1997), 328.

21. Arnold Toynbee, *Christianity Among the Religions of the World* (New York: Scribner's, 1957), 111.

22. Hick, *God and the Universe of Faiths*, 131.

23. Cited in Race, *Christians and Religious Pluralism*, 37.

universal self-revelation of God. Because this view is unfamiliar, it is worth quoting a number of writers who make this connection, for example, Archbishop William Temple, who wrote:

> By the Word of God—that is to say by Jesus Christ—Isaiah and Plato and Zoroaster and Buddha and Confucius conceived and uttered such truths as they declared. There is only one divine light; and every man in his measure is enlightened by it.[24]

John Hick writes:

> The different religions have their different names for God acting savingly towards humankind. . . . If selecting from our Christian language, we call God-acting-towards-humankind the Logos [Greek: word, sense, meaning], then we must say that *all* salvation, within all religions, is the work of the Logos, and that under their various images and symbols men and women in different cultures may encounter the Logos and find salvation. . . . The life of Jesus was one point at which the Logos—that is, God-in-relation-to-man—has acted; and it is the only point that savingly concerns the Christian; but we are not called upon, nor are we entitled, to make the negative assertion that the Logos has not acted and is not acting anywhere else in human life.[25]

Raimundo Panikkar, a Christian who has a deep knowledge of Hinduism, takes a similar position:

> The Christ the Christian comes to proclaim is Christ *present, active, unknown,* and *hidden within Hinduism.* The same Christ who lives and acts in the Hindu is the one whom the Christian recognizes as Jesus of Nazareth. This Christ present, active, unknown and hidden may be called "Iswara," "Bhagavan," or even "Krishna," "Narayana," or "Siva" [these are names of different Hindu deities].[26]

Kenneth Cracknell himself adds a reminder that religion is deeply ambiguous and can mask as well as reveal the light. He then suggests that:

> If it is truly the case that all human beings are created in and through the eternal Word, the *Logos,* we can hardly suppose that it can be the view of the author of the Fourth Gospel that because the Word has

---

24. William Temple, *Readings in St John's Gospel* (London: St Martin's Library Edition, Macmillan, 1961), 9.

25. John Hick, *God Has Many Names* (London: Macmillan, 1980), 75.

26. Author's italics, article in *New Blackfriars,* 1969. See also E. H. Cousins, *Christ of the 21st Century* (Shaftesbury: Element, 1992), 73–104.

become flesh and lived among us, that primary relationship has come to an end. On the contrary, the argument must surely be "how much more" are all human beings likely to be related to God through the one who is now risen and ascended.[27]

These views may find support in John 1:9. This says that the light, which is the Word of God, "was in being, light absolute, enlightening every man born into the world." At least that is the marginal reading in the New English Bible and agrees with the translation of the King James Authorized Version of the Bible. It suggests that the Light of God is eternally present, enlightening every person who is ever born. As the nineteenth-century Anglican scholar Bishop Westcott wrote,

> The words must be taken simply as they stand. No man is wholly des-titute of the illumination of "the Light." In nature, and life, and con-science it makes itself felt in various degrees to all. The Word is the spiritual Sun. . . . This truth is recognized here by St. John, but he does not (like Philo) dwell upon it. Before the fact of the incarnation it falls into the background.[28]

The same words can, however, be translated, as they are in the main text of the New English Bible, "The real light which enlightens every man was even then coming into the world," which applies the words specifically to the incarna-tion. This, argues the New Testament scholar C. K. Barrett, is the meaning, and the verse should not be used to support belief in a universal revelation:

> When the prologue is interpreted in terms of Hellenistic religion, and the Logos (word) thought of in Stoic manner, it is natural to see in the present verse a reference to a general illumination of all men [*sic*] by the divine Reason, which was subsequently deepened by the more complete manifestation of the Logos in the incarnation. . . . Whether John's words do in fact bear this meaning is open to doubt. In the next verse he emphasizes that "the world did not recognize him"—there was no natural and universal knowledge of the light. It was those who received Christ who received authority to become children of God. In the rest of the gospel the function of light is judgment; when it shines some come to it, others do not. It is not true that all men have a natural affinity with the light.[29]

---

27. Cracknell, *Towards a New Relationship*, 107.

28. B. F. Westcott, *The Gospel According to St John* (Edinburgh: John Murray, 1908), 13–14.

29 C. K. Barrett, *The Gospel According to St John* (London: SPCK, 1976), 134.

The question is at what point does John start to speak of the incarnation—at verse nine or earlier? The Greek allows for both translations and interpretations. Even John 14:6, in which Jesus claims to be the "Way, the Truth and the Life" may not be so exclusive as it is usually understood. The Dutch Catholic theologian Arnulf Camps writes:

> Religions are not first and foremost institutionalized systems but Ways. Aren't the Old and New Testaments full of talk about the Way of the Lord? Weren't the first Christians called followers of the Way (Acts 9:2)? Doesn't the first Sura [i.e., reading section] of the Koran talk about the straight Way? Doesn't Hinduism know three Ways to salvation? Doesn't Buddhism talk about the Eightfold Path [ultimately leading to liberation from self and world]? Here it seems to me, we have a good starting-point for dialogue.[30]

The term "way" was also common not only in the Judaism of the first century, but in Stoicism, Platonism, Hermetic, and Mandean literature, as well as in Gnostic dualism. Cracknell suggests that for those who are Christian theologians, "other religious traditions are counterparts to Christianity."[31] They set their followers' ideals and encourage them in moments of crisis. They claim to relate to the "way" of the universe—the cosmic order in which individuals are to find their own ways. Yet, Cracknell continues, "The Christian community believed then, as it must still do, that this Way of God has been most clearly discerned in the way that Jesus followed . . . the path of rejection and suffering, of abandonment and death."[32]

Another verse often quoted to support an exclusive view is Acts 4:12: "Salvation is found in no one else, for there is no other name under heaven given to men by which we must be saved." The verse is the climax of the narrative in chapters three and four, which begins with a healing miracle. Peter has said to the man who was lame from birth, "in the name of Jesus Christ, walk" (Acts 3:6). Peter then explains to the people, "It is Jesus' name and the faith that comes through him that has given this complete healing to him, as you can see" (Acts 3:16). Peter's address to the people alarmed the religious leaders. He was taken before the high priest and asked, "By what power or what name did you do this?" Peter answered that the healing was by "the name of Jesus Christ of Nazareth." The word translated here as "salvation" could also be translated "healing," and of course the two are closely linked. Yet, if Peter's answer is translated: "There is no healing in anyone else at all . . . there is no other

---

30. Arnulf Camps, *Partners in Dialogue: Christianity and Other World Religions* (Maryknoll, NY: Orbis Books, 1983), 84.

31. Cracknell, *Towards a New Relationship*, 79.

32. Ibid., 85.

name . . . by which we must be healed," it relates more closely to the context of a miracle of healing.

There must also be doubt whether Peter would so early make such a staggering claim for the unique salvific role of Jesus. It seems a statement of Lucan theology. Further, as Kenneth Cracknell says, even if Jesus is the name through whom the Christian experiences salvation, "this does not preclude the possibility that the grace and love which Jesus represents for us might be found under the names of the other religious traditions."[33] It is clear that those Christians who reject an exclusive interpretation of John 14:6 and Acts 4:12 in no way wish to minimize the Christian claim that the revelation and saving power of God is experienced in Jesus Christ, but they are open to the possibility that a knowledge of God's saving love may also be experienced in other communities of faith.

Balancing Particularity and Universality

This leads to the wider discussion of how to do justice both to the particularity of religions and to what they have in common, and, for the Christian, of how to hold together belief in the unique revelation of God in Jesus Christ and affirmation of God's universal activity and care for all people.

At the 1893 World Parliament of Religions, which was held in Chicago, Swami Vivekananda, one of the Hindu participants, said, "We accept all religions as true."[34] In this, Vivekananda was echoing the teaching of his master Sri Ramakrishna, who claimed to have reached the same mystical experience of unity with the Divine by following various spiritual paths. From this, Ramakrishna argued that the differences between religions were merely a matter of the language and the cultural conditioning of different mystics. Ramakrishna's claims have occasioned wide discussion about the nature of mystical experience. Walter Stace, in his *The Teachings of the Mystics*, supported Ramakrishna's claim: "The same mystical experience may be interpreted by a Christian in terms of Christian beliefs and by a Buddhist in terms of Buddhist beliefs."[35] The Indian philosopher Sarvepalli Radhakrishnan also said, "The seers describe their experiences with an impressive unanimity. They are near to one another on mountains farthest apart."[36]

This view, however, has been disputed. R. C. Zaehner, who was Spalding Professor of Eastern Religions and Ethics at Oxford, argued, in his *Mysticism, Sacred and Profane*, that there are different types of mystical experience. My own

---

33. Ibid., 10.

34. John Henry Barrows, ed., *The World's Parliament of Religions*, vol. II (Chicago: IL: Parliament Publishing Company, 1893), 977.

35. Walter Stace, *The Teachings of the Mystics* (New York: New American Library, 1960), 12.

36. S. Radhakrishnan, "Fragments of a Confession," in *The Philosophy of Sarvepalli Radhakrishnan*, ed. Paul Arthur Schilpp (New York: Tudor Publishing, 1992), 62.

feeling, as I have suggested elsewhere, is that there are differences of mystical experience, but, unlike Zaehner, I hesitate to assert that the theistic experience is higher than the monistic experience.[37]

Vivekananda's words at the 1893 World Parliament of Religions were a particular challenge to Christianity. The nineteenth century was the great age of Christian mission—especially by Protestant churches—in Asia and Africa. Christian triumphalism, with its claim to the unique and final revelation of God, was also evident amongst many in Chicago. In place of such aggressive Christian evangelism, Vivekananda seized the moral high ground by implying that the missionaries' call for conversions was irrelevant and narrow-minded. Instead Vivekananda appealed for universal tolerance. In his reply to the welcome, part of which has already been quoted, he declared:

> I am proud to belong to a religion which has taught the world both tolerance and universal acceptance. We believe not only in universal toleration, but we accept all religions as true. I am proud to belong to a nation which has sheltered the persecuted and the refugees of all religions and all nations of the earth.[38]

The importance of mutual respect between members of different religions is now widely recognized. Yet the relation of religions to each other is still a subject of vigorous debate. At least at the level of their teachings and practices there are significant differences between religions. For example, some religions claim that human beings have only one life on earth, others suggest that the soul comes back again and again in different bodies. There is sharp disagreement on whether God has a Son. Religious rituals are very varied. Is there a common or unifying spiritual experience? Can we indeed speak of universal human experiences?

My own view is that there is one God who made and loves all people and seeks from them an answering love and obedience. The great religions of the world are channels of that divine love and human responses to it. Because they are human responses, all are flawed. I do not think religions are all the same. Rather they are shaped by a creative experience of the Divine and by centuries of tradition and reflection. Each religion, as the American Catholic Robert Edward Whitson put it, is therefore "unique and universal: unique in that the core of each is a distinct central experience—not to be found elsewhere—and universal in that this core experience is of supreme significance for all men."[39] Each religion has a particular message or "gospel" for the whole world. As we learn from

---

37. See further my *Spiritual Experience That Crosses Religious Divisions*, 2nd series Occasional Paper 20 (Oxford: Religious Experience Research Centre, 1999), passim.

38. Barrows, *The World's Parliament of Religions*, 102.

39. Robert Edward Whitson, *The Coming Convergence of the World Religions* (New York: Columbia University Press, 1963), 97.

each other, our understanding of the Divine Mystery will grow. There are, in my view, more and less adequate pictures of God and understandings of the divine purpose. For example, traditional Christian teaching about hell—especially as a punishment for nonbelievers who never heard of Jesus—cannot be squared with belief in a God who loves all human beings.

Fr. Bede Griffiths, a Catholic priest who explored the meeting of Christianity and Hinduism at his ashram [a monastery-like center of/for spiritual life] in South India, expressed a similar approach when he wrote:

> The Buddha, Krishna, Christ—each is a unique revelation of God, of the divine Mystery, and each has to be understood in its historical context, in its own peculiar mode of thought . . . each revelation is therefore complementary to the other, and indeed in each religion we find a tendency to stress first one aspect of the Godhead and then another, always seeking that equilibrium in which the ultimate truth will be found.[40]

Yet his views may seem inadequate to many Christians who believe that Jesus is the unique and only Son of God and Savior of the world. The New Testament claim is that the Word of God was incarnate in Jesus Christ, and that in him, God is made known. The experience of faith is to have been met by the grace and love of God in Jesus Christ. The question is whether that experience is only in Jesus. A number of Christian thinkers acknowledge that members of other faiths may have a similar experience of divine grace and forgiveness, but some, like Karl Rahner, will claim that it is in fact an experience of Christ, although he is not known by name. Cardinal Francis Arinze, as President of the Pontifical Council for Interreligious Dialogue,[41] affirmed: "All human beings are included in the great and unique design of God in Jesus Christ, even when they are not aware of it."[42] That is to say there is one saving act—the death of Christ—for all people, but there are those who benefit from it without conscious faith in Jesus Christ.

Cardinal Arinze's remarks raise questions about how Christians understand the work of Christ, often known as the Atonement. A traditional belief is that Jesus Christ died on the cross for the sins of the whole world. If that is thought of as an objective event, which altered humanity's standing in relation to God, then the belief itself implies that it is significant for all people. An alternative understanding of the meaning of the death of Jesus is to think of it in a more personal and subjective way. By his willingness to die on the cross, Jesus showed

---

40. Bede Griffiths, *Return to the Centre* (London: Collins, 1976), 86–7.

41. Cardinal Arinze, a Nigerian, born 1932, was one of the principal advisors to Pope John Paul II and President of the Pontifical Council for Interreligious Dialogue from 1984-2002.

42. "The Christian Commitment to Interreligious Dialogue," *L'Osservatore Romano,* July 17, 1989, para 3 and para 9.

that there is no limit to God's love for us. To believe this is to experience an inner change that frees the believer from fear and, by deepening his or her compassion, makes the believer sorry for his or her selfishness and lack of love. In gratitude the believer makes a self-offering to the service of the Lord.

For myself, the story of Jesus' death on the cross is the place where I have known most vividly the unlimited love and forgiveness of God, which has helped to free me from self-doubt and fear and has enabled me to grow in love for others. I am glad to witness to this divine mercy and long for others to experience such forgiveness and peace for themselves. I do not, however, feel the need to pass judgment on the spiritual journey and experience of others. The interfaith sharing for which I long, of which there is still too little, is to speak to each other of our experience of the grace of God—"telling one another our beautiful names for God."[43] As the blind man in St John's Gospel says, "One thing I know, that whereas I was blind *now* I see" (9:25). If others can say the same, then we should rejoice together and learn from each other's story.

Some Christians, especially in the Orthodox Churches, have tried to balance the particular work of Christ and the universal love of God by emphasizing the role of the Holy Spirit. His Beatitude Archbishop Anastasios of Tirana, in a striking passage, wrote:

> "Present everywhere and filling all things," in the words of the prayer preceding almost all Orthodox services, the Holy Spirit continues to act for the sanctification of all persons and the fulfilment and completion of the salvation of the whole world: as the Spirit of holiness transferring the breath, love, and power of the trinitarian God to human existence and the universe: as the Spirit of power, dynamically renewing the atmosphere in which human beings live and breathe (it is the Holy Spirit who burns up whatever is rotten—concepts, ideas, institutions, customs, demonic structures—and offers new energy for the transforming and renewing of all things in creation); as the Spirit of truth, working and inspiring human beings in their longing and search for truth in any religious setting, every aspect of truth, including scientific, related to human life (this revelation of truth culminates in the decisive knowledge of the mystery of Christ who is the truth *par excellence* and it is the Spirit who reveals Christ); as the Spirit of peace calming the hearts and helping to create new relationships among human beings, bringing understanding and reconciliation to the whole of humankind; as the Spirit of justice giving inspiration and power for people to long and struggle for peace.[44]

---

43. This refers to the pious Muslim tradition that teaches of the "ninety-nine beautiful names of God."

44. *Current Dialogue*, WCC, n. 26 (June 1994), p. 46.

Seeing the Other as a Fellow Pilgrim

We should learn to see members of other faiths as fellow pilgrims. There are all too many people in our world who have little awareness of spiritual realities, and religious communities have a responsibility to make known their teachings. It is entirely proper to witness to one's experience of divine mercy. There is nothing to apologize for mission if it is such witness. It is natural to tell others of good discoveries we have made. If, however, mission becomes religious recruiting or proselytism, it fails to reflect God's own respect for human freedom and it is likely to be resented and to become divisive. People should, however, be free to change their religion if they feel this will help their spiritual growth, although those who change their religion, or who wish to marry a member of another faith community, often experience strong opposition and rejection.

When there is so much conflict in the world, often inflamed by religious differences, theological discussion may seem rather remote. But the more practical work of trying to remove prejudice and build up understanding, as well as encouraging communal harmony and cooperation, will, in the long run, only be successful if we change the image of the other, so that we no longer see them as "heathen" or "unsaved" or "non-Christians," but as fellow pilgrims and children of the One God.

A common liturgical response at Christian services is "Lord, have mercy upon us." Who do we mean by us? Members of the same congregation, members of the same denomination, all Christians, or all humanity? If we mean anything less than all people, our compassion fails to reflect the love and mercy of God, "who makes his sun rise on good and bad alike, and sends the rain on the honest and the dishonest" (Matthew 5:45).

5

Inter-religious Living in an Age of Globalization

Religion in the Third Millennium[1]

Martin Forward

EDITOR'S NOTE

The Methodist Rev. Martin Forward is a professor of religious studies at Aurora University in Illinois and Executive Director of its Wackerlin Center for Faith and Action. He taught Islamic studies at the Universities of Leicester, Bristol, and Cambridge. He founded the Centre for the Study of Jewish-Christian Relations at Cambridge, U.K. and served as the Director of Interfaith Relations for the Methodist Church.

Forward first came to realize the importance of inter-religious dialogue when working in the South of India. After his return to England, Forward, faced with the challenge of an extremely broad multi-religious surrounding in Britain, further reflected about inter-religious dialogue and began to publish widely on this topic.

The writing chosen for our selection here is the opening chapter of his book *Inter-religious Dialogue: A Short Introduction*. In this chapter, Forward gives a very general, broad description of religion, defining it as the "Human quest for Transcendent reality," which, throughout the history of human-kind, received different answers in what became established religions. In a more elaborate second section, Forward spells out the necessity to become inter-religious people by living together, by personal bonding, and by culti-vating friendships across religious divides, interspersing his argument with

Continued

---

1. Martin Forward, *Inter-religious Dialogue: A Short Introduction* (Oxford: Oneworld Publica-tions, 2001). Partial reprint of chapter 5 with kind permission by the copyright holder.

EDITOR'S NOTE *Continued*

several, mostly autobiographical, stories. Forward does not just appeal to good will and hospitable openness, however. He also makes the point that, since religions are dynamic entities that "grow and develop over time," religious people urged to live up to the challenge of multi-religiosity today must also address "areas of darkness where religions have . . . fallen short in their understanding of the will of Transcendent grace."

Conventional wisdom suggests that the power of religion is ebbing away in Western Europe. Although it is certainly the case that institutional Christianity is in deep decline, in other respects conventional wisdom could not be more wrong. This can be illustrated by a glance at a recent work: Rachel Morton's *One Island Many Faiths*, with its subtitle *The Experience of Religion in Britain*. This book contains seventy photographs of religious Britons and some random comments from them about the importance of their faith. It includes not only representatives of mainstream religions such as Christianity, Judaism, Islam, Hinduism, Sikhism, Buddhism, Jainism, Zoroastrianism, the Baha'i Faith, and Taoism, but also members of modern reconstructions of faith like Rastafarianism, adherents of indigenous pagan and New Age movements, and those who would describe themselves as nonaffiliated seekers after truth.

The human quest for Transcendent reality does not easily ebb away, not even in the face of the flood of skepticism and materialism that has engulfed the West in recent centuries and been exported elsewhere. In my *Religion: A Beginner's Guide* I describe how that human quest for something more than meets the eye can be discerned in humankind's earliest history or even prehistory.[2] Although the origins of the human and natural sciences, especially from the mid-nineteenth century onwards, were usually avowedly antireligious, seeking an origin for religion in, for example, sociology and psychology rather than in any genuine revelation from a Transcendent source, this reduction of theology to anthropology has by no means won out as many devoted followers of atheism hoped and believed it would. To be sure, it has wounded mainstream Christian and even Jewish religious observance, but no religion has lasted forever, a fact that fanatical devotees of one sort of faith or another (including secularists) would do well to keep in mind.

Although the thought that religions fade away and die is a hard one for their adherents to bear, it is demonstrably true in the sense that they flourish, sometimes for centuries and longer, but then die. Transcendence is eternal, whereas

---

2. Martin Forward, *Religion: A Beginner's Guide* (Oxford: Oneworld Publications, 2001), see especially in chapter 1.

human ways of obedience have their moments in the sun, then fade and expire. A case could be made that the longest lasting of all faiths was ancient Egyptian religion, which flourished from the third millennium BCE and finally petered out in about the fifth century CE.

However, there is another way of looking at the transience of religions. If one moves away from the boundaried definitions of religion so beloved of the Enlightenment West,[3] one can see that contemporary Chinese, Indian, Semitic, primal and other religions, although they have altered and adapted greatly over many centuries and even millennia, have some links with their origins in the dim and distant past in the second millennium BCE, if not earlier. Religions are living organisms, not desiccated relics, so it is entirely understandable that each religion has many and varied forms and interpretations. It is even possible to admit that dead religions cast their shadow upon living ones and may even have shaded, almost imperceptibly, into them. So, for example, modern Hinduism, Buddhism, and Jainism are all heirs to the nexus of Indian religion in the first millennium BCE, but they formulated different answers and sometimes even radically different questions to that religious milieu from which they sprang. Once we take clearly the point that religions are not static entities but are affected by culture and even by new and momentous revelatory acts of Transcendent grace, then the variegated expressions of faith in the contemporary world should be seen as natural and explicable in the context of rapid changes.

It is clear that if religions do not renew themselves so that fresh generations of people find them to be transforming institutions, not only will they ebb away, they will deserve to do so as anachronistic and irrelevant phenomena. To be sure, individuals are quite capable of taming and domesticating religions, outwardly embracing them but actually interpreting them in ways that remove their challenge to human self-centeredness. This means that not all expressions of religion are authentic. Some are indeed shallow and superficial, reflecting the wish of some of their adherents for fast-food religion. Religion, however, characteristically yields its secrets to those who are deeply committed to it and who work at appropriating its insights. For this reason, some guardians of faith and practice frown upon any change at all as innovative attempts by people to undermine religious authority and power and to sanction their own evil deeds. But this is mistaken disapproval.

The test of true religion is whether it puts people in touch with a Transcendent energy that transforms them and makes their attitudes and actions more just and loving. Does religion truly liberate us, as the Buddha taught? Does it actually help us love God, and our neighbor as ourselves, as Jesus commanded? Does it commend appropriate and energizing relationships in society,

---

3. For a fuller discussion of religions as boundaries systems, see the section on "Dialogue: a Definition" in chapter 1 of *Inter-religious Dialogue: A Short Introduction*; and also chapter 1 of my *Religion: A Beginner's Guide*.

as Confucius believed it should? The genius of religions is not that they simply offer good advice about how to live well, but that they also prescribe how this may be done. Moreover, our ability to accept and follow that guidance depends upon our willingness to look beyond shallow and surface phenomena to see deeply into the true meaning of life. Theistic religions describe this as a personal God to whose renovating power this world is porous. Buddhism and some other religions reject or ignore the idea of such a being, but are still convinced that the world works in a particular way to which most people have not yet woken up, and that it is necessary to go with the grain of the way the world works if true fulfillment and contentment are to be found.

Accordingly, if religion is to be relevant, it must make sense of the world in which we find ourselves, testing its assumptions but also willing to accept new insights and respond to them in ways that help us to flourish as individuals and in community. This means that religion is not simply the judge of new situations, asking whether they measure up to the standards that religious past precedent has set. Religion has to be humble enough to ask whether our rapidly changing world sets each faith the task of examining its own assumptions to see whether they are meaningful and beneficial for the needs of the third millennium.

Becoming Inter-religious People

In our interconnected world, it is more and more likely that people will live lives that are influenced by more than one religion. It is becoming harder, though it is far from impossible, to live in ghettos [i.e. secluded isolation]. Many people live next to neighbors of another faith. Perhaps their children will marry someone from another religion and so, like it or not, be heirs to more than one way of discerning Transcendence.

Broadly speaking, two particular areas of religious transformation are currently observable in pluralistic societies. The first is the mutual influence that comes from meeting and making friends with people of other faiths. The second is the more unusual yet increasingly common occurrence of what John Berthrong has called "multiple religious participation"[4] and Julius Lipner has designated "hyphenated religious identity."[5] We shall look at both of these in turn, though we shall see that they shade into each other.

I can illustrate the first of these in a personal way. When I first went to India in 1975, as a young man of twenty-three, I had already studied to become a Methodist minister. There I was ordained deacon in the Church of South India, though my ordination to presbyter orders was scheduled for 1978, after my return to the United Kingdom. In the Methodist ordination service to the

---

4. J. Berthrong, *The Devine Deli* (Maryknoll: Orbis Books, 1999), passim.

5. See Forward, *Ultimate Visions* (Oxford: Oneworld Publications 1995), 167. Lipner describes himself there as a "Hindu-Catholic."

presbyterate or priesthood, each candidate for ordination assents to the notion that the holy (Christian) scriptures contain all that is necessary for salvation. Upon my arrival in India, I interpreted that view to mean that Christian faith had nothing to learn from other claimed revelations of Transcendent reality. I think that I was inclined to see negative things about other religions rather than positive things. By the time I was ordained presbyter, I had returned to England and interpreted the words from the ordination service rather differently. By that time, the grace and goodness of so many friends and acquaintances of diverse faiths in India predisposed me to seek what I believed to be the best in another's interpretation of Transcendence. I had also to admit, which I did so freely and gladly after some initial and heart-searching reflection, that they had taught me to look at God in significantly different ways than hitherto. Up till then, I had been influenced by 1960s and 1970s Christian teaching in England that Jesus was your best friend. In India, I learned to modify this rather sentimental and one-sided view, though it is still widely held by some Christians. My Muslim friends taught me much about God as wholly other than humans—a God whose will is to be obeyed and whose nature remains shrouded in mystery though he is the merciful Lord of mercy. My Syrian Orthodox Christian friends from India's state of Kerala taught me that, despite God's utter holiness of being, far removed from sinful humans, we can nevertheless grow into goodness and godliness. To be sure, I could have learned both these insights from my own Methodist branch of Christianity, but I did not. It would be churlish as well as false to maintain otherwise.

So I came to believe that the words at the ordination service that the holy scriptures contain all things necessary for salvation did not mean that Christians (still less, only Methodist Christians) know everything that is to be known about God. I should have learned that from the apostle Paul when I read how, in sending a letter to the Christians at Corinth, he observed that "now we see in a mirror dimly, but then face to face" (1 Corinthians 13:11). I now interpret the ordination words to mean that the Christian scriptures witness to and reveal God as God essentially and relationally to human beings. Christians do not know everything about God. But they know enough to rely upon his grace. So do many people of other religions—if my experiences in India, England, and many other places are to make any sense to me.

To believe that God speaks positively and lovingly to other people than those who are members of one's own group does not mean that everybody believes the same thing about Transcendent reality. We do not. Jews and Buddhists do not conceive of Transcendence in the same way. The Muslim belief in one human life and then divine judgment of individuals to heaven or hell is very different from Hindu views of many rebirths of the soul until it is extinguished in Nirvana. There are intrafaith as well as interfaith bickerings and disagreements. The Methodist interfaith theologian and dialogician Kenneth Cracknell has been known to observe that he worships with people of other faith every Sunday in a Methodist church! Later in this chapter, we shall examine the importance of religious truth for and in a religiously diverse world.

Whatever we discover about the importance of truth, surely it cannot deny what we see with the evidence of our own eyes: the holiness of ordinary people of many faiths as they go about their everyday lives. "Holiness" does not mean an abstract kindliness and goodness. Rather, it means a recognition that this world is porous to Transcendent grace and goodness, which allures us into growing into its likeness. Since, in religiously diverse societies, we are bound (unless we choose to live in geographic or mental ghettos) to come into contact with people of quite different religions than ours yet who strive after holiness, we shall almost certainly be drawn into learning from each other about the ways of Transcendence in our world.

I have already described my own Indian journey into deepening dialogue and understanding. It may be helpful to offer another illustration from my own experience. When my daughter Naomi was born, she came nine years into my married life, much wanted and yet unexpected. Our friends were delighted for us. Hindu friends urged my wife and me to bring her to the local temple. When we did so, a holy woman was visiting from India. She gathered Naomi in her arms and took her into the shrine dedicated to two Hindu deities, where she blessed her and placed the sacred *tilak* [a paste-powdered mark] on her forehead. It crossed my mind that early missionaries to India like Henry Martyn and William Carey would have regarded this as an appalling and unfaithful act. (There was an amusing irony in that this event took place in a building that had once been the William Carey Memorial Baptist Church.) But this was 1989, not 1789, and, as we have noted, religions grow and develop fresh insights. I was not embarrassed by what happened, and too timid to rescue my daughter. Nor did I decide to put up with what happened for the sake of friendship: I have always believed that what you believe and what you do must go hand in hand. So I was glad and much moved that Naomi was blessed by a representative of another tradition of faith in a Hindu temple. Naomi was born in late December, so I was reminded of the visit of the wise men to the infant Jesus. It pleased me to assume that they were Zoroastrians, Persian scholars of religion who, though they returned home to their books and their learning, knew goodness and holiness and a revelatory act when they saw it; as did I, watching my baby daughter receive her blessing from a representative of a culture and a faith that had, to some extent, nurtured and sustained her father and his faith.

This need to reflect upon and work through why we do what we do in a multifaith society is crucial to the integrity of those engaged in dialogue. Many Westerners would do well to reflect that, in other parts of the world, people have long had more positive interfaith dialogical relations. In India, for generations Muslims, Hindus, Sikhs, and people of other faiths have lived cheek by jowl in friendship and mutual interaction until a recent rise in an exclusive form of Hinduism that closely identifies India with Hinduism and so marginalizes Islam and other faiths. In my edited book, *Ultimate Visions,*[6] in which people reflect on the religion to which they belong, the late Paulos Mar Gregorios, Metropolitan of Delhi and the North in the Malankara Orthodox Church, wrote, "I went to school [in India's Kerala state] where about a third were Christians, the others following Islam or different varieties of Sanatana Dharma [Hinduism]. As a child I was not brainwashed by Western missionary thinking forcing me to regard and condemn non-Christians as unsaved."[7] In a similar vein, reflecting on his Christian childhood among Buddhists and Hindus of Sri Lanka, Wesley Ariarajah, who once directed interfaith work for the World Council of Churches, has recorded that he felt "that it would be unfair on the part of God to receive us, the Christian family, into heaven and send our next-door Hindu neighbors to hell. It was inconceivable to me; it was clearly unfair. I wouldn't want to be in a heaven where our neighbors were not."[8]

Because of immigration, many people in Western countries now face these issues of squaring an outdated theology with their new circles of friends from diverse faiths, as a matter of urgent practice. Practitioners of dialogue in Britain often come across elderly white people in predominantly Asian areas of town who witness to the quality of their neighbors' faith, and their own. One such person—let us call her Mary—who is typical of many others, will speak warmly of how her Hindu friend Rama takes her shopping or invites her to dinner or to a religious festival that the family is celebrating. She will let slip the comment that she looks after the children while Rama and her husband are at work. Often, she will be puzzled and even dismayed because she has not been taught a theology, a view of God, that matches her experience of others' radiant faith and transparent goodness. Her pastor will tell her that Rama and her family are in deep darkness rather than the light of faith, or else will be unable to resolve the tension between the exclusive and parochial view of God imbibed at theological college and its unsuitability for assessing the holiness of Rama. Admittedly, things are changing. The ignorance of church pastors about other faiths is now more invincible than excusable, since, in recent years, people like me have taught quite another view of God to those being educated as Christian ministers. Still, we need to move on even from that improved situation, where we give sympathetic and objective information about other religions, to asking whether it would not make best sense of our experience to tackle the great issues of faith and belief from an interfaith perspective and with the participation of people from other religions.

---

6. Forward, *Ultimate Visions.*

7. Ibid., 113.

8. W. Ariarajah, *Not Without My Neighbour: Issues in Interfaith Relations* (Geneva: World Council of Churches, 1999), 4.

Mary remains a Christian, but is deeply impressed by Rama's faith and struggles to measure it against the tradition she has hitherto accepted that Christians have all or most of the light of truth. Her inter-religious dialogue has taught her to be skeptical of this tradition, however venerable it is. She may even begin to think that Rama's faith has something in it that her own lacks. Perhaps, she reflects, it is better to believe in many lives leading to the liberation of Nirvana [i.e. the blessed state of non-being; the ultimate goal of religious exercises and piety, especially in Buddhism] than to believe there is only one existence and then God's judgment, since, if true beliefs lead to good practice, then Hindus certainly seem to look after their old people better than many Christians do. What Mary needs is a theology, a belief about Transcendent reality, that enables her to respect the convictions of other people yet also helps her to choose what she can learn from them but also what she can, and maybe even must, disagree with. Through this process of inter-religious dialogue, Mary is on the move toward a way of believing and living her faith that is more appropriate—truer about God, herself, and her neighbor—than the one she had.

There are many people like Mary, not just in the Christian religion and in Western culture. I have listened to people of many faiths explain to me how an austere, exclusive, and condemnatory interpretation of their religion's attitude toward outsiders no longer makes any sense to them, even though they continue to cherish that religion. I was much moved when a Muslim friend told me that he had dreamed that he was dying and I was there to say prayers for him as he passed from this world to the next. Friendship enables and spurs us to talk openly about things that matter to us, including religion; it makes us see unexpected links and disagreements and encourages us to cope with working at what they mean.

The stories of my daughter and of Mary and Rama have moved us, almost imperceptibly, from the first area of mutual religious influence to that of hyphenated religious identity and multiple religious participation. Let us try to explore the area where the one area shades into another.

The urgency to puzzle through where Transcendence is to be found in the midst of religious diversity is an issue for all faithful people, but is particularly acute for some. Nowadays, more people than ever marry outside their religion. Most religions have frowned upon this, and some have not allowed it. Islam forbids Muslim women to marry non-Muslim men, but is nevertheless powerless to stop it happening in many places. Judaism, in its Orthodox form, determines who is a Jew through the mother's line, so, if a Jewish man marries outside his religion, his children cannot be regarded as Orthodox Jews unless their mother converts before the birth of the children. One result of religious authorities insisting on maintaining traditional beliefs is that such inter-religious families, who may want to be identified with religious belief and practice, feel let down and alienated. Very rarely are such religious authorities asked to justify their actions. Many people assume they are simply being faithful to their faith's fundamental meaning. Yet there are good reasons to doubt this. All religions grow and develop over time. The history of religions allows us sometimes to take a skeptical view of religious leaders, who often, no doubt unintentionally for the most part, miss the wood for the trees. We may recollect the Buddha's critique of certain Hindu leaders of his day, or Jesus' condemnation of religious men who interpreted faith in ways that laid burdens on others' backs.

When such exponents tell us that God forbids certain things, that permits us to deduce certain things about their portrayal of God. Is it a worthy or credible interpretation of God in the third millennium CE to maintain that God disapproves of interfaith or multicultural marriage?

When people who live and love in religiously diverse societies do what they feel they must, irrespective of backward-looking religious grandees, then they are drawn into a new kind of faithful living. An Indian Christian friend of mine, almost my sister, is married to a Hindu. They recently bought land to farm. They then participated in a Hindu rite to bless and sanctify the new enterprise upon which they were engaged. At about the same time, after years of lacking much formal contact with a church, my friend formally joined a nearby church. She provides an example of multiple religious participation: she belongs, in some sense, to more than one religion. Of course, she has done so for many years. People like her face these issues in relation to such matters as how to bring up children. Since religions, though they change and adapt, are essentially conservative, not only in negative ways but in the positive sense that they conserve and pass on tried and tested patterns of faith and practice, it is not easy for people to break the mold and set out on courses that have rarely been explored before and that have been regarded with suspicion if not outright hostility. But nowadays more people than ever are attempting to interpret their faith in the light of the choices they have made in a plural society that have hitherto been condemned or hardly ever tried and tested.

John Berthrong has pointed out, in his wise, witty, and entertaining work, *The Divine Deli*, that to a great extent "MRP-ing," [multiple religious participation] as he calls people's involvement in more than one religion, is a fact of life in North America. (He addresses specific situations there, but would agree that MRP-ing is increasingly visible in Europe and other areas where it has hardly ever existed before.) People borrow from variant readings of truth; they get caught up in matters of marriage, meditation, and the environment, and blend together different views from a variety of religions to locate and live out their convictions. To be sure, MRP-ing may be little more than cocktail religion for the chattering classes, for whom idle conversation is a substitute for deep commitment. That may very well be the future of religion for many people in the contemporary Western world. Still, it would be unfair to accuse all MRP-ers of that. One may criticize the gullibility of many young people who, mainly in the 1960s and 1970s but also today, have sought light from the East to clarify the meaning of their materialistic lives, and who often found conmen and con-women who brewed a potent blend of sex, money, yoga, and drugs and relieved them of their money. Gita Mehta's hilarious exposé, *Karma Cola: Marketing the Mystic East*, is a read impossible to put down. Still, the sincerity of most of these young people and their unwillingness to accept stale and irrelevant faith can hardly be denied.

MRP-ing has been a fact of life in some parts of the world for millennia, not least in China and Japan. In Nigeria, my wife's native country, not only do Christians, Muslims, and practitioners of African traditional religion live cheek by jowl; often the same family will have representatives of each of these faiths and think nothing much of it. (This is, problematically, changing, in the face of more fundamentalist interpretations of Islam, a resurgence of self-confident traditional religion, and postcolonial Christian self-absorption.) When I was a pastor in London, I was occasionally asked to bless the marriage of Japanese couples, who mostly did not speak English and were on their honeymoon. They felt, although they were Shintoists, that it was appropriate for a wedding to be conducted in a Christian church and that the bride should wear white. This is an updated variation on a traditional East Asian theme that people engage with different religious practices for different rites of passage, at birth, marriage, and death, and yet these various customs are refracted through a particular, overriding commitment. So, in Japan, a couple may be Shinto but still want a Christian blessing on their marriage, and in China a man may be essentially a Confucianist in his allegiance yet participate in Buddhist and Taoist rites at various times in his life. Even if it is the case that one religion provides the focus of MRP-ing, Berthrong writes that "it is not uncommon for East Asians to claim that they participate faithfully in more than one tradition even if this seems impossible from a Western perspective."[9] He goes on to ask in what sense he can regard himself as a Confucian-Christian, given his life experience.

So we encounter hyphenated religious identity. We have seen that some people, by virtue of their marriage, the customs of their ancestors, or for some other reason, engage for much of their lives with more than one expression of religious identity. Others take this a step further: by reason of deep personal commitment, they are devoted to more than one religion. A close friend of mine calls himself a Parsee-Christian. Brought up as a Parsee, he became attached to Christian faith as a young man. Yet the memory of his loving Parsee grandmother, whose affection and tenderness arose from her strong faith, still remains with him many years later. He has no wish to describe his religious journey as a movement from darkness to light. Somehow he has to hold both religions in tension to make sense of who he is and what he is becoming.[10]

---

9. Forward, *Ultimate Visions*, 24.

10. See also Julius Lipner in Forward, *Ultimate Visions*, 167–175.

I have argued that dialogue must be done as an interfaith effort and that such dialogue is essential to discern what Transcendence is like and how it regards us. The great and prophetic voice in this area has been that of Wilfred Cantwell Smith, the Canadian historian and theologian of religion who died in 2000. He argued that, if Christians affirm that theirs is a monotheistic faith in one creator, God, there can be no parochial Christian theology. It makes no sense at all for believers in one God to talk of "my God" and "your God." Theology must therefore be done dialogically and with an interfaith perspective so as to understand the divine reality that most Christians confess as Trinity but others differently affirm. To explore this insight was the purpose of Smith's remarkable book, *Towards a World Theology: Faith and the Comparative Study of Religion*,[11] which can be seen as the natural development of his concerns over forty years of academic and humane work. Smith believed that such a global theology was what great Christian figures like Aquinas, Calvin, and Luther believed they were exploring. They were interested in articulating a universal theology, not a sectarian one.[12] In our contemporary context, how can we embark on such an enterprise without reaching across boundaries and exploring with others? The scale of that endeavor may be greater, but it is not entirely new. The great medieval theologian, Thomas Aquinas, was deeply indebted to translations of Arab and Greek works by Muslim authors, and Wesley was persuaded of the case for a universal theology not least because of his conviction that faith and works are fruitfully and mutually related in godly living and godly dying.

If there is truly a need for a universal theology, we must be willing to join with a number of other voices in articulating it. And if it is truly universal, it must address and mend areas of darkness where religions have usually stumbled and fallen short in their understanding of the will of Transcendent grace.

---

11. Wilfred Cantwell Smith, *Towards a World Theology: Faith and the Comparative Study of Religion* (London: Macmillan, and Philadelphia: Westminster, 1981).

12. K. Cracknell, *Wilfred Cantwell Smith: A Reader* (Oxford: Oneworld Publications, 2001), passim.

Apologies to an Unbeliever[1]

Thomas Merton

EDITOR'S NOTE

Thomas Merton, OCSO (1915–1968), known also as Father Louis, was an influential Anglo-American Trappist monk, poet, and best-selling spiritual writer. Out of genuine spiritual concern, Merton engaged in interreligious dialogue with people of the religious traditions of Asia. Merton opposed any form of violence in resolving conflict, including taking an outspoken stance against violence during the racially charged civil rights movement of the 1960s. At the height of the Vietnam War in 1968, fully aware of the political crisis, he published an article proposing interreligious dialogue as a spiritual discipline and declared the Vietnamese Buddhist monk Thich Nhat Hanh to be his "brother."

In his "Apologies to an Unbeliever," Merton dialogues with an imagined counterpart, who might be an atheist or a devotee of another religion. Far from claiming to speak for all Christians, Merton admits that he himself is a conscious believer who takes his "own faith seriously" because, after all, he is "not a priest for nothing." However, urged by the distortion of the Christian witness to God's unconditional love for all, Merton feels driven to apologize to anyone outside the Christian fold for proselytization or for blunt refusal of dialogue by Christians. Convinced that "a faith that is afraid of other people is not faith at all," Merton pleads for dialogue as the way to communicate genuine faith "intelligently."

This is not going to be an easy tune to sing. To begin with, it is not one of the currently popular numbers. Still less one of the older and more timeworn routines. But I see you are already suspicious. I do not dispute your perfect right to be so. You should be suspicious. That is the first thing I have to say. Not that you need me to say it. But perhaps I need myself to say it.

---

1. "Apologies to an Unbeliever," by Thomas Merton, reprinted in *Faith and Violence: Christian Teaching and Christian Practice* (Notre Dame: University of Notre Dame Press, 1968). Used by permission of the Thomas Merton Legacy Trust.

However, if you distrust the word "apologies" and if you think that I am trying to afflict you with apologetics, please set your mind at rest. By "apologies" I mean simply what the word says. I recognize that I have been standing on your foot, and I am now at last getting off it, with these few mumbled sentences.

"But who," you say, "is behind that pronoun: who do you mean when you say 'I'? Do you mean 'the Believer'? Do you mean your Church? Do you mean the clergy? Do you mean your monastic order? Or do you just mean yourself?"

Well, in the first place, I am not entitled to speak in anybody's name but my own. I am quite sure that what I want to say will not be endorsed by many of the clergy, and it certainly is not the official teaching of the Catholic Church. On the other hand, I take my own faith seriously and am not a priest for nothing. I am a Believer, though not the aggressive kind. I would not say these things if I thought they were not in the deepest sense true to what I believe. At the same time I am conscious of the futility of being a mere respectable and secure "Believer" with a capital "B."

So I am apologizing to you for the inadequacy and impertinence of so much that has been inflicted on you in the name of religion, not only because it has embarrassed me, and others like me, but because it seems to me to be a falsification of religious truth. In fact, I am secretly grateful to you for refusing to accept so much of the arrogant dictation that they have tried to foist on you. And here you notice that I have a tendency to slip out of my rank among the capital *B*-Believers, and even to edge over a little toward your side, not because I don't believe, but just because things sometimes seem to me a little quieter and more thoughtful where you are.

But in any case, I am definitely speaking from the Christian side of the fence, at once identifying myself with the other Believers—Catholic and Protestant— and reserving the right to disagree with them and even to scandalize them a little. In these terms I speak to you, an unbeliever—or at any rate, one who cannot find it in himself to stomach what I seem to have swallowed without difficulty.

Though it is true that day by day you care less and less what I may have swallowed, and though I am in fact apologizing for the fact that there is still such an exaggerated obsession with the difference between us, I think the time has come (at least for me) to take a new attitude toward our relationship.

At this point, let us get clear about *your* identity. You are, they say, an Unbeliever. On the other hand you are not a professional and militant Unbeliever. The militant Unbeliever is, in fact, a Believer—though perhaps a Believer-in-reverse. I will take care not to patronize you by seeming to doubt your unbelief—though technically it would be more accurate to say that you are a *Non*-Believer rather than an *Un*-believer. You are one who neither rejects belief nor accepts it. In fact you have given up thinking about it because the message of faith does not reach you, does not interest you, and seems to have nothing to do with you at all. Or if it does reach you and does seem somehow relevant to you, yet you do not understand how one can know there is such a thing as a divine revelation. The concept of "revelation" is, to you, meaningless.

It is to you that I now say, with all the honesty at my command, that you are a sorely affronted person. Believers have for centuries made a habit out of reviling and disparaging you. Have they perhaps done this in order to fortify themselves against their own secret doubts? Do all these Believers believe in God, or are they more intent upon believing that they themselves are Believers? Are you—the Unbeliever—more useful to them in this devout exercise than God himself?

They not only claim to know all about you, they take it upon themselves to expose the hidden sins which (according to them) explain your unbelief. They exert themselves to make you insecure, to tell you how unhappy you are—as if you needed them to tell you, and as if they were any happier themselves! They weave a thousand myths about you, and having covered you with shame and discredit, they wonder why you do not run to them for comfort. Seeing their failure they try a different approach. Currently they are playing a game called "God is Dead."[2] But do not take this too seriously. This is only another card in an ideological card game, and what they want, in the end, is the same thing as before: to get you into their Churches. I confess I myself fail to see how the claim that "God is dead" constitutes an argument for going to church.

At this point I am making a public renunciation, in my own name at least, of all tactical, clerical, apologetic designs upon the sincerity of your non-belief. I am not trying to tamper with your conscience. I am not insinuating that you have "spiritual problems" that I can detect and you cannot. On the contrary, I am writing this for one purpose only: to apologize for the fact that this kind of affront has been, and still is, daily and hourly perpetrated on you by a variety of Believers, some fanatical, some reasonable; some clerical, some lay; some religious and some irreligious; some futuristic and some antique.

I think this apology is demanded by the respect I have for my own faith. If I, as a Christian, believe that my first duty is to love and respect my fellow man in his personal frailty and perplexity, in his unique hazard and his need for trust, then I think that the refusal to let him alone, the inability to entrust him to God and to his own conscience, and the insistence on rejecting him as a person until he agrees with me, is simply a sign that my own faith is inadequate. I do not (in such a case) believe in the love of God for man, I simply itch to impose my own ideas on others. Claiming to love truth and my fellow man I am really only loving my own spiritual security, and using the Gospel as a gimmick for self-justification.

---

2. Merton, writing in 1968, refers here to the 'death-of-God' theology (indebted to philosopher F. Nietzsche) emerging in American Protestant theology in the 1960s and reported about in a cover story in *Time*, April 8, 1966.

Let me be quite frank about it; the current fuss and shouting about whether or not God is dead, whether or not the Church (or Churches) can make the grade in twentieth-century society, whether or not the Church can regain the attention of modern man (either by guitar playing or liturgical gamesmanship), all seems to me to be rather trivial and beside the point. Where authentic religious concern degenerates into salesmanship it becomes an affront to the honest perplexities of the vast majority of men. I think, frankly, that you are entitled to be left unbothered by the sheer triviality of so much religious vaudeville.

This of course requires much more explanation than I can give it here. For instance, I do not intend to call into question all attempts at religious renewal. If I doubted for a moment that Christianity was alive and developing I would not bother my head with it at all. Yet at the same time I think a great deal of the fuss, argument and publicity in which the renewal seeks to express itself is very ambiguous. Are the Believers trying to convince themselves of their singular importance by selling a new image of themselves? I certainly do not feel that the question of religious renewal is as relevant to you as Church news releases imply. I appreciate your sometimes sympathetic curiosity, your cautious gestures of approval. Yet I think too many churchmen are still toying with the vain hope that their various institutions are going to continue to play dominant roles in society. I very much doubt it! I think the existence of the Christian in the modern world is going to be more and more marginal. We are going to be "Diaspora" Christians in a frankly secular and non-believing society. This is not necessarily as tragic as it may sound, if I can judge by the quality of the Christians from Czechoslovakia,[3] for instance, that I have met!

As you see, I am apologizing because *you* have to suffer from our illusions.

This does not make life very comfortable for you, particularly when, as may happen, you are yourself serious enough about "beliefs" to think twice about adopting one. You hesitate to believe without motives that seem to you to be really worthy of such a perilous commitment. Others are less scrupulous about it. They can have the luxury of peaceful consciences, at very low cost, and they can look down on you into the bargain. (What makes them so sure that they are God's good friends and you are not? Some theologians I know are beginning to speak differently. They are saying that you others may be closer to God and potentially more "Believing" than many of us. This is not new either. Paul had something of the sort to say to the Athenians!)

There was a time when we pursued you everywhere with foolproof arguments for religion in which, as it turned out, you were not interested. We assumed this convicted you of bad faith. More recently, the sharp insights of a Sartre[4] have reminded us that knowing all the answers in advance can itself

---

3. At the time of Merton's writing, Czechoslovakia still existed as a communist country of the European Eastern bloc states. It dissolved into the Czech Republic and Slovakia on Jan. 1, 1993.

4. French novelist-philosopher Jean Paul Sartre (1905–1980).

be evidence of bad faith. Some of us have begun to find routine argumentation rather hollow. Obviously, clear insight is a matter of intelligence and reasonable judgment, not emotion. Yet such insights are not the fruit of argument and cannot be pounded into another by debate. Perhaps if we had debated less, you would have been better disposed to receive these insights in the silence of your own conscience. Faith comes by hearing, says St. Paul[5]: but by hearing *what?* The cries of snake-handlers? The soothing platitudes of the religious operator? One must first be able to listen to the inscrutable ground of his own being, and who am I to say that your reservations about religious commitment do not protect, in you, this kind of listening?

The "absence of God" and the "silence of God" in the modern world are not only evident, but they are facts of profound *religious* significance.

What do these metaphorical expressions mean? They refer obviously to another metaphorical concept, that of "communication" between man and God. To say that "God is absent" and "God is silent" is to say that the familiar concept of "communication" between man and God has broken down. And if you are an Unbeliever it is often enough because such communication is, to you, incredible. We, on the other hand, have insisted more and more that communication with God was credible and was in fact taking place: when *we* spoke, *God* spoke. Unfortunately, the terms in which we have continued to say this did little to make the idea acceptable, or even conceivable, to you. We keep insisting that we and God deal with each other morning, noon and night over closed-circuit TV. These pious metaphors are permissible with certain reservations, but to try to force them on you can border on blasphemous idiocy. Thus our very language itself (to many of us still adequate) has tended to become an important element in the absence and the silence of God. Does it occur to us that instead of revealing him we are hiding him? As a matter of fact, the Second Vatican Council[6] formally admitted this. In the Constitution on the Church in the Modern World we read that "Believers can have more than a little to do with the birth of atheism" when by their deficiencies "they must be said to conceal rather than reveal the authentic face of God and religion" (no. 19).[7]

Whatever one may choose to make of this absence and this silence of God they have to be accepted as primary religious facts of our time. There is no use trying to ignore them, to act as if they could not possibly have happened, or to blame them all on somebody else. Much as I might wish that all men shared my faith—and I wish they did—there is no point in my sitting and dreaming about it, when in fact I live in a world in which God is silent, from which he is apparently absent, in which the conventional routines

---

5. See Romans 10:17.

6. The Second Vatican Council was held in Rome during the years 1962–1965.

7. *Gaudium et Spes*, promulgated Dec. 7, 1965.

designed to celebrate his presence only make the spiritual void all the more embarrassing. Some Christians still cling desperately to the idea that if one *admits* all this, one loses everything!

To admit that this is a world to which God seems not to be speaking is not a renunciation of faith: it is a simple acceptance of an existential religious fact. It should not disconcert anyone who knows, from the Bible and from the mystics, that the silences of God are also messages with a definite import of their own. And this import is not necessarily reassuring. One thing it may imply, for instance, is a judgment on the self-righteousness of those who trust in themselves because they are fully respectable and "established." It may imply a judgment of their affirmations, and suggest that a great deal is being said by God in language that we have not yet learned to decode. Not that there are new dogmas being revealed: but perhaps things that we badly need to know are being told us in new and disconcerting ways. Perhaps they are staring us in the face, and we cannot see them. It is in such situations that the language of prophetism speaks of the "silence of God."

To turn to such a world, in which every other voice but the voice of God is heard and merely to add one more voice to the general din—one's own—is to neglect the ominous reality of a crisis that has perhaps become apocalyptic. In "turning to" this kind of world, I think the Catholic Church intends to respect the gravity of its predicament, and to do a little listening. There is certainly an enormous difference between the solemn anathemas of Vatican I[8] and the more temperate and sympathetic appeals of Vatican II for dialogue.

My apology can be summed up in this admission: we self-styled believers have assumed that we are always right, you were always wrong; we knew, you did not know; we had everything to tell you, but you would not listen. In actual fact while I certainly believe that the message of the Gospel is something that we are called upon to preach, I think we will communicate it more intelligently in dialogue. Half of talking is listening. And listening implies that the other speaker also has something to say.

I know, you do not trust this admission as it stands. There are still plenty of Christians who see the dialogue between the Believer and Unbeliever more or less as that between the old-fashioned psychiatric counselor and his client. The Unbeliever is a madman who must be listened to tolerantly until he is softened up (his "confidence is won"). Then he can be tactfully led to discover the right answers.

Without prejudice to the truth of the Gospel and to the Church's authority to teach and interpret the message of Christ, that message still demands to be understood in an authentic human situation. In this situation, men meet one

---

8. The First Vatican Council was held at Rome 1869–1870. It condemned in 'anathemas' certain convictions, threatening those who held them with excommunication.

another as men, that is to say as equals, as "fellow servants." Equals listen to one another because they have a compassionate respect for one another in their common predicament.

My own peculiar task in my Church and in my world has been that of the solitary explorer who, instead of jumping on all the latest bandwagons at once, is bound to search the existential depths of faith in its silences, its ambiguities, and in those certainties which lie deeper than the bottom of anxiety. In these depths there are no easy answers, no pat solutions to anything. It is a kind of submarine life in which faith sometimes mysteriously takes on the aspect of doubt when, in fact, one has to doubt and reject conventional and superstitious surrogates that have taken the place of faith. On this level, the division between Believer and Unbeliever ceases to be so crystal clear. It is not that some are all right and others are all wrong: *all* are bound to seek in honest perplexity. Everybody is an Unbeliever more or less! Only when this fact is fully experienced, accepted, and lived with, does one become fit to hear the simple message of the Gospel—or of any other religious teaching.

The religious problem of the twentieth century is not understandable if we regard it only as a problem of Unbelievers and of atheists. It is also and perhaps chiefly a problem of Believers. The faith that has grown cold is not only the faith that the Unbeliever has lost, but the faith that the Believer has kept. This faith has too often become rigid, or complex, sentimental, foolish, or impertinent. It has lost itself in imaginings and unrealities, dispersed itself in pontifical and organizational routines, or evaporated in activism and loose talk.

The most hopeful sign of religious renewal is the authentic sincerity and openness with which some Believers are beginning to recognize this. At the very moment when it would seem that they had to gather for a fanatical last-ditch stand, these Believers are dropping their defensiveness, their defiance, and their mistrust. They are realizing that a faith that is afraid of other people is no faith at all. A faith that supports itself by condemning others is itself condemned by the Gospel.

PART

INTERFAITH DIALOGUE
The View of Different Traditions

All are monks, but of different religious traditions; one is likely a Christian while the others are Buddhists. Maintaining their distinctiveness, they talk amiably face to face, unafraid of the exotic other and thereby displaying one of the principal virtues for engaging in genuine interreligious dialogue.

CHAPTER

The Importance
of Interfaith Dialogue
A Buddhist Perspective[1]

Venerable Havanpola Ratanasara

EDITOR'S NOTE

The Venerable Havanpola Ratanasara (1920–2000), author of the following contribution, was a Sri Lankan Buddhist monk with a master's degree from Columbia University and a PhD in education from the University of London, who lived in California since 1980. Concerned about uniting the broad varieties of Buddhist traditions present in the United States—due to immigration from numerous Asian countries the most diverse in the world—Ratanasara founded the Buddhist Sangha Council of Southern California and organized in 1987 the American Buddhist Congress. Seriously engaged in interreligious dialogue from early on, too, he served as president of the Interreligious Council of Southern California and was the official Buddhist representative to Pope John Paul II on the latter's visit to Los Angeles in 1987.

The text here reproduced is his address given on occasion of the historic "Gethsemani Encounter" (July 22–27, 1996) between Christian and Buddhist monastics held at the monastery of the late Thomas Merton at Gethsemani in Louisville, Kentucky. In plain speech, one admires the familiarity of this Buddhist with the Christian tradition, not only with biblical accounts but also with magisterial sources and contemporary documents of the World Council of Churches. Yet, what is most interesting to see is that Ratanasara explicitly

Continued

1. Venerable Havanpola Ratanasara, PhD, "Interfaith Dialogue: A Buddhist Perspective; An Examination of Pope John Paul II's *Crossing the Threshold of Hope*," a talk given at the Gethsemani Encounter, an inter-monastic dialogue hosted by the Abbey of Gethsemani, Trappist, Kentucky, July 1996. Used by permission of the Catholic Office of Ecumenical and Interreligious Affairs, Archdiocese of Los Angeles.

EDITOR'S NOTE Continued

marks some basic misperceptions of Buddhism by Christians and points to severe differences within Buddhism. However, he also emphasizes that there is no other way to come to a proper understanding than by dialoguing and dispels the fear "that by participating in it [interreligious dialogue]" the faithful "may be compromising their own beliefs." His contribution gives an impressive proof that it is otherwise.

In his published work, *Crossing the Threshold of Hope*,[2] His Holiness, Pope John Paul II, made some observations with which I, as a Buddhist, wholly agree: The Holy Father reminded us all that "What unites us is much greater than what separates us. . . . It is necessary . . . to rid ourselves of stereotypes, of old habits and above all, it is necessary to recognize the unity that already exists." Since all of you are already knowledgeable about the history of interreligious dialogue, it isn't my intention to bore you by rehashing it. But I think it is worth our while to pause every now and then, to "step back" and remind ourselves just how far we've come in the last three decades. The evidence, which confirms the Pope's observation of a "unity that already exists," is most encouraging. Formal interfaith dialogue, however, does not materialize, fully developed, out of a vacuum. It evolves gradually, in response to the needs and aspirations of the broader community of which its participants are members. The "unity that already exists," of which the Pope speaks, is the life of the community, and a tacit consensus that "what unites us" is at least as important as "what separates us." On the other hand, this pre–existing "unity" must be recognized, and positive steps taken to build on it. No less encouraging, therefore, is the evidence that what was begun some thirty years ago continues with increasing momentum.

Brief History of the Development of Interreligious Dialogue

While in recent times interfaith dialogue has become not only national but international in its scope, I cite the experience of Los Angeles as but one example, because it is the one with which I'm most familiar. Almost from the very beginning, dialogue in Los Angeles included Buddhists, Hindus, Muslims, Jews, and Christians. Since it is unique in being a truly "global" community, Los Angeles provided an ideal environment for such dialogue. Over 120 languages are spoken there. And all religions and ethnic groups are represented as well, including all major Buddhist traditions, each with its own language and customs.

---

2. New York: Random House: Knopf, 1995.

Formal dialogue, however, required a catalyst, and it was the Catholic Church which, by the enlightened leadership of its pontiffs, provided it. As early as 1964, in his first encyclical letter, *Ecclesiam Suam* [On the Church], Pope Paul VI already emphasized the need for interreligious dialogue, an attitude which was further underscored in *Nostra Aetate* [In Our Time], which was wholly dedicated to the subject indicated by the title.[3] It was *Nostra Aetate*, however, that set the stage for the beginning of genuine interreligious dialogue. This decree initiated a fundamental change in the way the Church viewed other religions. For the first time, it encouraged dialogue with them.

For its part, the Catholic community in Los Angeles lost no time following the guidelines set by *Nostra Aetate*. In 1969 the Catholic Archdiocese of Los Angeles, together with representatives of the Catholic and Jewish communities, founded the Interreligious Council of Southern California (ICSC). In 1971, Buddhist communities joined in. This became the focal point of the Los Angeles dialogue. In 1974, the Catholic Archdiocese formed the Commission on Ecumenical and Interreligious Affairs (CEIA) to coordinate and expedite its relations with other religious communities. The work of both of these organizations continues, sponsoring ongoing dialogue, but also (and just as important), informal contacts among the various participating religious organizations. These activities have enhanced considerably mutual understanding and a lessening of conflicts among religions.

Development of dialogue after these first steps was impressive. *Nostra Aetate*, to its great credit, called upon Catholics to repudiate anti–Semitism in all its forms. It also encouraged them to promote dialogue between Catholics and the Jewish community. In 1977, in Malibu, an all-day conference, the first of its kind, brought together about 50 Catholic sisters, with about as many Jewish women. Since that auspicious beginning, conferences have been held annually. It's worth noting too, that in Los Angeles, the Catholic and Jewish communities had already developed strong ties prior to *Nostra Aetate*, indeed as far back as the 1920s. And in the 1950s and 1960s Loyola University (now Loyola Marymount) became a meeting place for members of the two faiths, and the American Jewish Committee did much to encourage this. During this period, however, such contacts were mostly informal, but nonetheless important. Most significant, as well, have been the activities of the National Conference of Christians and Jews, which has its headquarters in Los Angeles and is dedicated to combating racial and religious bigotry.

Through the initiatives of both of the organizations I mentioned earlier (ICSC and CEIA), meaningful informal exchanges with the Buddhist community were begun, and have continued apace. A highlight of this process was a visit by Pope John Paul II to Los Angeles in 1987. In 1989, the Los Angeles

---

3. Second Vatican Council, *Nostra Aetate*, Declaration on the Relation of the Church to Non-Christian Religions, promulgated October 28, 1965. For the full text see *www.vatican.va/ archive/hist_councils/ii_vatican_council/documents/vat-ii_decl_19651028_nostra-aetate_en.html.*

Buddhist-Catholic Dialogue began. It marked the beginning of a formal Buddhist-Catholic communication. It was sponsored by the Buddhist Sangha Council of Southern California and the Catholic Office of Ecumenical and Interreligious Affairs. A commemorative pamphlet published in 1991 described this as a "very early and preliminary dialogue, with a great need for mutual patience and simply getting to know one another."

This is certainly true. But what I think is most significant is that this formal dialogue in fact conferred recognition on what had already been happening more informally for almost twenty years. And this "informal" communication continues to the present day, alongside more formal or "official" dialogue. This suggests that the mandate for our dialogue, far from being "imposed from on high," whether by *Nostra Aetate* or anything else, is an expression of a genuine respect and friendship, which, I would like to think, would be happening anyway. As a document prepared by the Vatican's Secretariat for Non-Christians puts it: "Dialogue does not grow out of the opportunism of the tactics of the moment, but arises from reasons which experience and reflection, and even the difficulties themselves, have deepened." This is not to suggest, of course, that *Nostra Aetate* did not provide the impetus to get it going; it surely did. But if the will to carry it forward had not existed, I think we would not be meeting here today.

Also encouraging is the evidence of international interreligious dialogue. In 1979, The World Council of Churches first published its *Guidelines on Dialogue with People of Living Faiths and Ideologies.* In the index to the fourth edition of that publication, I counted 75 major international meetings concerned with interreligious dialogue, from 1969 to 1989. And most recently, in summer 1995, the Vatican Pontifical Council for Interreligious Dialogue organized a Buddhist-Christian Colloquium in Taiwan. It was attended by ten Christians and ten Buddhist scholars, as well as four members of the Pontifical Council for Interreligious Dialogue, and many monks and nuns from a monastery in Taiwan, as well as some of the Catholic bishops in Taiwan. The attending scholars came from Japan, Taiwan, Sri Lanka, Thailand, Italy, and the United States. The very fact that an international colloquium at such a high level was taking place at all seems to me a most auspicious development.

The Prospects for an Ongoing Dialogue

Perhaps the only mistake we can make now is to allow our optimism to become complacency. While it is true that much has been accomplished by way of interfaith dialogue, there remain significant stumbling blocks to its longevity. One of the most enduring impediments to dialogue is the belief by members of the various religions that by participating in it they may be compromising their own beliefs. I would like to address this concern.

In his book which I cited at the beginning of this address, the Holy Father, with characteristic eloquence, makes another point with which any Buddhist would find it hard to disagree, and which states an important principle on which dialogue can go forward: ". . . there is basis for dialogue and for the growth of unity, a growth that should occur at the same rate at which we are able to overcome our divisions—divisions that to a great degree result from the idea that one can have a monopoly on truth." For a Buddhist, his or her faith is no bar to dialogue with other religions. The reason is that Buddhism is neither a system of dogmas, nor a doctrine of "salvation" as that term is generally understood in theistic religions. The Buddha exhorted his disciples to take nothing on blind faith, not even his words. Rather, they should listen, and then examine the teachings for themselves, so that they might be convinced of its truth.

Once, when the Buddha was visiting a market town called Kesaputta, the local people, known as the Kalamas, sought his advice. Wandering ascetics and teachers used to visit the town from time to time, and were not reticent about propagating their own particular religious and philosophical doctrines, and at the same time disparaging the teachings of others.

The Buddha advised them in this way:

> "It is proper for you, Kalamas, to doubt, to be uncertain, to not be led by reports, or tradition, or hearsay. Do not be led by the authority of religious texts, nor by mere logic or inference, nor by considering appearances; nor by delight in speculative opinions, nor by seeming possibilities, nor by the idea, this ascetic is our teacher. But rather, when you yourselves know [that] certain things are unwholesome and wrong, [that such] things are censured by the wise, and when undertaken, such things lead to harm, [then] abandon them. And when you yourselves know [that] certain things are wholesome and good, [that such] things are approved by the wise, and when undertaken such things lead to benefit and happiness, [then] enter on and abide in them."

What the Buddha's teaching offers, then, is an intellectual and spiritual "crutch" that we may use until we are able to tread the path to liberation and Enlightenment alone. While the teachings of other religions do have much in common with Buddhism, the latter is unique in its emphasis on this point. As the Buddha put it: "One is indeed, one's own savior, for what other savior could there be? When one is in control of oneself, one obtains a savior difficult to find." The Buddha compared his doctrine, the Dhamma [Pali: the teaching of the Buddha], to a raft which one uses to cross over a lake or stream, but is left behind when one reaches shore. It would make no sense to continue lugging the raft about, once it had served its purpose. So attachment to doctrine for its own sake, be it religious, political, or ideological, is illogical from a Buddhist's point of view. It follows, then, that a Buddhist needn't fear "losing" his faith by coming into contact with the faiths of others.

This principle of "eclecticism" has, in my view, two corollaries. The first is that differences between faiths should not be overdrawn, or created where none exist. For example, in his book, the Pope characterizes Buddhist soteriology [the Buddhist concept of salvation] as almost exclusively negative.

This he explains in the following way:

> "We do not free ourselves from evil through the good which comes from God; we liberate ourselves only through detachment from the world, which is bad. The fullness of such a detachment is not union with God, but what is called nirvana, a state of perfect indifference with regard to the world. To save oneself means, above all, to free oneself from evil by becoming indifferent to the world, which is the source of evil. This is the culmination of the spiritual process."

Now, it seems that such "indifference" to the world, were it true, would be but a step removed from contempt for the world. And nothing could be farther removed from the Buddhist attitude. In fact, it was out of love for the world that the Buddha spent 45 years of his life teaching. Nor was he reticent about involving himself in what today, we would call "social issues." On one occasion, in fact, he intervened to prevent what started as a petty squabble over land ownership, from developing into armed conflict. And many Buddhist traditions emphasize the Bodhisattva ideal. This means that even one who has achieved liberation vows to remain in samsara (the cycle of birth and death), until all sentient beings have been enlightened. It is difficult, in Buddhist terms at least, to imagine an altruism more encompassing than this.

The second corollary is that we must be no less candid about our differences than we are sanguine about our similarities. Sometimes Buddhists who are highly regarded in the Buddhist community, and whose words therefore carry an aura of authority, lose sight of this principle. In a misguided zeal to promote an ecumenical atmosphere, they misrepresent the Buddhist position, by making it more compatible with the beliefs of other religions than it actually is. For example, in his 1995 work, Thich Nhat Hanh attempted to attenuate the doctrine of "not-self" (*anatta*) by suggesting that the Buddha did not really mean what he said.[4] Such attempts to water down basic Buddhist principles tends to have the opposite effect of that intended, because other participants will then express opinions on Buddhism, based upon what they have heard, believing that they have it on good authority. As a result, their remarks will appear to their Buddhist colleagues as ill-informed or disparaging of Buddhism.

What I am actually talking about here are canons of sound scholarship, which all participants in the dialogue should recognize and try to honor. When non-Buddhists express opinions on Buddhism, they should take care

---

4. *Living Buddha, Living Christ* (New York: Riverhead Books, 1995).

to do their homework. Uninformed comments not only engender ill feelings, but an attitude of condescension on the other side. Genuine dialogue, however, is possible only in an atmosphere of mutual respect, based upon a consensus that it is being conducted among equals. And, this is obviously no less true when Buddhists talk about Christianity or other religions. At the same time, it is necessary that all of us remain committed to an open forum, where the participants are free to express ideas and views without fear of recrimination for "political incorrectness." It may happen that certain religious communities who are only recently part of the dialogue and therefore new to its ways will be unable to "find their tongue" when others make criticisms, which seem to them unjustified or ill-informed. Their first inclination, then, will almost naturally be to want to silence their critics. This is all the more reason why the representatives of each faith should be aware of the special needs of others. And again, this means each member should recognize a responsibility to learn the traditions of the others.

These caveats, however, are not merely a paraphrase of the old saw, "If you can't say something nice, don't say anything at all." As Buddhists, we cannot and do not close our eyes to the evil and injustice in the world. We are no less bound than our Christian, Jewish, Muslim, and Hindu brothers and sisters to take a stand on it. The easy part, of course, is staking out a position when we agree with each other. No religion that deserves to be taken seriously condones slavery or oppression in any form. Both the Pope and his predecessors have issued encyclicals sternly condemning political and religious persecution, as well as reproving the excesses of all forms of economic organization, capitalist, socialist, or communist. And Buddhists would be the first to agree. The hard part is taking a stand, when we disagree with each other. And this I identify as a second potential stumbling block to interfaith dialogue. Buddhists have often said what everyone knows, but is all too easily forgotten, that harsh or idle words, once uttered, cannot be retracted. They remain "out there" to poison the ambiance in which dialogue takes place, and may, in the few seconds required to utter them, undo what has taken years to accomplish. On the other hand, we cannot and will not always agree; and none of us can hope to enjoy the approval of everyone all the time. As the Buddha reminded us, "there never was, there never will be, nor does there exist now, a person who is wholly praised or wholly blamed." The very fact we are here, however, and expressing our willingness to talk to each other, suggests that we—all of us—must be doing something right!

Reflection on this second potential impediment to dialogue at once reveals a second reason why it should continue. In the WCC's booklet, *Guidelines on Dialogue*, to which I alluded earlier, the author remarks that it "is easy to discuss religions and even ideologies as though they existed in some realm of calm quite separate from the sharp divisions, conflicts and sufferings of humankind." I wholly agree, and not only me, but all Buddhists would agree with the author when he suggests that "religions and ideologies often contribute to the disruption of communities and the suffering of those whose community life is broken."

Religious differences have often been the most deeply rooted and destructive of all. If we, as representatives of the world's major religions, can show the rest of the world that we can communicate with each other, they just might come to realize that there is no reason why they cannot do the same.

In Buddhism, virtuous conduct (*sila*) includes "right speech" (*samma vaca*). And by practicing the virtue of right speech in the context of dialogue, we will be setting an example for the larger community to emulate. As I pointed out earlier, dialogue already takes place as a part of the life of the community, even before it becomes formal. The many problems which beset our communities, indeed all humankind, at the close of this century [the twentieth century] are articulated in the political forum—the environment, nuclear proliferation, international terrorism, human rights, urban violence, social justice, and the like. Representatives of the religious communities, therefore, are drawn into the fray. The only question is whether we will rise to the occasion.

I would like to focus upon just one of these issues—one, indeed, that must concern us as representatives of the world's religions—religious intolerance and persecution. Not only has it not disappeared, but it is actually on the rise in many parts of the world and has shown itself in shameful incidents, even in our own country, and even within the last few weeks.

A recent spate of Church bombings has elicited a formal response from the White House and has alarmed the public out of its characteristic lethargy. In fact, on the very day that I was working on this address, I happened to glance at the daily paper, only to see on the front page a heart-rending picture of a 92-year-old black minister standing in front of what was left of his church in Boligee, Alabama. Let me put it in his words:

> "The last Sunday we were in [our church] I had a real good sermon. And there wasn't any quarrel in the church. My sermon was about turning over a new life, to start a new thing, to start living better, to start working together, to live in the Spirit of God, to get along. Four days later they called me. My daughter drove me back out there. And it was all burned down. It was gone. The church was all down in ashes, just one wall and one corner still standing. The other walls had fallen in, and there was nothing left but ashes. So I said a prayer, and I asked the Lord to take charge. I asked the Lord to take control of it. I asked him two things. I asked him to help me build another church. And I asked him to tell us who did it. Because he's the Lord. He knows."

The very same day the *Times* reported that a church in South-central Los Angeles had received its second arson threat.

As a Buddhist, who with great sadness must watch what is happening to his Christian brothers and sisters, I am reminded of the words of the Buddha: "*Yo appadutthassa narassa dussati suddhassa posassa ananganassa. Tam eva balam pacceti papam sukkhumo rajo pativatam' va khitto.*" (Pali: "Whoever harms a harmless person, one pure and guiltless, upon that very fool the evil recoils like a fine dust thrown against the wind.") When I see things like this happening, I find it difficult to forgive the perpetrators, even though I know I must. The Buddha told his monks that "even if bandits were to sever you savagely limb by limb with a two-handed saw, he who gave rise to a mind of hate towards them would not be carrying out my teaching." As a Buddhist I do not profess to know whether Christ ever really healed the sick, raised up a cripple, made the blind see, the deaf hear, or raised the dead. But I do know that he never made anyone lame, or blind, or mute; nor did he ever put anyone to death. He was at the very least a good, compassionate, and virtuous human being; he was, indeed, everything that the Buddha was, and taught us what we should be. Even though we (and I speak now not only as a Buddhist, but as a Christian, a Jew, a Muslim, a Hindu, as a human being, as one of you) . . . I say, even though we may wonder whether we can find it in our hearts to forgive those who harm us, who beat us, kill us, defame us, or burn our churches and temples, we must remember that Christ himself had no second thoughts about those who persecuted him, beat him, spat upon him, and even killed him. He forgave them from the cross; can we do less?

And this is why we must continue our dialogue; this is why we must talk! The only alternative to talk is the buildup of resentment and anger, which in time must inevitably become open hostility and conflict. Nor can religions take the attitude that they will start talking, when they have "settled scores." As the Buddha reminds us, "In those who harbor such thoughts as 'he abused me, he beat me, he defeated me, he robbed me,' hatred is not appeased." In Buddhism there are few instances of "eternal truths," and so, when the Buddha himself declares something so to be, we have to assume that he really meant it. In an often quoted verse, the Buddha stated that "hatreds never cease through hatred in this world; through love alone do they cease. This is an eternal law." And did not Jesus say, "Love your enemies and pray for those who persecute you"? And again, in St. Paul's letter to the Romans, we read: "Bless those who persecute you; never curse them, bless them, resist evil and conquer it with good."

Concluding Note

The Pope's conviction, then, that what unites us is greater than what separates us offers firm ground upon which to continue building an edifice in which all faiths can feel at home. I, as a Buddhist, believe that Buddhism is a "universal" religion, in the sense that it is concerned with the fundamental human condition, and thus with the problem of suffering, first and foremost. The Buddha said, "It is suffering I teach, and the cessation of suffering." But in this respect it is like other religions, and Christianity in particular. For it, too, is concerned with the problem of suffering. As the Pope himself reminds us, "*Stat crux dum volvitur orbis.*" (Latin:

"The cross remains constant while the world turns.") For Christians (as well as other theistic religions), this observation has at once led philosophers and theologians to seek an answer to a most perplexing question: since there is obviously evil in the world, how can God permit it? The Buddhist is no less aware of, and concerned about, the reality of evil and suffering. But for us, the question is not how God can permit it, but rather, what are we going to do about it?

In any case, the corollary of the universality of suffering is not that we claim that everyone should be a Buddhist, but rather that, with respect to the fundamental problem with which Buddhism is concerned, everyone already is a *"Buddhist,"* whether he accepts that name or not. Referring to Hinduism and Buddhism, the Holy Father states that "the Catholic Church rejects nothing that is true and holy in these religions. The Church has a high regard for their conduct and way of life, for those precepts and doctrines which, although differing on many points from that which the Church believes and propounds, often reflect a ray of that truth which enlightens all men." On this point, I must mention a comment by Francis Cardinal Arinze, President of the Vatican's Pontifical Council for Interreligious Dialogue [from 1984 to 2002]. In one of the most gracious gestures of the Church in our memory, a letter sent this year [1996] to the Buddhist community, the Cardinal extended his wishes for a "Happy feast of Vesakh." Vesakh is the day on which Buddhists commemorate the birth, Enlightenment, and death of the Buddha. True to the spirit of its founder, Buddhism has been renowned throughout its history for its tolerance of other beliefs and values. But as the Cardinal reminds us, this is not enough. He points out:

> "The pluralistic society in which we live demands more than mere tolerance. Tolerance is usually thought of as putting up with the other, or at best as a code of polite conduct. Yet this resigned, lukewarm attitude does not create the right atmosphere for a [truly] harmonious existence. The spirit of our religions challenges us to go beyond this. We are commanded in fact to love our neighbors as ourselves."

And in the Dhammapada [one of the core Buddhist scriptures] the Buddha exhorts us: "Conquer anger by love, conquer evil by good; conquer avarice by giving; conquer the liar by truth."

Now, it seems to me that since we are so ready to embrace each other and claim that we are already honorary members of each other's religion, there is really no reason why we cannot continue talking. We are alike in that we all suffer, and our primary concern is the end of suffering; this is what we call liberation. As His Holiness the Dalai Lama has put it: "I am interested not in converting other people to Buddhism but in how we Buddhists can contribute to human society, according to our own ideas." And I have always maintained, and maintain today, that if we had enough in common thirty years ago to begin talking to each other, then we have enough in common to continue.

8

CHAPTER

We and You

Let us Meet in God's Love [1]

Seyyed Hossein Nasr

EDITOR'S NOTE

The following text is a pointed address delivered by eminent Iranian scholar of comparative religion and Islamic philosophy, Seyyed Hossein Nasr, University Professor of Islamic Studies at Georgetown University, on the occasion of a papal audience for participants of the first conference of the Catholic-Muslim Forum, held in Vatican City, Rome, in 2008.

Nasr's speech shows all the typical marks of a conventional religious talk by a pious Muslim—praise of Allah, blessing of the Prophet and of all "friends of God"—while also showing respect for the distinguished audience, Pope Benedict XVI. Stressing the common concern for peace and calling for joint action "against the desacralizing . . . antireligious forces of the modern world" so that secularism does not become "a source for . . . further distance between us," Nasr also mentions the conflicts between Christianity and Islam past and present and highlights some controversial theological and political understandings. Asserting that "we cannot claim that violence is the monopoly of only one religion," Nasr is convinced that despite all these differences and "memories of historical confrontations," it is possible to meet honestly and learn from one another in dialogue, provided one meets the other "in God's love."

Bismi'Llah ai-Rahman ai-Rahim: In the Name of God, the All-Good, the Infinitely Merciful, and blessings and peace be upon the Prophet Muhammad and upon all the prophets and messengers.

---

1. Seyyed Hossein Nasr, "We and You Let us Meet in God's Love," *The Islamic Monthly* (April 8, 2009). Used by permission of *The Islamic Monthly*.

Your Holiness, Eminences, Excellencies, Distinguished Scholars: It is asserted by the Word of God, which for us Muslims is the Noble Qur'an, "And God summons to the Abode of Peace," and by Christ (may peace be upon him), who is the Word of God in Christianity and also a prophet and messenger of the highest order in Islam, "Blessed are the peacemakers." The goal of attaining peace is thus common between our two religions and we are here precisely with the hope of attaining peace between Christianity and Islam. Furthermore, what can be more important and foundational in the quest for peace than creating peace between our religions? For only from this peace will it be possible to establish peace between peoples and nations, more specifically the Islamic world and the West. Whether we are Christians or Muslims, we are beckoned by our religions to seek peace. As people of religion meeting here at the center of Catholicism [i.e., the Vatican], let us then dedicate ourselves to mutual understanding, not as diplomats, but as sincere religious scholars and authorities standing before God and responsible to Him beyond all worldly authority.

When one ponders over the remarkable similarities between Islam and Christianity, one wonders why there has been so much contention between the two religions over the centuries. As Muslims we share with Christians faith in the One God, the God of Abraham, and see in the beginning of the Catholic declaration of belief, *credo in unum deum* [I believe in one God], the deepest confirmation of the first *shahada* [the basic Muslim creed] or testimony of our religion, namely *la ilaha illa'Llah* (there is no divinity but God), which we consider to be foundational not only to our religion, but to every authentic religion. Our religion and yours share, therefore, the same foundation and basis despite differences among us in the interpretation of the doctrine of *tawhid*, or unity [of God], that is so central not only to Islam, but also to Christianity since the doctrine of the Trinity certainly does not negate Divine Unity in mainstream Christian theology.

Moreover, for us God is the Creator and Sustainer of the universe, at once Transcendent and Immanent, as He is for you. Over the many centuries of our history men and women of our two communities have stood in awe before the majesty of God as Transcendent and felt His closeness as the Immanent, for as the Noble Qur'an asserts, God is closer to us than our jugular vein. And there have been those in our two communities who have smelled the perfume of Divine Proximity, have become immersed in the Ocean of Oneness, and have been blessed by the beatific vision of God.

For both of us God has a personal dimension and we can address Him as the "Thou" to whom we both pray. For Muslims as well as Christians, God is both Merciful and Just, and the harmonization of these two apparently contradictory qualities has been the subject of countless studies by both your theologians and ours. And of course we both associate God with love with different interpretations of this central divine quality in our two religions. Christians speak of the love of God and some view Islam as lacking in emphasizing this quality. Muslims would respond that, with God being infinite, surely His love for His creation could not have become exhausted by the advent of Christianity. Some of that love must in fact have remained to be manifested in Islam and we, no less than Christians, live the life of faith in the glow of Divine Love. That is why one of the greatest spiritual masters of Islam, Jalal ai-Din Rumi, identified God with the Beloved, as did so many other Sufis [members of a mystic branch of Islam known for their circular dancing], and could utter in a poem:

> Hail to Thee O our Love with goodly passion,
> O physician of all our ailments,
> O remedy of our pride and honor,
> O Thou our Plato and Galen besides.

Both you and we believe that God has created the human soul, which is immortal, and reject all those views that consider man as a clever machine brought about through accidental and haphazard biological events. We both associate human dignity with men's and women's eternal souls. Consequently we both emphasize the ethical character of human life and believe that having been given free will to act, we are responsible to God for our earthly actions. Our theologians may have debated about free will and determinism for many centuries, but both religions have always insisted upon morality and the ethical nature of human actions with consequences beyond the grave. We all affirm the reality of good and evil and their basic distinction, without which belief in ethical action and its effect upon our immortal soul would be meaningless. And our ethical norms are in fact similar in so many ways. That is why we both seek to avoid what classical Catholic theology calls the seven deadly sins. That is why on the social plane we both emphasize the importance of the family and, on the individual level, the crucial significance of sexual ethics, which, although dealing primarily with the individual, has such a major impact upon society at large.

For both you and us it is our common eschatological beliefs, in their general principles and not details, that provide the framework for the religious understanding of human actions and their consequences upon our souls. We all believe in the reality of posthumous states, in various paradises, infernos, and at least in the case of Catholic Christianity, the purgatories. All of us expect to meet God and rely on His mercy and forgiveness. We even have fairly similar historical eschatologies with of course some differences, but in any case we both expect the second coming of Christ, who is at once the center of Christianity and such a major figure in the Islamic religious universe.

We Muslims and Christians, like followers of other religions, pray, and although the external forms are different, there are remarkable similarities in our prayers. Some of us say "O God forgive us our sins," and others *"astaghfiru'Llah,"* that is, "I ask forgiveness of God." The life of the pious person, whether Christian or Muslim, is intertwined with prayer, and both religions are witness to a vast spectrum of prayers, from the simple petition to God for some need or want, to the prayer of the heart, of the saints who only want "Thy will be done," or "I want not to want."

Also over the centuries both Christians and Muslims have made pilgrimages and many continue to do so: Christians to such places as St. James of Compostella, Lourdes, and in earlier Christian history, Canterbury; and Muslims primarily to Mecca and Medina, but also many other sites including Jerusalem, which has been shared by both Muslims and Christians as a site of pilgrimage. Indeed, the external forms are different but how similar was and is the inner experience of pilgrimage in our two religions!

"How precious is the gift of faith!" Such an assertion can be made equally by a Christian and a Muslim. Whether one speaks of *fides* [faith] or *iman* [belief], one is dealing with a most profound reality shared by Muslims and Christians alike. Moreover, both religious communities have encountered the relative significance of faith and works in their religious life. Remarkably enough, every theological position taken in Christianity as a whole on the question of the relation and relative significance of faith and works has its equivalence *mutatis mutandis* [with certain marginal variations] in Islam.

Such is also true of the question of free will and determinism. Islamic thought is not confined to Ash'arism [a theological school within Islam stressing the importance of rational reflection], nor Christianity to Calvinism. It is false to assert that Islam is fatalistic and deterministic while Christianity is based on free will. In reality the rich theological and philosophical schools of both religions present a full spectrum of views on this crucial subject. Nor could this have been otherwise, for the followers of both religions experience in an immediate way, as do all human beings, their freedom to act. Yet along with Jews, they stand before the God of Abraham, whose Will reigns supreme.

How strange that Muslims have been accused of being opposed to reason while it was a Muslim philosopher and jurist, Ibn Rushd or Averroes, who is considered to have been the single most important figure in the introduction of rationalist arguments into medieval Christian theology. The reality of the matter is that both Christians and Muslims have presented and held many diverse views concerning the relation between reason and faith or reason and revelation and practically every view in one religion finds its counterpart in the other, except that of course Islam did not encounter Enlightenment rationalism in the eighteenth century and did not surrender to its tenets as did certain strands of Christianity. In any case, persons of faith in both religions stand before the Majesty of God and His all-powerful Will as well as all-encompassing knowledge. And among them those who have had philosophical and theological tendencies have had to ponder over the relation between reason and revelation and have come often to similar conclusions. It is true that in Christianity God is a mystery hidden from man and in Islam it is not He who is hidden and a mystery but man who is hidden from God. And yet, the question of the relation between reason and faith, far from being a source of contention between the two religions, is a source of common accord if one considers the full spectrum of the traditional theologies and philosophies of Christianity and Islam.

Both religions, having been sent by God to lead human beings back to Him, Christianity and Islam are channels of grace and make possible not only salvation, but also the experience of sanctity as well as the attainment of inner illumination. The pious life of both religions has, through the centuries, been involved with the reality of sanctity in one way or another despite the eclipse of this dimension of religious life in recent times in both religions, in Western Christianity due to the advent of secularism, and in Islam as a result of the rise of what has now come to be known as "fundamentalism." One can only ask what the relation between Christianity and Islam would be if saints, men and women whose being are rooted in God, represented each religion in dialogue. In any case, the reality of sanctity as well as spiritual leadership—whether associated with an imam [the spiritual head and leader of worship in a mosque] or a superior of a Catholic order—are shared between us. In Shi'ism and certain schools of Sunnism we speak of *walaya*, which means spiritual power, sanctity and inner guidance. Surely Christians would find in this concept and reality deep similarities to their own doctrines.

It is also important to recall that both Islam and Christianity have created major civilizations with their own social structures, sciences, philosophies, arts, etcetera. Both have created sacred architecture of the highest order whether it be Chartres or the Mezquita [the Mosque-Cathedral][2] in Cordova. Both have produced most outstanding examples of literature imbued with the values of the religions in question. Outward forms differ but the inner meanings of traditional Islamic and Christian arts and sciences—and not the humanistic and modernistic distortions of the traditional norms—are very close and should be a means of bringing the two religions closer together.

Speaking of Christian and Islamic civilizations, it must be noted that the name of both religions has been associated with violence in certain periods of their history. To associate only Islam with violence is to overlook the fact that over the centuries many more Muslims have been killed by Christians than Christians by Muslims. If there is more violence today carried out in the name of Islam than of Christianity, that is not due to the support of violence by one

---

2. In Cordoba, Spain, on the site of a Roman temple, the Mezquita was built as a mosque by Islamic architects over two centuries beginning in the eighth century, where it became one of the largest sacred buildings in the Islamic world. It was converted into a Christian cathedral in the thirteenth century and is currently the cathedral of Cordoba.

religion and opposition to violence by the other, but rather the result of the relative strength of each religion today. If Christianity in the West is no longer associated with violence, it is because of the weakening of Christianity before the onslaught of secularism. One could hardly imagine calling French or British soldiers to war these days in the name of Christianity, in contrast to older days from the Crusades to the destruction of natives in the Americas when Christianity being strong, was used oftentimes by political forces to legitimize wars and violence. To associate Islam simply with violence and Christianity with nonviolence is to make virtue out of necessity. The task to confront and oppose violence in all its forms is in fact a task in whose realization both Muslims and Christians must work hand in hand.

When we ponder over what unites us, we are confronted with the issue of human dignity. The views of the two religions are indeed close in this crucial matter. Traditional and classical Christianity and Islam both believe in human dignity because as both religions have asserted, "God has created man in His image," whatever different meanings we attach to the word "image." Furthermore, God has breathed into us His Spirit and that is the origin of human dignity we both accept and the source of human rights. To base human rights and freedoms on humanistic, evolutionary and secularist conceptions of man is merely to espouse a position that is based on sheer sentimentality bereft of any theological foundation and opposed by serious theological thought, both Islamic and Christian.

These are but a few of the realities shared by us and you. Why then has there been such confrontation and opposition between Christianity and Islam? One must consider first of all the fact that Islam appeared after Christianity and from the dawn of Islam Muslims have had respect for Christianity as a revealed religion, and have protected the Christians living among them and as they continue to in sizeable numbers in several Islamic countries. In contrast Christianity preceded Islam and its mainstream religious thought did not accept and for the most part does not accept even now Islam as an authentic religion revealed by God and given the power to bring about salvation to its followers. There are also formal differences, many of which were divinely ordained in order to keep the two religions distinct. Had not those providential distinctions existed, we would not be speaking to each other as followers of two religions today, both of which have not only survived but possess a global presence to this day, a situation surely willed by God for those of us who accept God as the Almighty whose Will rules supreme. Let us then turn to some of those differences.

Islam emphasizes above all else Divine Unity for, as the Noble Qur'an asserts, "Say God is One" (*ahad*). Being the One, who is also the Absolute, God's reality cannot be compromised by any relationality, for that would imply relativity; hence the Islamic rejection of the Trinitarian doctrine and the possibility of Divine Sonship. Christianity on the contrary emphasizes the Triune nature of

God while, like Islam, accepting His Oneness. Likewise, the two religions differ in their account of the end of the life of Christ who plays such an important spiritual role in the Islamic religious universe as well as being the heart and center of Christianity. The question between the two religions that remains is the following: was Christ crucified or not? And the answer to this crucial question is not the same as far as Islam and Christianity are concerned.

On the social plane, Islam emphasizes the centrality of the Divine Law (*al-Shari'a*) whose main sources are the Noble Qur'an and the Sunnah or wonts of the Prophet of Islam while for Christianity the law of Christ is a spiritual law and in everyday affairs Christianity incorporated much of Roman law and later Germanic common law. The result is different views concerning the significance of laws that govern human society. Likewise, on the social plane Christianity preached giving unto God what is God's and unto Caesar what is Caesar's. This meant the complete separation of spiritual and temporal authority, although in practice after Constantine [the Great, Roman Emperor, 272–337], the two became intertwined, resulting practically in a situation not very different from that of Islam, which has never accepted the separation of the domains of God and Caesar. Today both religions struggle with this question but for different reasons.

When we come to the organization of religion we again detect important differences. In Catholic Christianity there is the ordained priesthood and only priests can perform certain ritual actions, especially the consecration of the Eucharist. In Islam every man [i.e., male] is a priest and there is no religious hierarchy as we find in Christianity in general and Catholicism in particular. Even the hierarchy found in Shi'ism is not the same as that found in Catholicism and a Shi'ite, like his Sunni brothers, is a priest in being able to conduct all the rites of the religion from performing or leading the daily canonical prayers to leading the prayer for the dead.

What or who is the Divine Word? To this question a Christian would answer Christ and a Muslim the Noble Qur'an, although in certain schools of Islamic thought each prophet including Jesus has been identified with an aspect of the Divine Word. In any case, for Christians the body of Christ is the "container" of the Word, while for Islam it is the Qur'anic Arabic language which, as the result of the Islamic revelation, became by God's Will the sacred language of Islam and the "container" of God's Word. Christianity has had many liturgical languages, including, besides Latin, Aramaic, Greek, Russian, Slovanic and even Arabic, which is thus the sacred language of Islam as well as the liturgical language of Arab Christians. This different understanding of the role of language in religious rites has had many significant consequences. Not only Arabs, but all Muslims, whether Malay, Indo-Pakistani, Persian, Turk, or African, all having mother tongues other than Arabic, pray five times a day in Arabic, whereas in the West after nearly two millennia of the use of the beautiful Latin liturgy, it was put aside in favor of vernacular languages after Vatican II.

Many have said that for Christianity, Islamic teachings have been too close for comfort and there is what one might call family enmity toward Islam that Christianity has not had toward other religions, the case of Judaism being an exceptional one. Yes, Christians read in the Holy Bible about Noah, Abraham, and Moses, all of whom along with many other prophets are also mentioned in the Noble Qur'an. Christians, especially Catholic and Orthodox, venerate the Virgin Mary and so do Muslims. For Christians, Jesus is the Son of God, who was born miraculously from a virgin mother and who performed many miracles. For Muslims he is not the son of God but one of the foremost prophets dedicated to spiritual guidance, the prophet of inwardness, born miraculously of a virgin mother. Yes, Muslims also venerate Mary, the only woman after whom a chapter of the Qur'an is named (Sura 19). Moreover, they not only accept the virginal birth of Jesus as do Christians, but also affirm his performance of miracles. Despite differences, the similarities are great enough to have aroused suspicion and special enmity among many Christians against Islam even after the political threat of Islam to Europe had disappeared.

There are also significant differences between Islam and Christianity due to their very different encounters with modernism and secularism. Obviously in dealing with Christianity today, we Muslims are not confronted with St. Thomas Aquinas, Dante, and the builders of the Cologne Cathedral, however real these dimensions of traditional Western Christianity might still be. Rather, we face a Christianity that bears the deep wounds of five centuries of battle with forces opposed to religion, from the secular humanism and skepticism of the Renaissance to the materialism associated with the seventeenth century Scientific Revolution and the subsequent secularization of the cosmos to the rationalism of the Age of Enlightenment, to the historicism and evolutionism of the nineteenth century to the current post-modern critique of religious texts and the virulent atheistic attacks being made recently in the West against religion as such. Western Christianity has had to face such figures as Montaigne, Bayle, Feuerbach, Marx, and Freud, all of whom were products of the West and not from a land far away, as has been the case of Islam in its confrontation with such figures. Islam, moreover, did not experience various phases of modernism in a gradual manner as did Western Christianity, but experienced it rapidly and in quick order. Of course there are those in the West who claim that the problem is precisely that Islam did not experience in depth modernism and especially the Enlightenment to which Muslims would respond, "Thank God that this did not happen to us." Otherwise the number of Muslim worshippers performing the Friday prayers at the Sultan Hasan Mosque in Cairo would be the same as the number of Christians participating in the Mass on a Sunday at the St. Sulpice Church in Paris.

In seeking to come together we must be fully aware of the differences created by the advent of modernism. Western Christianity has fought against but also in many cases surrendered to the foe as we see in the abandonment of the cosmos to a secularist science or the adoption of certain Marxist themes in some of the currents of liberation theology. As for Islam, its encounter with modernism has been confined to a short period. Within the span of a century Muslims have had to face the challenges of five centuries of European antireligious thought. Their reaction has, therefore, been different from that of Western Christianity. Islam's encounter with modernism has not produced an army of influential secularist thinkers, nor a strong wave against religion as we see in modem European history. But there have been severe reactions, sometimes unfortunately violent, to modernism throughout the Islamic world recently, resulting in what is called problematically in the West fundamentalism, which however also has its equivalents in both Judaism and Christianity, not to speak of Hinduism.

Let us understand the roots of our differences not only as based in scripture and tradition, but also as resulting from our very different experiences of modernism and secularism. Simple criticism of the other without understanding and empathy cannot bring accord despite all the elements common between Islam and Christianity to which some reference has already been made. We are situated in the same boat floating over very dangerous waters. The vilification of the other through accentuation of differences without deeper understanding of causes of these differences and disregard for all that unites us, especially the love of God and the neighbor, cannot but lead to our own perdition.

Forgetting and casting aside the remarkable accord on so many basic doctrines and values, and exaggerating differences used often to bring about purposefully discord and opposition have characterized much of the history of relations between our two religions. As we now all stand at the edge of a precipice it is time to turn a new page and seek to come together in the bosom of Divine Love. Of course our coming together does not and should not mean the destruction of divinely ordained formal structures of each religion. You and us: we must in fact be able to continue our distinct religious lives without constant threat of the destruction of our faith from the other side before even embarking upon dialogue. That is why we Muslims oppose aggressive proselytizing which seeks to reward conversion with worldly advantages. We wish to preserve our religion, as do the Jews, who in 1988 passed a law in Israel banning religious proselytizing, as would Christians if they were placed in our situation. To be friends requires that we first exist as ourselves. The other must be respected as the other, not as potential material for conversion from the category of otherness. Yes, both Christianity and Islam envisage for themselves a universal message, but if we are to live together in peace, we cannot try to destroy the religious identity of the other at all costs, imposing what we consider to be our right on the other, and disregarding his right for self-preservation.

Our attitudes in this matter as in so many others will change if we realize not only theoretically, but also concretely, that we belong to the same family of religions, worshipping the same God. The great tragedies of the twentieth century have helped to expand the usage of the term "Judeo-Christian." It is now time to realize that we have to speak of "Judeo-Christian-Islamic" if we are to be honest, and also reverential toward Abraham, who is the father of mono-theism. It was God's Will that the Abrahamic tradition should be comprised of the three religions of Judaism, Christianity, and Islam. You cannot sever bonds that have been forged by God. If we are to accept in our hearts, and not only dip-lomatically, that we are members of the same religious family (seen in the pos-itive sense of family based on accord and not discord), then we must discourse with each other as family members and respect each other in every way without hatred and above the fray of family feuds. Our dialogues must not be based on suspicion, hidden agendas, and duplicity, but on sincerity and honesty, which are so much needed in our world. We are not each other's enemies, but members of the same divinely ordained family. Therefore, we should not try to destroy each other, but seek to vie with each other in goodness, as the Noble Qur'an asserts.

One might understand that a thousand years ago, when we both lived in a world impregnated by faith, some Christians might have called Muslims their enemies, and vice versa, although even then many Christians and Muslims lived as friends, as can be seen in the long history of Christian communities in the Islamic world. In any case, we no longer live in a traditional world of faith and are confronting other enemies. We live in a secularist world in which religions are each other's best friends. In any case, today our enemy, which in fact is com-mon between us, is the materialistic, hedonistic, nihilistic and God-negating worldview that is so widespread, the worldview that negates the spiritual nature of humanity, denies the sacred and the transcendent, and seeks to shatter our hopes for a blessed life everlasting. We have much to offer to each other in the central battle between truth and falsehood. But the offer can only be accepted if we first recognize each other as friends and not as enemies.

In this effort to reorient ourselves toward each other, all of us, Christian and Muslim alike, can play a role. But there is no doubt that the main responsibility lies on the shoulders of religious leaders, thinkers, and scholars, those whom we call *'ulama'* in Islam. Those who are guides and trailblazers in religious matters must come forward and seek to bring about understanding to those in their own communities who hearken to their call. They should bring about further knowl-edge about the other whom they should present as friend, not enemy, to be loved and not vilified. And surely the carrying out of such a task on our part is one that is not always easy. It requires—besides the necessary knowledge—selflessness, honesty, and truthfulness in conjunction with love and compassion.

We as Muslims from different schools of Islamic thought and countries have come together to extend to you our hand of friendship, seeking to meet you in God's love, beyond all our theological differences and memories of his-torical confrontations. Surely we, who respect and love Christ as you do, can meet and come together under the banner of what he has stated to be the two supreme commandments: to love God and to love the neighbor. We can also seek to extend, often in harmony with each other, the border of the definition of neighbor to include not only you and us, but also the whole of humanity, and even beyond that the rest of God's creation. As the Holy Bible asserts, "With God, all things are possible." We submit to Him and ask for His help and affirmation in carrying out this momentous task of meeting with you in friendship and peace under the banner of that common word that unites us. There can be no more blessed act in our times than the creation of deep accord between God's religions, especially the two religions that have the largest numbers of followers in the world, namely Christianity and Islam. Indeed, God summons us to the Abode of Peace, and blessed are the peacemakers.

Hindu-Christian Dialogue

A Hindu Perspective[1]

K. L. Seshagiri Rao

EDITOR'S NOTE

K. L. Seshagiri Rao is a distinguished veteran of religious studies and interreligious dialogue, emeritus professor of religious studies, University of Virginia, and editor-in-chief of the multivolume *Encyclopedia of Hinduism* (published in 2011). As a committed Hindu, Seshagiri Rao has been engaged in interreligious dialogue for decades. He acquired his remarkable familiarity with Christianity while in college in Mysore, India, where students, inspired by Mahatma Gandhi (1869–1948), studied the Bible as well as Hindu scriptures, and later while doing doctoral studies and teaching in the United States. "I deeply cherish my tradition," Seshagiri Rao acknowledges, "but I do not wish it ever to be the only religion in the world. Nor do I . . . turn a blind eye to its shortcomings."

Briefly sketching the traumatizing history of nineteenth-century Christian missionary encounter with the religions of India (Hinduism), an encounter tainted by imperial colonialism, Rao welcomes the more recent initiatives by Christians for mutual exchange in dialogues, in several of which he actively participated. Fully aware of substantial differences between both religious traditions, Rao is nonetheless confident that "dialogue and cooperation" between Christians and Hindus "will bring greater light and deeper understanding," which will help in overcoming conflicts and violence in today's globalized world and society.

I got my early lessons in Hinduism from my parents, who were devout Hindus. I was born seventy-two winters ago, and imbibed from my domestic and social environments aspects of Hindu tradition and practice. My first acquaintance

---

1. "Hindu-Christian Dialogue: A Hindu Perspective," by K. L. Seshagiri Rao, in *Journal of Hindu-Christian Studies Bulletin* 14 (2001): 7–12, is used by permission.

with Christianity was in the late forties, when under the influence of Mahatma Gandhi, a number of students in Indian colleges took to the study of the Bible and the Gita [the Bhagavad Gita]. In my case, the study continued, and came to a focus when I accepted a fellowship from the Gandhi Peace Foundation, Delhi, to study Gandhi's religious thought. In that connection, I came into contact with and learned much from Hindu as well as Christian followers of Gandhi. I also had the opportunity to study, in some detail, other world religions. Further, as a doctoral student at Harvard University in the early sixties, I took a number of courses in Christian theology, history, and ethics; they have helped me to understand Christianity in the proper context.

I deeply cherish my tradition, but I do not wish it ever to be the only religion in the world. Nor do I see any need to turn a blind eye to its shortcomings. Actually, I am glad that there are other great religions which are, like mine, trying to stem the tides of violence, terrorism, war, and materialism on one hand and trying to bring happiness and fulfillment through moral and spiritual instructions on the other.

Past

In India, as in many Asian countries, Christianity came into effective contact with non-Christian traditions during the days of colonial expansion of Western powers: Portuguese, French, Danish, and British. For Asian peoples, Christianity came mixed with and vitiated by imperialism, colonial domination, a degree of racism, and a dose of Western culture. Even the architecture and music of the churches in the colonies imitated Western styles. These historical factors created difficulties for a proper appreciation of Christianity. During the period of struggle for Indian independence, I remember the question was frequently raised: "Why should Christianity be presented to the Hindus? Does the West desire to 'dominate' Indian spirituality in the same way as it controls India's politics and economics?"

Christian missionaries used to make scathing attacks on Hinduism and dismiss it as a religion of superstition and crass idolatry, not to be taken seriously. They referred to the Hindus as polytheists, pagans, and heathens. They implicitly believed that the Western nations possessed a superior religion and culture. Hence they went out to give and not to receive; their objective was to spread Christianity. The technique frequently adopted was to exaggerate the so-called vulnerable points in Hindu thought and practice with little appreciation of the positive elements in them. The works of philanthropy, social uplift, medical aid, or educational services were often used as means for winning converts.

Hindu response to such criticisms was typical: praising one's own faith and blaming the faith of others are due to lack of sympathy and understanding. Each religion, like every geometric figure, has its own inherent logic and inner consistency. Unless one understands the inner logic, one cannot appreciate that religion. For example, Hindus worship one God (who is beyond names and forms) who makes Himself available to His devotees in many names and forms. From the time of the Rgveda[2] (which says that: Truth is one, sages call it by many names) to Sri Ramakrishna and Mahatma Gandhi, the validity of many names and forms of the one God is asserted. In the absence of appreciation of this basic Hindu principle, criticisms such as the one above, miss the point altogether.

For all its hopes and opportunities, "Christian triumphalism" of the Colonial era did not succeed. Christianity continues to be, by and large, a minority religion in Asia; it has to live with and amidst a majority community of another faith. Western Christians do not fully realize the enormous cultural and national pressures faced by the Christian minorities in Asia. Asian Christians clearly see the practical situation and recognize that human community is religiously pluralistic. They see no signs of immediate or even distant displacement of all other religions by Christianity.

Present

I know that in recent times, a number of Christian thinkers and groups are trying hard to eliminate the burdens of the past, to redefine their attitudes to other cultures, religions, and peoples, and to dissociate themselves from certain unhappy historical associations; however, Asian peoples are still handicapped in their appreciation of Christianity by what has been done to them in the past by Western nations.

Traditional theology, developed in religious isolation, has now become inadequate. Historically, Christianity, like every other world religion, is a particular religion, but it has a universal message. Each religion has to transcend itself to become universal. The Christian faith is challenged daily from within to enter into dialogue with the followers of other religions. "In my Father's house are many dwelling places. If this were not so, I would have told you" (John 14:2). Peter, the leader of the Apostles, declares: "In truth, I see that God shows no partiality. Rather, in every nation whoever fears Him and acts uprightly is acceptable to him" (Acts 10:34–5). There are scholars in recent decades who have not felt shy of visiting other dwelling places in God's mansion. Thanks to the efforts of farseeing leaders like Paul Devanandan, Stanley Samartha, John Taylor, and Dom Bede Griffiths, the atmosphere is now much better. The World Council of Churches (WCC) has struggled as a pioneer in the area of religions dialogue.

I have been involved in scores of important interreligious conferences and Hindu-Christian dialogues organized by the World Council of Churches, Temple

---

2. The Rgveda is the oldest religious Indian text.

of Understanding, World Conference of Religion and Peace, World Congress of Faith, and others. For example, I was invited as a Hindu guest to participate in the Fifth Assembly of the World Council of Churches in Nairobi in 1975. I was the cochairman of the International Hindu-Christian Consultation organized by WCC at Dehradun, India in 1981. I was a nonvoting Hindu delegate to the World Conference on Mission and Evangelism convened by the WCC in San Antonio, Texas in 1989. By engaging in vigorous dialogue for the last three decades, the WCC has shown that Christian faith stands to gain by spreading the testimony of Christ to others, and by receiving valuable insights from them. In my dialogue with Christians, I have understood much about Christianity, but also much about my own religious tradition.

It took some time for me to understand the diversity in Christian tradition. It certainly is difficult to make judgments on Christianity on the basis of a single sect or movement. Within Christianity, there are Catholics, Protestants, followers of Eastern Orthodoxy, and within each branch, there are many denominations, not always harmonious with one another. In the late fifties, I once went into a Christian section of a South Indian village, in the course of my fieldwork. I met the members and their families. On inquiry, I came to know that they belonged to seven different churches, and they scarcely knew about their church histories. Some were Roman Catholics, but did not know where Rome was, some others were Anglicans, but did not know where England was, and so on. I wondered at that time what the European ecclesiastical struggles had to do with the communication of Jesus Christ to villagers in India. Thankfully, ecumenical dialogue is going on among these churches. As a Hindu, I pray for the ecumenical unity of Christian churches. United Christianity is a spiritual gain to the world. It will also enable Christian activities to be coordinated for the benefit of humankind and of all creation.

I cherish my associations with enlightened Christian thinkers who have sought to realize that God is at work in events beyond the boundaries of the Christian church. God is already present in his world; we need only to recognize and respond to his presence. When Christ is exalted, whatever is universal in any religion is also exalted. I believe that Christ aimed at changing lives of persons, not their religious labels. In a multireligious society, my dialogue with Christians has made me realize that there is need to recognize that God is one, religions are many. Creative theological formulations are needed to do justice to religious pluralism. Further, the spiritual traditions of the world have a great role to play in arresting the tides of violence, materialism, skepticism and scientism that are challenging all religions. In this sense, Christianity and Hinduism have to work together, not against one another, in humanizing humanity.

In my understanding of the New Testament, God's love embraces the whole world. Churches may be exclusivist; Christ is universal. The Kingdom of God includes the entire humanity. The resemblances between Hindu and Christian parables and scriptural passages came as a pleasant surprise to me. Let me illustrate the point with the Song of Praise, in which Mary discloses to Elizabeth God's purpose:

> For he who is mighty has done great things for me, and holy is his name.
> and his mercy is on those who fear him from generation to generation.
> He has scattered the proud in the imagination of their hearts,
> he has put down the mighty from their thrones,
> and exalted those of low degree;
> he has filled the hungry with good things,
> and the rich he has sent empty away. (Luke 1:49–53)

Compare this with what Lord Krishna says about the purpose of avatar (incarnation of God on earth) in the Bhagavad Gita:

> When righteousness is weak and faints
> and unrighteousness exults in pride, then my Spirit arises on earth.
> For the Salvation of those who are good, for the destruction of evil in men,
> for the fulfillment of the Kingdom of righteousness,
> I come into this world in the ages that pass. (Bhagavad Gita IV. 7–8)[3]

Incidentally, Hinduism and Christianity are the only world religions which reveal the doctrine of Incarnation, though their interpretations of the doctrine are different.

Hindu View of Christ

Jesus Christ is an ineradicable part of modern Hinduism. The power of the cross is felt in the lives of many Hindus in different walks of life. Hindus adore Christ. The way in which Christ has touched their lives, and their responses to him are varied: some Hindus acknowledge Jesus as an avatar [embodiment of Lord Vishnu]; some others consider him as a yogi [a holy man], a satguru [the true, enlightened spiritual guru] and so on. Mahatma Gandhi, for instance, showed great reverence to Jesus Christ and publicly acknowledged his indebtedness to him, but refused to limit Jesus Christ to the boundaries of this or that church.

Hindus look upon Jesus without the appendages of theology, dogma, or doctrine. They give attention to his life of love and forgiveness. In the majesty of pure living, in the breadth of his sympathy, in the unselfish and sacrificial outlook of his life, and in pure disinterested love, he was supreme. What strikes a Hindu above all is his complete obedience to the will of God; the more he emptied himself the more he discovered God. The cross is not something to be

---

3. Quoted according to the Bhagavad Gita, translated from the Sanskrit by Juan Mascaro, with an introduction by Simon Brodbeck (London: Penguin Classics, 1962).

believed in and subscribed to as a dogma, but something to be lived and borne in life and experience. Jesus signifies to the Hindus the transcendence of the ego as the whole purpose of morality and spirituality. The enlightened person gains release by the surrender of his little self and its vanities by the purity of self and devotion to God.

The New Testament symbol of the Kingdom of God made a powerful appeal to modern Hindu reformers. It showed them the Christian message in its moral aspect. The teachings of the Sermon on the Mount were not speculative; they were exemplified in the life of Christ. They were impressed that the "Kingdom of God" belongs to the humble and the poor, that the "persecuted and the meek" are its citizens; that the "pure in heart" see it, and that the "Kingdom" is not meat and drink, but "righteousness, and peace and joy in the Holy Spirit." On the social side, the Kingdom of God involved the establishment of right relationships between institutions and communities of people. Modern Hindu reformers felt that this aspect of Christ's teaching was much needed in India. They tried to inculcate that spirituality did not consist in turning away from poverty, misery, and ignorance, but in fully facing and fighting them.

I found that Gandhi's understanding and practice of the cross brought out fresh aspects of Jesus' life and character which the West had not so clearly perceived. He demonstrated how the soul force fights and overcomes evil only with the weapons of Truth and love. Although *satyagraha* [passive, nonviolent political resistance] was used by Gandhi, a Hindu, against governments run by Christians (whether in South Africa or Britain), many Christians all over the world recognized that his movements were in truth Christian, a reviving and reinterpretation of the cross. Dr. Stanley Jones, the well-known American missionary, observes: "Never in human history has so much light been shed on the Cross as has been through this one man, and that man not even called Christian. Had not our Christianity been so vitiated and overlain by our identification with unchristian attitudes and policies in public and private life, we would have seen at once the kinship between Gandhi's method and the Cross."[4]

Hindus do not accept the Bible as the only scripture and Jesus Christ as the only instance of God's self-disclosure. And yet the Hindus accept the Bible, and the scriptures of other religions along with the Vedas [the ancient religious texts of India] as God-given. Despite this theological difference between Hindu and Christian approaches, practical cooperation with one another is possible in overcoming violence, war, injustice, poverty and sickness in the world. In this regard, the following verses of the New Testament are very instructive:

> And John answered and said, "Master, we saw one casting out devils in thy name; and we forbade him, because he followeth not with us." And

---

4. E. Stanley Jones, *Mahatma Gandhi: An Interpretation* (New York: Abingdon-Cokesbury Press, 1948), 105.

Jesus said unto him, "Forbid him not: for he that is not against us is for us." (Luke 9:4–50)

May I say that Hindus are not against Jesus Christ; they love him and adore him. Further there are many devils to be cast out; Hindus and Christians should come together to vanquish them.

Hindu Approach

Hindus have expressed an ecumenical spirit in religious matters throughout history. Never have they claimed to be exclusive possessors of truth. It is not necessary to be or become a Hindu to obtain salvation. They recognize revealing and saving powers in all great religions. Hindus respect all prophets and sages who come to guide humanity. In the context of the diversity of human needs, they hold that the great religions of the world are not only relevant but also necessary. Hindus have shown willingness to learn from other traditions. They are at liberty to draw inspiration from any source in their spiritual quest. Actually, the Hindu tradition encourages its followers to celebrate each other's way of God-realization. Reverence for other religions is an essential element of the Hindu spiritual vision.

Hinduism has witnessed the vicissitudes of history. It has periods of growth and stagnation which have brought many valuable and some questionable elements to life and society. New conditions bring new challenges to its adherents, while the age-old shortcomings are still to be addressed. But it has also shown remarkable powers of revival. Saints and sages have continued to call the Hindus to reform themselves and their society by purging old abuses, by throwing out undesirable accretions, and by conserving valuable insights and practices. In this endeavor, Christian contacts and even criticism have been very helpful. Hindus have been resilient, open, and have succeeded in several areas. For example, in my teenage days, it was inconceivable for people of different castes to eat together and work together, but now these prejudices have dissipated.

Hindus have never been an organized ecclesiastical body, nor do they seek to convert humanity to any one set of beliefs. In this sense, they have never been and will never be in competition with Christianity or with any other religion. They have been generally accommodating and cooperative. The Hindu tradition has provided historical examples of this attitude. When Jews (after the second destruction of the Temple in Jerusalem by the Romans) and Zoroastrians (in the seventh century when Persia was invaded by Muslims) sought shelter in India, they were received in their midst with warmth and understanding and were granted freedom of worship. The same spirit continues through the ages. Recently in 1961, India offered refuge to Dalai Lama and 100,000 of his followers from Tibet from the threat of the Chinese Communist army. For those who questioned the wisdom of this action, Dr. Radhakrishnan, the former President of India, said, "We cannot go against our own tradition and history."

Hindus point out that Yoga is not in competition with any religious tradition. Yogic meditative techniques have helped spiritual aspirants across religious borders. They help a Hindu to become a better Hindu, a Christian a better Christian, and so forth. Men of other faiths have testified that their own dormant faith has come alive as consequence of yogi practices.

The Christian Church does not admit the theory of reincarnation: rebirth of a soul after death with a new body. In recent years, however, a number of Christian thinkers have considered reincarnation as a valid phenomenon, while at the same time remaining firmly within the Christian faith. They also believe that it was acceptable in the Christian tradition in early times, and that it does justice to the Christian God of love and compassion. An errant child is given enough opportunities to correct his mistakes; God wishes that no soul be lost. In Hinduism, spiritual liberation is obtained through many lifetimes. Each lifetime is a god-given opportunity for further spiritual progress.

The theory of reincarnation is closely related to the doctrine of Karma, which emphasizes the principle of moral causality. Not only does a person reap what he sows, but what he is reaping is the result of what he has already sown. Man is the maker of his destiny. All sects and schools of Hinduism have realized the truth and value of this doctrine. The present-day revival of the subject in philosophical, religious, and popular circles in the West points to its importance. According to a recent Gallup poll survey, 23 percent of North Americans and Europeans believe in reincarnation.

Future

1. Historically, the dialogue of religions has broadened and deepened religious insights. Active dialogue and cooperation between Christianity and Hinduism will bring in greater light and deeper understanding.

2. Truth is many sided and our understanding of truth is fragmentary. Therefore, it is desirable to go deep into one's own religious tradition and adhere firmly to it, while keeping an open mind regarding the Truth that may be available in other traditions.

3. Hindu-Christian dialogue has led to a stronger sense of the essential dignity of a human being as a human being. The caste system in India has considerably weakened. The integration of the "untouchables" into the mainstream of Hindu Society, started by Gandhi, has recorded enormous success. Social obligations have assumed a greater importance.

4. In as much as God is one, the world is one, and humanity is one, it is possible for Hindus and Christians to meet and cooperate at these vantage points and reinforce the religious life of humanity.

5. Hindu-Christian dialogue is necessary: a) to overcome misconceptions entertained about each other's tradition; b) to achieve a clearer understanding of the similarities and differences between the two traditions; and c) to promote spiritual and moral goods in them.

6. Hindu-Christian dialogue recognizes that a) religious indifference is bad, religious prejudice is worse; b) proselytism is bad, conversion to a higher way of life is necessary; and c) no religious tradition should present its message in a way that may lead to conflict and violence in societies.

10
CHAPTER

Spirituality of Hinduism and Christianity[1]

George Gispert-Sauch, SJ

EDITOR'S NOTE

Indian Jesuit George Gispert-Sauch is professor emeritus of systematic theology of Vidyajyoti (Sanskrit for "Light of Knowledge") College of Theology in Delhi, one of the oldest and most respected institutions of higher learning run by Jesuits in India. He is a classic example of a competent interlocutor between Christianity and Hinduism because, over the course of his priesthood, he has acquired an intimate knowledge of Indian sacred traditions by studying the holy scriptures in their original languages and dialoguing with their representatives. He has published widely on topics of interreligious dialogue and his experiences.

    The article "Spirituality of Hinduism and Christianity" demands a lot of someone not familiar with the subject, not just because of the many allusions to Indian history, religion, and philosophy; what is also challenging to an outsider is the dense style in which he writes and the language he uses, a language imbued with theological terminology. However, the study of this text is worth the effort, because its author not only discusses several important topics of interreligious dialogue and relates these to the magisterial teachings of the Roman Catholic Church, he also cites impressive examples and "models" of such dialogue that have left their mark. In addition, Gispert-Sauch shows how meditation, political activism, and the "intertextual" reading of Holy Scriptures can lead Christians "into Indian spirituality." He thereby does not plead for "syncretism" but for "symbiosis," that is, the "living" and "acting together," which "works at the subconscious level," as "the work of the *Spirit of Love.*"

---

1. George Gispert-Sauch, SJ, "Spirituality of Hinduism and Christianity," *Geist und Leben* 83, issue 5 (Sept./Oct. 2010): 361–77; English version at *www.con-spiration.de/texte/english/2010/gispert-sauch-e.html*. Reprinted with permission of the author.

The relations between the followers of the many world religions and even of smaller religious traditions and Christian believers have now entered a stage beyond "confrontation," "encounter," and comparative "dialogue," to a search for sharing spirituality. Actually this may be the entry to an authentic "dialogue." For what often passes for dialogue is nothing but a "duo-logue," or a "poly-logue," where two or more "words" are exchanged between different traditions, with the hope that each "logos" is understood and perhaps captured by the other(s), regardless of whether it has an influence on them or not. Etymologically "dia-logue" implies not many words, but *one* word that goes across (*dia-*) to the other(s) and nestles in their hearts, so to say, where it induces a spiritual transformation and leads to a sense of "belonging" together. There is an implicit demand of reciprocity in the idea of dialogue. Of course many "words" and other signs are involved in this exercise, but in essence they are all meant to establish "a *common* word" that unites and ennobles the participants in the dialogue.

1. Beyond Dialogue?

The hope involved in sharing spiritual experiences at this level is that this dialogue will lead to growth or personal enrichment in assimilating the Word of God to humanity in a more comprehensive form. It may also lower the walls of alienation between various denominations, and consequently create greater peace and harmony among the many religious traditions. At this stage, "*other*" religions are no longer [regarded as] adversaries, or fortresses to be conquered, or even simply the "*other*," but as places where the Divine Power has manifested itself for the sake of strengthening the bonds of the human family. That dialogue belongs to the very structure of the Church is clear from the contemporary magisterium ever since the first encyclical letter of Paul VI, *Ecclesiam suam*,[2] August 6, 1964, and the *International Eucharistic Congress* in Bombay, which he attended four months later.

Further theological trends in the community as well as statements from various episcopal bodies have spelled out different levels of dialogue, like the *dialogue of life* where members of many religious traditions cooperate in activities aimed at advancing the common good, the *dialogue of theological sharing* where the themes of the religious traditions are explored and their values brought up for mutual edification. This may take place at the popular level or at more sophisticated levels of scholarship where concepts are explored among duly trained participants. Beyond that, there is the *dialogue of sharing in prayer and religious experience.*

There are surely problems involved in any claim to praying in common with members of other religions: can we "pray together" when a Buddhist partner has

---

2. Pope Paul VI, "*Ecclesiam suam*, Encyclical of Pope Paul VI on the Church" (Vatican: The Holy See, Aug. 6, 1964).

no faith in a God to pray to? However, experience and reflection say that there is a form of contemplative "prayer" based on being consciously together in the Presence of the Absolute Goal of our existence that can be shared by most religiously minded people.

The *Guidelines for Interreligious Dialogue* issued in 1989 by the Dialogue Commission of the Catholic Bishops' Conference of India spoke of this as "sharing in prayer and contemplation. The purpose of such common prayer is primarily the corporate worship of the God of all, Who created us to be one large family. We are called to worship God not only individually but also in community." This is how the Christian would interpret the value of such prayers. Other religious people may have a different articulation. The text appeals to the practice and testimony of Mahatma Gandhi for whom "congregational prayer is a means for establishing the essential unity through common worship" (*Guidelines*, no. 82, p. 68).

The search for deeper bonds of fellowship with religiously minded brothers and sisters has led some Christians to open themselves to a kind of "mystical dialogue," if the expression is not self-contradictory, to a sharing of spiritual lights, which may often include a large measure of shared silence! They revive the oft-forgotten appeal of Vatican II to members of religious institutes to "attentively consider how the ascetic and contemplative traditions, whose seeds have at times already been planted by God in ancient cultures, even prior to the preaching of the gospel, may be incorporated into Christian religious life" (*Ad Gentes* 18, see also 11).

Even the Congregation for the Evangelization of Peoples has spoken of four types of dialogue, the last of which wants "to share the spiritual experiences in order to participate in the spiritual treasures of each other's religions."

2. Can There Be an Eschatological Faith?

The acceptance of forms of spirituality coming from different traditions within our commitment of faith appears to many Christians as a necessary antidote to the unease not seldom felt in professing the Christian faith proclaimed as the eschatological Word of God in a world where eschatology[3] is not yet a visible reality and where many religious people, and others too, evidently are unable to accept that there can be a "final" word before the end of history. In this post-modern world that has rejected any all-encompassing epic visions, Christians may ask themselves whether they are victims of a hubris when they profess the Christian creed as the expression of God's definitive Word to the human family with the total certainty implied in the act of faith. Would the expressions of the "absoluteness" of Christianity, its "transcendence," its "eschatological"

---

3. Eschatology is a topical subject in theology dealing with things ultimate namely the resurrection of the dead, judgment day, and life eternal.

character, be perhaps the fruit of the post-Enlightenment culture rather than of the gospel of Jesus?

This unease and the doubts it raises even in believing hearts lead us to a reflection about the meaning of our profession of faith. They may lead us to accept a distinction between what we believe *on principle* and what we have made our own, or assimilated; between our creed and our spirituality. The distinction does not seem to lack natural validity. We all hear declarations of love in weddings: "I promise to be true to you in good times and in bad, in sickness and in health. I will love you and honor you all the days of my life." The promise is not false. The love on which it is based is authentic. But we also know that the fulfillment will take many years of living together and will pass through many ups and downs.

The love lived day after day does not often measure up to the quality of love professed at the time of marriage. In our faith life, too, much as we may profess a total commitment to the Lord revealed to us as the "eschaton" of history, and however much as we mean it sincerely, we never succeed in fully living up to it.

This is the reason for Christian humility. However ultimate be the revelation to which we surrender, we are never sure that our lived faith corresponds to the quality of the Word given to us. Experience also teaches us that at least some believers who profess different creeds live up to their own commitments to an extraordinary degree. One may think of Mahatma Gandhi, or many similar models. Only God who scrutinizes the heart can measure our commitments, however true in intention the commitment itself may be. Perhaps this is the lesson we must draw from the scene of the last judgment, described for us in Matthew 25: we are ultimately judged by our concrete lives, not by our creeds.

3. Creed and Faith

This however does not mean that our creed is either invalid or futile. If nothing else, it reminds us that the value of the Christian faith is not measured by the quality of our response to God but by the reality of the Divine Love communicated to us through it. There are also other presuppositions in the "dialogue" of spirituality. The first is that God has spoken to our ancestors and speaks to us in many partial and different ways. The opening sentence of the letter to the Hebrews says this clearly. There are many translations of the first word, but it surely states the fact of a long history of the divine address to the human family. The etymology of the [Greek] word (*poly-meros*) seems to suggest plurality of *partial* words, or words partially revelatory, more than plurality of times. This "plural" word is contrasted with the fullness of the word spoken "in a son" who is the "heir" of all.

This text is a basic source for all theologians who have in recent times reflected on theology of religions. Few however seem to pay attention to the contrast and the finality that the letter gives to the word spoken through "a son": Jesus. The important thing for them, which we should not forget, is that God has spoken often in the past. It is true that in the immediate context of the letter these revelations of God may refer to those recorded in the Bible itself. But chapter 11 will recall the saving "faith" professed by personages who did not belong to the Jewish ancestry as such: Abel, Enoch, Noah. And in chapters 6 and 7 Melchizedek, a "pagan" priest, is presented as a type of priesthood foreshadowing the meaning of Jesus Christ, who is surely the eschatological Word. Today many theologians see without hesitation in this affirmation of Hebrews 1:1 a larger truth than the revelatory nature of the whole Jewish tradition. Luke's Peter says it in Acts: God never left himself without witness (Greek: *a-martyron*) in the long history of humanity (Acts 14:17). God has spoken and continues to communicate both with individuals and with communities in many ways. It is obvious that each one of us must respond to the Divine Voice in the way It calls us.

A second presupposition of interfaith dialogue which many Christians today take for granted is that God calls us now to listen to his voice as it is echoed in the beliefs and practices of his faithful from other than our own religion. This may sound strange, but is implied in the universal character our faith gives to the revelation in Christ. If universal, it must be open to all. Many Christians feel called to try religious paths that have been trod for centuries and millennia, many of which to all evidence have produced magnificent fruits of kindness and holiness. If God really has been calling people in various ways, then why should God's voice to them not be relevant and valuable for us too? The present stage of human evolution, where people of many families sit together at the table where the common political and social issues are discussed, creates a desire for harmony and cooperation in order to overcome the fissiparous trends that result from human pride and sin. There is an urgent need of an effort toward spiritual openness and convergence. This need not deny the plurality of paths, but may make us aware that somehow they are related to one another.

4. Is Double Religious Identity Possible?

In a recent article in the *Vidyajyoti Journal* (July 2009) Indian theologian Michael Amaladoss studies the question of the double religious identity. He makes a distinction between double belonging and double identity. Belonging is essentially a social category, and therefore must respect the social laws involved. Based on ultimate socioreligious commitment, membership to one religion seems to exclude the membership to another religion, the object of whose ultimate commitment is seen to all appearances as divergent and not seldom incompatible. This is true also in the political world. Yet even there, where patriotic commitments seem to exclude plurality, there is now a growing number of cases where, by mutual agreement, people are entitled to a double nationality. Should we speak of a primary political commitment and secondary ones? The question is not so clear and needs further experience and study.

At the level of spiritual commitment, however, there seems to be in theory less objection to multiple identity. In fact in some way this is everybody's experience. We all know of multiple schools of spirituality within the Christian tradition. Apart from the fact that the four Gospels represent different perceptions of Jesus Christ, we have in the New Testament itself different stresses in the response to God in authors like Paul, Matthew, Luke, Mark, the author of Hebrews, John. . . . Later, in some form the various "particular churches" within the "Roman" Church represent specific forms not only of church organization but also of spirituality. There is surely an oriental spirituality, an Orthodox spirituality, and patristic, Franciscan, Dominican, Jesuit forms of spirituality.

We may identify with the spirituality of several traditions: as Christians we are all shaped by the spirituality of our Jewish ancestry, although reinterpreted in the light of our faith in the Lord Jesus. And we cannot ignore in our faith any form of spirituality suggested by the various biblical writings. Marcion[4] was rejected for doing that. Among all the biblical authors, no spirituality is totally different from others.

There is a center in all Christian spirituality, and it is the person of Jesus Christ, crucified and risen, revealing to us the mystery of the God who is love in Trinitarian self-communication.

Some in the Church insist that because Jesus is the perfect and final expression of the Father in our history, all forms of spirituality must be included in the New Testament and therefore the Christian needs not to appeal to any other tradition. This may be true if we speak in the *eschatological perspective*: the end sums up whatever was experienced in the means. But our immediate experience is historical, the *eschaton* remaining in the horizon of our faith in the resurrection. Although in our faith we hold on to this *eschaton*, we however live it through historical consciousness. And historical consciousness is always limited and provisional, always open to growth, to more. From this perspective we cannot but be limited, and we can surely learn from the ways in which God has spoken throughout history and other believers have responded to the Divine Word. And this is what the Indian Church is ready to explore.

Some Models

One of the early models for living such dialogal spirituality based on a double identity is Brahmabandhab Upadhyay [1861–1907], a Bengali convert to Catholicism in the late nineteenth century. Called at his birth in 1861

---

4. Marcion of Sinope (85–c. 160), excommunicated church leader who discarded the God of the Old Testament and accepted as true God only God as the Father of Christ.

Bhavanicaran Bandyopadhyay, this son of a police officer of the British Raj [the political authority in colonial British India] passed in his youth through many stages of interaction with the Western culture, by then in the process of getting rooted in renascent India. He ended as a marginal member of the Catholic Church and an extremist revolutionary against the British rule. In the peak years of his theological and spiritual output, in the nineties, he repeatedly professed himself a "Hindu-Christian": Hindu by birth and culture, Christian by faith and baptism.[5]

From the time of his conversion in 1891 he never hesitated about this double affiliation. He somehow found a way of explaining it intellectually by making a clear theological distinction between nature and grace or, in a sociological perspective, between culture and choice. He did pass through various stages of criticism and rejection of part of the Hindu heritage: Vedanta,[6] the bhakti popular traditions,[7] the contemporary revivalist movements. . . . Eventually he recovered most of the traditions he had criticized (he never lost his basic grounding in the Hindu cultural world) and seemed happy to walk alone on the uncomfortable tightrope he had stretched for himself between the Hindu tradition he loved viscerally and the Jesus he had discovered and to whom he had surrendered sincerely. He left many expressions of his double spiritual identity in many writings, the best undoubtedly being his "Hymn to the Blessed Trinity" under the Indian invocation of *Saccidananda*, where his Christian faith appears enriched by many references and allusions to the Hindu tradition at various levels of its history.

Upadhyay's was a lonely journey, but not ultimately futile in its scope. His political commitment to India's independence would find fruition beyond his dreams forty years after his death when, thanks to the leadership of Mahatma Gandhi, India affirmed its total independence [in 1947] and in 1950 declared itself to be a "sovereign democratic republic." Upadhyay's spiritual endeavor and theological reflection produced, soon after his death, a movement of sympathetic study of the Hindu theological world, and eventually of all Indian religions, that resulted in numerous philosophical and theological studies, often on the pattern of comparative studies. The so-called Calcutta School of Indian Theology, led by P. Johanns, G. Dandoy and others who edited *The Light of the East* (1922–1946) was much indebted to Upadhyay. These trends led to a search in the spirituality that had produced such rich theological expressions as we find in Hinduism.

The movement led to an integration of Indian spiritual traditions into the Christian search. Many tried to assimilate the Indian traditions of renunciation

---

5. See references in J. Lipner, *Brahmabandhab Upadhyay. The Life and Thought of a Revolutionary* (Delhi: OUP, 1999), 161 and passim.

6. Vedanta is one particular school of Hindu philosophy.

7. Bhakti popular traditions are pious Hindu religious traditions that emphasize emotional faith commitment.

or *sannyasa* within a Christian frame of reference. This was the original intention of Swami Abhishiktananda (the Benedictine Dom Henri Le Saux [1910-1973]), who, however, wrestled valiantly with the perceived incompatibility between Vedanta and the Christian faith.

His is the best-known case, because he wrote much about an integration of "Ermites du Saccidandnanda: *Sagesse hindou, mystique chrétienne*" (the title of one of his books, English translation under the title *Saccidananda*).[8] In its original French version this book ends with a commentary on Upadhyay's hymn to the Trinity. Abhishiktananda himself followed the *sannyasa* way of life [i.e., renouncing the world] and his diary reveals both the insights he obtained from his adoption of this form of Indian spirituality, and the tension he felt in not being capable of explaining to himself and to others how the truth of the *Upanishads*,[9] as he understood them, could coexist with the truth of Jesus Christ, as his Christian faith taught him. A disciple of his, Sister Sara Grant,[10] would also testify that her way was to hold in tension within her heart and mind the truth of both traditions, Advaita[11] and Jesus Christ Son of God and savior, letting the conceptual tension between these two worldviews remain taut in her soul and allowing this tension to produce a (subconscious?) spiritual wisdom.

Not all those inspired by Upadhyay followed the path of renunciation. Others took rather his path of involvement in the political world that was developing in the long gestation of Indian political freedom in the first half of the twentieth century. Some associated themselves with the Gandhian movement: the best-known figure in this was the Anglican missionary C. F. Andrews [1871–1940], a great friend and supporter of the Mahatma in his *satyagraha* campaign [i.e., nonviolent resistance] and his negotiations with the British Raj. Even today the thought of the Mahatma, who himself felt the attraction of Jesus Christ, inspires many activists in their political commitments. Other activists have followed a path more to the left, although generally keeping the nonviolent style, working for social justice and equality of both classes and castes. Many of their names have been more or less directly associated with Bangalore-based CISRS (the Christian Institute for the Study of Religion and Society), the best-known thinker and activist of whom was perhaps the protestant M. M. Thomas [1916–1996], Moderator of the Central Committee of the World Council of Churches (WCC) in Geneva, 1968–1975. This trend has also produced a movement particularly concerned with restoring dignity to the outcastes of India, which

---

8. Paris: Casterman, 1956; English translation: *Saccidananda: A Christian Approach to Advaitic Experience* (Delhi: ISCPK, 1984).

9. Upanishads provides ancient interpretations of the Vedas, regarded as holy tradition in Hinduism.

10. Sister Sara Grant, RSCJ (1922–2002), British Indologist, Christian missionary, and one of the pioneers of interreligious dialogue in India.

11. Advaita is a nondualistic Indian philosophy based on the Upanishads.

receives the general title of "Dalit Theology." This is both a social and spiritual movement, and like other Christian movements in India is deeply ecumenical.

5. Paths Leading into Indian Spirituality

There are many paths through which Christians seek to integrate Indian spiritual traditions into Christian practice. Let me outline a few: the path of meditation, the path of political activism in the form of *ahimsa* [nonviolence] and *satyagraha*, the path of intertextual scriptural reading.

Meditation

The Indian forms of meditation have been in the market place for many decades already. In 1956 a "Yogin of the Christ" (J. M. Déchanet, OSB) could claim in the booklet *La voie du silence* that the exercises of Yoga were well known in the West. In effect, orientalists and Indian swamis [holy men] had already publicized this tradition of spirituality. Numerous Christians began to adopt what came to be called "Christian Yoga," though yoga can hardly bear any qualifier. Some people did find help in the various exercises of yoga, not only for mental relaxation but also for spiritual preparation for prayer and as a spiritual path by itself. Its Japanese counterpart may be even better known in Germany thanks to the work of Fr. Enomiya Lassale [SJ, 1898-1990]. The basic idea is well known: to seek interior silence, to empty the mind of its constant flow of images and emotions, even "religious" ones, so as to lead it to rest and to let the deeper level of the psyche surface and produce its fruit of quiet, peace, [and] supra-conceptual vision.

How far this Indian trend has had direct influence on the spiritual traditions of meditation in the modern West (e.g., John Main, Thomas Merton) is a matter for investigation. Whether the association of breathing with the exercise of concentration was already present in the ancient traditions of the Fathers of the Desert, and whether it had an influence from the Yogic *pranayama* [particular Yogic practice of extending the *prāṇa* or breath] are again historical questions that need not concern us here. Even St. Ignatius recommends in the first form of prayer at the end of *The Spiritual Exercises* that one associates mental prayer with the rhythm of one's natural breathing.

Recent studies on the Ignatian contemplative tradition also stress the importance of "stopping where one finds satisfaction" in what one is meditating, thus preparing "the way of silence" and letting grace work directly on the soul, beyond the mediation of concepts. Is this trend due to any Indian spiritual influence?

Without going specifically into the ways of Yoga or Zen, Fr. Tony de Mello's books have been immensely popular in the Spanish- and English-speaking world in spreading various themes of the Indian spiritual traditions in the West. His first book, *Sadhana*, in 1978, dealt specifically in ways to prayer. Its popularity may be compared to that of another booklet, *Prayer*, by Swami Abhishiktananda, first published in 1967. Both authors have written abundantly in areas of Eastern spirituality. In general, Ignatian retreat directors propose exercises of inner quieting through body awareness, and specifically related to the exercise of breathing. In this, many find a way to deeper levels of contemplation. Another useful author well known in the German- and Spanish-speaking worlds is the Hungarian Jesuit Franz Jalicsz.

Obviously this spiritual path suggests also a certain adaptation of the metaphysical frame of reference. We are accustomed in the Christian traditions, at least in the West, to operate on a dualistic understanding rooted in a metaphysics of the person as a relational being. God is the Other, *"totaliter alius"* [the totally other], necessarily beyond any form as we experience them in the created universe. Yet the creature relates to this "Other" and, like in Indian bhakti, the relation may be conceived as that of the creature to the Creator, of the servant to the Lord and Master, or of the son/daughter to Parent (actually to Father), of a lover and the Beloved, perhaps even of a friend to the Friend, especially when mediated by the incarnate figure of Jesus Christ.

But in all cases it is an I-Thou relation, not always avoiding a certain implication of quasi-familiar camaraderie with the Divine and a danger of placing the Creator and the creature at the same level. Is a different "ontology," a sense of identity or "reflection," possible in the Christian perspective? The *advaita* tradition seeks a *subjective* knowledge of the *Absolute Brahman*, as "self" (*atmatvena*), as "subject," rather than an *objective* knowledge. Can this find a place in the Christian search traditionally patterned after the symbol of the "Son" of God? Where do we place the "Word" and where the oneness between Father and Son of which John's Gospel speaks?

In a series of lectures he gave in Delhi and other cities of India (later published as *Truth Is Two-Eyed*, London SCM, 1979) the Anglican bishop John Robinson suggested that we would be spiritually enriched if we take into consideration the "Eastern" presupposition of a certain identity between the individual self and the absolute Self, and hold this view together with the personalist or "dualistic" way of the West, without trying to find a metaphysical synthesis of the two. Any healthy bodily vision, he explained, requires two eyes: each perceives a different angle of reality. In a process beyond the conscious activity, the brain somehow fuses the two pictures into one where there is a sense of depth and proportion richer than in either eye's picture. Everybody has a primary "eyesight," the other acting as complementary. Such, he suggested, should be the meeting of East and West: a search for a richer vision in which the traditional Christian Western eye is enriched by a "different picture," letting the subconscious spiritual life fuse the two into one vision. And vice versa.

Of course the two-eye metaphor will need to be expanded: there is not only a so-called "Oriental" and a "Western" pattern of spirituality; there may be, there are other patterns (e.g., those of the indigenous peoples who live closer to mother earth). At any rate *advaita* has often been valued by Indian Christian theologians and spiritual masters. Upadhyay did it between the nineteenth and the twentieth centuries. In 1925 a priest in the Nilgiris, Rev. J. F. Pessein, published a book, *Vedanta Vindicated or Harmony of Vedanta and Christian Philosophy*, printed in the Jesuit Press of Trichinopoly. In 1950 an Indian priest from Bombay, Fr. H. O. Mascarenhas, suggested the spiritual significance of *advaita* in a booklet, *The Quintessence of Hinduism*, which was then heavily criticized and ignored.

Today many Christian theologians and committed Christians are in search of a kind of "Christian advaita." After Abhishiktananda, M. Amaladoss has often touched on this theme. The question remains as to what is the relation of the contemplation of the life of Jesus and the saints in the Christian tradition and the search for a supra-conceptual experience of the "Self" (in the Indian tradition) or the divine Spirit in us.

Political Activism

The first book Gandhi actually wrote as a text, and which he also translated from his mother tongue Gujarati into English, is known as *Hind Swaraj* [Indian Home Rule], and in 2009–2010 India celebrated the centenary of its first edition. Here as well as in other writings and in his whole political life, Mahatma Gandhi raised political involvement to the level of spirituality. He followed the Indian tradition that the four human goals (Sanskrit: *purushartha*) of life should be sought conjointly in a balanced manner: *artha* or wealth-cum-power (politics), *kama* or pleasure of the senses and the spirit, *dharma* or duty performance in social and religious relations, and *moksa* or the search for inner and ultimate liberation. The last represents the highest *purushartha*, but does not eliminate the validity of the other goals.

Following his interpretation of the *Gita* [Bhagavad Gita], quite different from that of his illustrious predecessor Sankaracharya,[12] Mahatma Gandhi heard the call of the divine to join the struggle, to "fight" for the well-being of humanity, but without violence, and without seeking personal rewards. In many ways the *Gita* is a search for a spirituality of detachment within a commitment to the moral and political struggles for the good. However, if we accept that chapter 11[13] is important, the experience of the Divine involved in the evolution of the universe may be considered the prophetic core, in the words of R. C. Zaehner,[14] of the moral teaching of this text.

In the Gandhian tradition this teaching finds expression in two important and interlinked themes: *ahimsa* and *satyagraha*. *Satyagraha* is the goal: "an

---

12. Sankaracharya, 8th/9th-century founder of the Advaita Vedanta school of Indian philosophy.

13. Chapter 11 of the *Gita* deals with the vision of the ultimate Cosmic Form.

14. R. C. Zaehner (1913–1974), British scholar of comparative religion and intelligence officer.

earnest holding on to '*Truth*'," which may be considered as close to what the New Testament means by "faith," with the obvious difference that while for the Christian writers the "Truth" is somehow expressed in Jesus Christ, for Gandhiji it was "social" justice, in concrete the struggle for independence and economic reform for India. Life has no meaning unless it is imbued with *satyagraha*.

Ahimsa on the other hand refers to the purity of means to be maintained in every endeavor of life. Basically it means absence of aggressiveness or the desire to hurt or kill. Gandhiji elevated this primary theme of ancient Indian ethics (with roots in Buddhism and Jainism) to a complete spirituality for political action. Often translated as equivalent to the British "Nonviolence," there is a danger in the translation that we turn the adjective into a noun. Actually Gandhian "Nonviolence" is a short form for "nonviolent action," with stress on the noun.

The political career of the Mahatma shows him in constant activity to checkmate the British Raj by all religious, social, and political resources available to him, excluding violence, which was the path that some of his younger contemporaries were advocating to obtain freedom for India. Gandhi saw the futility of violence. The post-Gandhian history has vindicated his stand, and the various movements for nonviolent political action, whether in South Africa, among the blacks of North America or the "Indians" of South America, or in Europe itself, this form of Indian spirituality has left a valuable legacy: Lanza del Vasto, Martin Luther King Jr., Octavio Paz, Perez Esquivel, Bishop Helder Camara, and Nelson Mandela.

Reading the Scriptures Intertextually

I come now to a third way by which Christians are attempting to open themselves more to the Indian spiritual traditions, related in some form to the meditative way mentioned above, but taking as its basis not the Yoga tradition but the sacred scriptures. I refer to the intertextual reading of sacred texts as sacred texts. Already in 1974 a group of theologians in India came together under the auspices of the Bangalore-based National Biblical, Catechetical and Liturgical Centre to study whether at least an occasional use of readings of Scriptures of other religions within the Christian liturgy or paraliturgies was meaningful, and whether we can theologically say that such Scriptures are in some way "inspired," taking into account the analogical way in which the adjective "inspired" is used in respect to the biblical books themselves.

The general agreement, with many qualifications, was clearly in favor of an analogical affirmation of such "inspiration" with all that it implies, and also the prudent use of such readings with communities that are prepared for it. Later on the theological faculty of St. Peter's Institute in Bangalore initiated a special course/seminar in the master's degree program on the "inspiration" of the non-biblical scriptures. The Third World theological trend has gone in this direction in the last thirty-five years. Today most theologians of Asia seem to think that in some way God has spoken to their communities especially through the texts that have been received and preserved as sacred and foundational. Retreats based on the *Gita* and similar texts are offered to Christian groups interested in closer relationships with other religions. Connected with this, there is also the growing trend of celebrating in some form the more important religious festivals of our neighbors. Even the Pontifical Council for Interreligious Dialogue sends greetings each year to the faithful of other religions on the occasion of their principal feasts like Ramadan, Diwali [the Hindu festival of lights], Vaishakh [the main Sikh festival], among others. Christians in India go further and celebrate—by themselves or in union with members of other religions—these festivals at the social and even at religious levels.

There is a special liturgy approved by the Holy See for the celebration of Diwali as a feast of "Christ the Light of the World." This is clearly a case of appropriation. Others prefer to preserve the original meaning and significance of these feasts, though always celebrated in the context of the Christian faith. Not only the feasts of the Great Tradition are thus celebrated but also the specific feasts of Tribal and Dalit communities.

Recently two significant books by a North American Jesuit indologist, Francis X. Clooney, have spelled out further implications of this way. He had earlier written abundantly on doing theology in India, but his last two books published in 2008 focus on the means and importance of intertextual reading of the scriptures. The books are *The Truth, the Way, the Life* (Peeters & Eerdmans) and *Beyond Compare* (Georgetown University Press). The first offers a very detailed Christian reading of a basic *mantra* [a sacred utterance, chanted over and over again] of South Indian Vaishnavism:

> *Om, Obeisance to Narayana!* Having completely given up all dharmas [activities], to Me alone come for refuge, from all sins I will make you free. Do not grieve. I approach for refuge the feet of Narayana [the supreme God] with Shri [supreme consciousness, which, again, is God]!

In his explanation, rich for its constant reference to the ancient Indian commentatorial literature, Clooney studies the possibility for a Christian of praying this *mantra* as it is, and the limitations he or she may find in repeating it, with sincerity and honesty to her or his Christian roots. He suggests that Hindus may equally want to use at times Christian prayers for their own meditation and repetition, reinterpreting them from their spiritual perspectives. This would open the door to a shared spiritual experience.

In *Beyond Compare* it is not a prayer that is shared between the two traditions, but two books that are read one in the light of the other so that there is, so to say, a mutual fecundation. The books are *The Essence of the Auspicious Three Mysteries* (*Srimadrahasyatrayasara*), a Sanskrit text by Venkatanatha, better known as Vedanta Desika (1268–1369), and the *Treatise on the Love of God* of St Francis de Sales (1567–1622). The common theme found in these two spiritual books is "loving surrender to God." Clooney makes a very detailed analysis of both texts and shows their stresses in the means they suggest to reach the peak spiritual experience. This Christian integration of the Indian spiritual tradition (and vice versa) as explained by Clooney can only be open to the few scholars that feel comfortable in the two worlds of the Hindu and Christian traditions, while other forms suggested above are open to a larger public. Even Mahatma Gandhi introduced the reading of scriptures of various traditions in his popular prayer meetings.

Conclusion

Few people will deny the need for the various religions of the world to come closer together and the possibility that Christians may be enriched by sharing the spiritual traditions of other religions. This is not syncretism where there is little concern for consistency of thought and action. It is rather what Sri Lankan Jesuit theologian Aloysius Pieris has called symbiosis, leading to a synergy, a "living together" with another and accordingly acting together. Such a process is not new: it has been operative from the beginning of history and the beginning of the Church. It requires the action of the Spirit of Truth, the Spirit of discernment that enables us to conjugate different and apparently irreconcilable traditions into one vision. Christians have from the second century at least made a symbiosis of the four Gospels into an integrated figure of Jesus Christ. It is not the primary concern of the spiritual person to propose a logical synthesis of the various traditions that one operates with simultaneously. The symbiosis works at the subconscious level, the work of the *Spirit of Love*. In the measure in which we grow *in* the love of all our brothers and sisters, even the most distant, in that measure there is bound to be a fusion of spiritualities, which should result in a source of energy for the world at large.

11

CHAPTER

Dialogue of Life

Celebrating our Commonalities, Understanding our Differences[1]

Auxiliary Bishop Barry C. Knestout

EDITOR'S NOTE

"The art of engaging well in interreligious dialogue is . . . a necessity," Auxiliary Bishop Barry C. Knestout, of the Archdiocese of Washington, DC, told an audience of young adult Muslim, Hindu, Sikh, and Christian leaders at the second Generations of Faith conference in November 2012. Only by dialogue do "understanding and mutual respect" come about. "Interreligious dialogue practiced by ordinary Muslims, Christians, Sikhs, Hindus, Jews, and Buddhists can serve our nation and the world in ways that professional diplomats cannot," he said in his keynote address. However, since addressing issues of differing "notions of divine revelation" requires a solid basis of trust, attention should first be paid to "the dedicated cultivation of relationships," because genuine dialogue implies "to present oneself as vulnerable to another." In addition to opening one to the other in dialogue, the capacity for attentive listening, for "listening well," is of "critical importance for effective dialogue," Bishop Knestout said, as it enables proper understanding of existing differences. "Listening," he said, "is a sacred gift that leads to the goal of dialogue, namely, a deeper communion that has the potential to emerge in a space of trust."

The conference was organized by the Secretariat for Ecumenical and Interreligious Affairs of the U.S. Conference of Catholic Bishops and held at St. Paul's North American College in Washington, DC.

---

1. Auxiliary Bishop Barry Knestout, "Dialogue of Life: Celebrating our Commonalities, Understanding Our Differences" (keynote address, Generations of Faith II conference, Washington, DC, November 10, 2012). Reprinted with permission of the author.

You young adults are the future of this important work of interreligious dialogue. The network of relationships you are building, which will no doubt be expanded by today's encounter with your peers, will be the key to building greater trust and understanding and mutual cooperation in the public square in the coming years!

We have high hopes for you—for you are the future hands and feet of God in the world! This task of interreligious dialogue, a task that requires your hands and feet, that is, your commitment to interreligious service and cooperation, as well as understanding and solidarity, is of immense importance at this point in history. Let me explain:

On the one hand, it is obvious to all that the world is quite small now and that interaction among peoples from around the globe is, literally, a mouse click away. This phenomenon of immediacy means, like never before in human history, that one is almost guaranteed to encounter people of different races, languages, cultures, and religions. Being exposed to such difference is integral, therefore, to positive interactions in this new world. And to that end, the art of engaging well in interreligious dialogue is, I would dare to say, a necessity.

On the other hand, it is equally obvious that while people your age and older have always craved knowledge of God and of truth, there is a special, urgent cry of the human heart in this age—an age in which God has been pushed to the margins of cultural forms and expression—to know and experience God. People need to know that despite the palpable sense at times of God's absence as well as the presence of suffering and sadness in the world, God IS—and that God cares for each of us and calls us to himself, and to one another, in the hope of establishing love and mutual respect among all his children.

The modern era presents one answer to the question of how to accommodate an increasing diversity of religious belief and expression in Western culture, a diversity that sometimes may lead to tension or conflict. It is the approach of secularism—the pushing of those with religious belief to the margins of or completely out of the civic space. However, there is another approach which is more effective and respectful of the reality of the spiritual dimension of life: dialogue, which has as its fruit understanding and mutual respect.

To that end, interreligious harmony is an important way, indeed a necessity, to facilitate rather than hinder the deepest need of every human heart, that is, the need of having the joy and love of God brought to all people. You must strive to cultivate a dialogue with "the other" such that you can help bring about a culture where the pursuit of God is celebrated, and not hindered, because of the differences of religious expression amongst us.

I believe that the young people of the present generation have qualities which are most conducive to fruitful dialogue. Some of you may have heard of the generational theories of Neil Howe and Bill Strauss, historians and social scientists who have written extensively on generational issues. They list seven core traits of what they have named the Millennial Generation—those at present who are roughly 30 years of age and younger. These traits include being special, sheltered, confident, team oriented, conventional, pressured, and achieving. I believe that two of these qualities serve well in dialogue—first, the confidence that is expressive of optimism about yourselves and your future. This positive outlook I believe makes you more open to dialogue. Second, team orientation gives this generation an instinct for collegiality—and a strong desire to not leave anyone out of participation in the culture. Also, being a very diverse generation, many the children of immigrants, you are used to dealing with a diversity of individuals in school and in other circumstances.

Pope Benedict XVI, in addressing the youth of all religions during a trip to Lebanon, captured well this sentiment:

> [We must strive] to be completely open to others, even if they belong to a different cultural, religious, or national group. Making space for them, respecting them, being good to them, making them ever more rich in humanity and firm in the peace of the Lord. . . . [This kinship] is a foretaste of heaven![2]

Seeing you, hearing your stories, and witnessing the seeds of friendship that you are planting among one another, I take heart that this important ministry of interreligious dialogue will thrive in your generation—and in ways rarely seen before!

For Catholic Christians, we are invited by the Pope—indeed by Christ himself—to cast our nets in search of truth, as well as to proclaim that truth which we have discovered in our own faith—but also to recognize and appreciate the expressions of truth that we perceive in other religious traditions!

The Declaration on the Church's Relations with Non-Christian Religions (*Nostra Aetate*), proclaimed by Pope Paul VI in October 1965 and published among the documents of the Second Vatican Council, expresses this thought this way: "The Church, therefore, urges its sons and daughters to enter with prudence and charity into discussion and collaboration with members of other religions. Let Christians, while witnessing to their own faith and way of life, acknowledge, preserve, and encourage the spiritual and moral truths found among non-Christians, together with their social life and culture" (no. 2).

---

2. Pope Benedict XVI, "Address of His Holiness Pope Benedict XVI" (Address at Meeting with Young People, Apostolic Journey to Lebanon, Bkerké, Lebanon, 15 September 2012).

Body of Speech

The importance and urgency of effective interreligious dialogue is an obvious fact of modern life—one need only consider religious tension that intensified in some places after 9/11. Obvious also, at least for professional ecumenists and interfaith officers in the church, is the fact that such dialogue must be focused on building and maintaining relationships before any serious conversation—say, over the nature of competing notions of divine revelation—can emerge. More specifically, for those who are tasked with the leadership of faith communities— this will mean you in the near future—the dedicated cultivation of relationships will allow for a space of trust to emerge that will not only facilitate authentic and fruitful theological debate but, more importantly, serve as an effective engine for positively connecting individual members of different faith traditions. One might say that good interpersonal relations among leaders produces tangible fruits not only among those in formal dialogue, but also for ordinary faithful Christians, Muslims, Hindus, Sikhs, Buddhists, and Jews.

That being said, one might ask what then makes for effective dialogue between leaders and, ultimately, between the faithful of different religions? However, before answering this question, it is helpful to begin with a consideration of the meaning of the word "dialogue" itself.

The word "dialogue" is derived from the Greek *dia-logos. Dia* is a preposition meaning "through" while *logos* is a complex word meaning many things but generally denoting reason, thought, mind, or word. When *dia* is prefixed to *logos* the word conveys the sharing of speech between two people that brings to expression the content of thought and so serves as a powerful vehicle for the disclosure of truth. In short, dialogue is an event that discloses truth (or, sadly, untruth) between people. It is essentially the sharing of what is in my mind with an "other" who shares what is in his or her "mind." Right away one can see that this interpersonal dynamic is a fragile business, a balancing act, one might say, between human beings as agents engaging in an exchange of truth that will shape our understanding of the other and, perhaps, determine our actions. Dialogue requires, therefore, the willingness to present oneself as vulnerable to another. One must choose to disclose oneself, one's "truth," to another in the hope that what is shared will be received with welcome, with care, with the feeling of safety.

For example, speaking from my own limited experience in interreligious dialogue, a Muslim or a Jew who cherishes a radically transcendent monotheism that precludes belief in the very possibility of Incarnation (God become flesh) must feel that his or her non-Muslim partner in dialogue will receive his or her (Islamic or Jewish) belief with an openness that suggests that his/her (Islamic or Jewish) belief will not be mocked, dismissed, pilloried, or, at least at first, challenged.

"You, my Muslim dialogue partner, will be listened to with respect," one must say. "You will be given a space to disclose your mind and heart. I will listen. I want to listen. I want to know you, and I promise to respect your thoughts as they unfold to me, the recipient of your trust."

Furthermore, "I" as the privileged subject-recipient of what you hold to be objectively true from your faith perspective—the content of your heart and mind—must also make a choice. In this case, I must choose to conduct myself with integrity by being an active listener that is perceptibly patient and warm. I must listen and not speak, at least not at first, and not until I am invited. I must, perhaps above all, present a welcoming countenance and mean it. I am, as it were, the active agent of the other before me—beckoning them to present themselves, that is, their true feelings and ideas, without fear, by means of the outward welcoming disposition of a trustworthy companion.

One can see how effective and true dialogue unfolds as an exercise in what Catholic thinkers would call the shepherding of being; that is to say, the drawing out of the shadows (in this case, the inner world of the dialogue partners) the true, good, and beautiful that we hold as dear, as precious, as inviolable, and which, when given a space, can bring about the positive transformation of the world. The Christian example, of course, is Jesus the Good Shepherd who welcomed others into the gift of the triune life of God, including especially those on the margins of that society who received him with trust and so were willing to share their own lives with him without fear. Think, for example, of the martyrs, saints, and countless legions of followers down through the centuries, not to mention his own contemporaries—who were able to serve as agents for the establishment of the church in the world.

In short, a good way of describing the nature of dialogue is to study the interplay between humans acting as subjects of the logos-word and objects of the logos-word. On the one hand, I as "subject" find myself to be in the position of one whose job in dialogue with another is to draw out of the other, the truth; and so, in a sense, I by virtue of being the subject find myself to be a shepherd of the truth.

On the other hand, I as "object" find myself under the gaze of the subject who is asking me to bear the truth of what I hold within. In short, will I, by virtue of being in this case that object, entrust my thoughts, my truth, to the other? Just as Christians are called in the first place to accept the invitation of Our Lord to trust him and so share our whole life with him, so too, in the same sense, we Christians are called to imitate his act of welcome to us by extending it to others.

As a Christian, one might suggest that true dialogue between humans is a representation of God's love communicated to us through (*dia*) Christ (the Logos). If one accepts this interpretation of dialogue, then one might further suggest that engaging in dialogue—precisely in the way I have outlined it here—is in fact mandated by God. Therefore, we strive to create a space for authentic dialogue in our families and in our friendships, but also, and especially, in the public square with the other, the stranger, and the person of a different faith tradition.

This give-and-take world of dialogue, therefore, can be thought of as a defining moment in the lives of individuals. To welcome the other, to encourage him/her to love and share his/her life with the world, and so to bring people into the light and out of the world of loneliness and fear, is the basis for transforming the world into an ever-greater sphere of positive action that will lead to the formation of healthy minds and the building of culture. In other words, dialogue is the key not only to bringing people from our own traditions closer to one another and to those "outside" our particular group, but also, and especially, to opening up the realm of grace, which alone brings healing and understanding, creativity and fruitfulness.

Since some might say that people of all religious traditions acknowledge that the grace (or gift) of God heals the divisions that separate us from one another, it is equally true that our choice to engage in authentic dialogue is a sign of our cooperation with God's grace to bring about such healing, and so dialogue is, to be sure, the key to making a space for God to bring about ever greater healing in the world.

Our commitment to an authentic and robust dialogue will foster understanding and peaceful coexistence. With respect to the tensions between faiths nowadays, one might assert that interreligious dialogue, practiced by ordinary Muslims, Christians, Sikhs, Hindus, Jews, and Buddhists, can serve our nation and the world in ways that professional diplomats cannot.

Celebrating our Commonalities

With respect to my main theme of "dialogue," it is clear that each of our traditions places a premium on the importance of cultivating a listening disposition in order to attain greater understanding that makes possible the emergence of an area of trust between persons.

To listen—to be mindful and attentive to the other is, I am convinced, a common thread to any successful dialogue in all the great faith traditions of the world. But what does this mean exactly?

My understanding of the notion of mindfulness and attentiveness is that they make possible a kind of "authentic recognition" of the other—that is to say, they manifest in me, the listener, a real commitment to the other, a commitment to providing a space in which you can disclose yourself. In disclosing yourself, you are therefore showing me your inherent dignity or worth, which Christians believe is a manifestation of the presence of God and therefore commands respect and reverence from me.

Understanding Our Differences

Dialogue in many ways presupposes difference (personal, spiritual, etc.) and these differences become the occasion for dialogue as well as the source of the matters addressed in dialogue. A recognition of difference is tied to our own identity and integrity as a distinct human person. We perceive the distinction between "I" and "thou." In dialogue, differences are explained to better reveal which differences are essential, which are accidental, and which are illusory.

Of critical importance for effective dialogue is the capacity to understand our differences, which requires the prior disposition of being a good listener. One cannot understand difference without listening and listening well. Listening, therefore, has the potential to produce tremendous fruits in dialogue—not least of which is the fruit of trust.

In other words, for you to know that you are truly listened to is a real gift—the gratitude for which usually entails ever-greater disclosure in direct proportion to an ever-greater degree of trust. Listening, therefore, is a sacred gift that leads to the goal of dialogue, namely, a deeper communion that has the potential to emerge in a space of trust.

So what about our real differences? Rather than talking directly to our differences, I would merely say this: that when one listens well to another, that is, listens with real compassion and attentiveness, then there is the possibility of trust. When there is trust, there is the potential for friendship. When there is friendship, there can be an honest discussion of differences. And, frankly, it should be our goal to reach this point of the dialogue. Why? Each of us holds his or her faith tradition to be the authentic revelation of God and truth for the world. This belief is the source of our hope and joy—why wouldn't we want to share this news with our friends? And so, while this advanced sharing should not be the first thing we bring to dialogue, it cannot be relativized or ignored.

In short, true dialogue, as I have tried to describe it from my own faith tradition, involves the prior disposition of listening, which leads to trust, which matures in friendship. This process makes possible an understanding of differences that does not lead to strife and discord.

What I mentioned earlier in my presentation bears repeating. The quote from the Declaration on the Church's Relations with Non-Christian Religions (*Nostra Aetate*), states that "The Church, therefore, urges its sons and daughters to enter with prudence and charity into discussion and collaboration with members of other religions. Let Christians, while witnessing to their own faith and way of life, acknowledge, preserve, and encourage the spiritual and moral truths found among non-Christians, together with their social life and culture" (no. 2).

Conclusion

For Roman Catholics, Pope John Paul II was an important figure for an entire generation of young people. Again and again he exhorted young people to draw closer to God, to learn to see him in all things, and so to take heart and to have hope, great hope, in a world that seems at times to have forgotten God.

But the search for God, John Paul taught, required that we see him in the human person—that is, that we acknowledge his abiding presence in each person regardless of class, culture, race, and religion. This is the world, he believed, that God desires.

To John Paul, it was as though this particular vision of what the world can look like, and ought to look like, is most realizable in youth. For young people have likely not been habituated to the ideas and behavior which militate against such an openness to the other.

On that note, I would like to conclude by referring to John Paul's 1985 speech to young Muslims in Morocco:

> You are charged with the world of tomorrow. It is by fully and courageously undertaking your responsibilities that you will be able to overcome the existing difficulties. It reverts to you to take the initiatives and not to wait for everything to come from the older people and from those in office. You must build the world and not just dream about it.[3]

---

3. Pope John Paul II, "Address of His Holiness John Paul II to Young Muslims" (Apostolic Journey to Togo, Ivory Coast, Cameroon, Central African Republic, Zaire, Kenya and Morocco, given in Casablanca, Morocco, August 19, 1985).

PART III

INTERRELIGIOUS DIALOGUE

SOME PRACTICAL SAMPLES

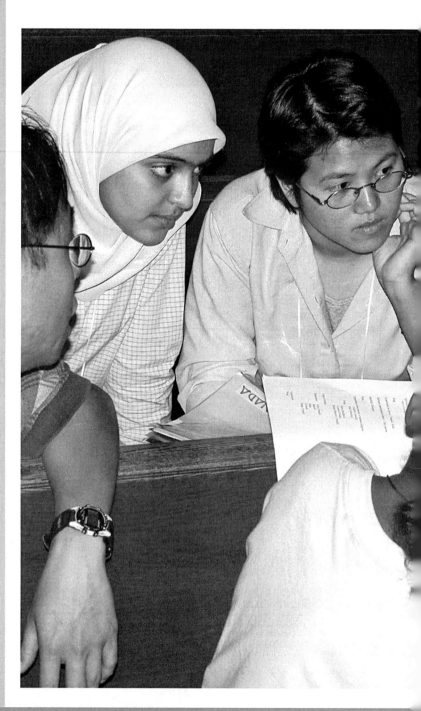

Attentive listening is one of the vital conditions for interreligious dialogue to succeed, displayed here in an informal encounter among people from distinct religious traditions.

12
CHAPTER

A Buddhist Monk as a Member of a Christian Mission College[1]

Andrew Wingate

EDITOR'S NOTE

Rev. Canon Dr. Andrew Wingate, OBE, is a minister of the Church of England with a long history of interfaith involvement. Canon theologian in Leicester, he was founding director of the St. Philip's Centre, internationally known for its interfaith work. Now consultant in Sweden on integration questions, he has served as the interfaith consultant for the Bishop of Leicester and the Director of Ministry and Training for the diocese. Leicester has the largest Hindu population in the United Kingdom as well as a substantial number of Muslims, Sikhs, and people of other faiths. Wingate was involved in theological education for 25 years—at the Tamilnadu Theological Seminary, in Madurai in southern India; as Principal of the West Midlands Course at Queen's College Birmingham, and as Principal of the College of the Ascension, a missionary training facility at Selly Oak, Birmingham, United Kingdom.

In the following article, Wingate shares his experiences as a teacher and principal of bringing a Buddhist monk from Sri Lanka to an international Christian community in training for missionary service. Wingate gives insights into the complexities of the religious situation in Sri Lanka today, his personal acquaintance with the monk, and the administrative struggles in securing the financial support for this three-month experiment. He includes many comments from individuals who experienced this living encounter with a monk from the Buddhist tradition and the mutual impact it had. While official events and classroom settings provided the formal stage for dialogue, it was the casual exchanges in the dining room, at the pool table, and in the computer

Continued

1. Reprinted with permission from the author. Original article published in association with the Network for Inter Faith Concerns of the Anglican Communion © 2013 Anglican Communion Office.

EDITOR'S NOTE *Continued*

room that made interaction between Christians from around the world and their Buddhist guest the most engaging and intensive. This "impact on the international Christian community," which was "very great," prompted Wingate to write the article, and his account gives vivid insight into the opportunities, challenges, and risks of getting involved in lived interreligious dialogue.

I first met the Venerable Sutadhara in 1999, when I was in Sri Lanka as a member of a Friends for Peace delegation of Churches Together in Britain and Ireland. As with every other outside visiting group, we were able to do little to further the cause of peace in this most intractable of civil wars, apart from gaining much more understanding of the complexity of a struggle which had ethnic, linguistic, social, and religious connotations.[2] Buddhists and Hindus were on different sides of this divide, as Sinhala and Tamil respectively. Muslims speak Tamil but felt deeply antagonistic towards the Tamil Tigers (the LTTE) because of the massacres Muslims had endured. Christians stood uneasily on both sides of the community divide; some took ethnic positions, while a minority tried to use their strategic position to work actively for peace.

As a community, Buddhists were much influenced by their monks. A few of these were actively engaged in peace efforts, while a number were actively militant in favor of the Sinhala cause. In between came the majority, who, like Sutadhara, continued their daily lives as best they could, willing peace, but not being politically active by temperament.

I met Sutadhara somewhat incongruously, in a bar in the rather nice hotel in which we were staying in Colombo. Dressed in the robes of his order, he seemed quite at home, as he had a cup of tea, and we discussed the possibility of coming to England to be the first official Interfaith Visiting Fellow at the United College of the Ascension, Selly Oak, Birmingham, where I was principal at that time. He had been recommended to me as someone for whom dialogue and listening were natural, and as someone who could be clear about his complex faith. He has a doctorate in linguistics and teaches in the university.

This first meeting revealed a man of great humility and graciousness. I also saw the first signs of an impish sense of humor that I was to get to know well later. Far from being rigid in his rules, he indicated he would be ready to adapt to our college in ways that surprised me. He did not normally eat after noon. I asked him whether he would expect his lunch early, and then to fast until the next morning, imagining that this would not endear him to our caterer. He said that this would not be necessary; as a guest he should adjust to our ways. I also

---

2. The Sri Lanka Civil War lasted from 1983–2009.

pointed out that the garb he was wearing, a saffron robe with bare arms, might fit our stereotype of a Buddhist monk, but might leave him shivering in our autumn and spring, yet alone winter. He said that putting a sweater over his shoulders would not invalidate his vows! More importantly, he said that, though he would share his faith with us, above all he wanted to learn about Christianity, a great religion that he knew little about, and that it was difficult to pursue such a study in his own context for communal reasons. He also wanted to learn about the way of life of Christian monks. Professionally, he would like to study local English dialects—quite a task in the West Midlands!

I came back determined to invite Sutadhara to England. There were some obstacles, as the proposal for an interfaith fellowship had to be approved by the Methodist Church, as well as my own Anglican Missionary Society, USPG. There was considerable discussion in the Methodist case. Could money donated in a Christian cause be used in this way? Was Christian mission not about converting Buddhists, but rather about learning from them? In the end, the proposal for an annual fellowship was approved in both cases.

My zeal to develop this program came from an earlier invitation I had been able to issue to a Hindu scholar who had been my fellow teacher in the Tamilnadu Theological Seminary in South India. He had been financed in a different way, but had shown the value of having a person of another faith living in the community. A devout Gandhian Hindu, he taught us much of Saiva Siddhanta, the Tamil religious philosophy of which he is a scholar. This is difficult to learn from books, but can be experienced through a visiting teacher. At the same time, he attended the chapel every morning. I asked him why he did this, when many of the Christian clergy did not. He said that the God he worshipped in Hinduism in India was the same God whom he met in the chapel. He believed that God left a space outside of his Hinduism each day to be filled with new knowledge and experience; here he filled it in our chapel and community. He used to listen especially carefully to the gospel readings, and wanted to discuss them each day at breakfast—not the norm among the Christian members of the community! He said that his Guru [spiritual teacher and role model] would be delighted that he was here. When I asked him who was his Guru, he said it was William Miller, former Principal of Madras Christian College, and a pioneer in Hindu-Christian interaction. I found this strange, as Miller died long before our Hindu was born. He smiled and said, "Yes that was so, but I found him such an inspiration when studying in his college, that I went daily to meditate, sitting beside his statue! That journey I am continuing here in Birmingham."

Sutadhara arrived on a cold January evening, looking as I had left him in the Colombo heat. He arrived in a taxi. As I welcomed him, I found that he was being cheated and an enormous fare was being demanded—a universal issue for those in a foreign land. I went out personally and negotiated a much lower fare. He was very impressed that, as a principal, I should engage in such action for him. His gratefulness continued daily for the three months he was with us, and his impact on the international Christian community was very great, hence this article.

These were some of the remarks made at his leaving party. A woman from the Philippines said, "He was not a monk to me, but a friend." A fellow Sri Lankan, a Christian priest, remarked, "As a monk, he ran up to me when I arrived and carried my case. This was an extraordinary experience for me. He is not just a functionary, doing religious actions for others; he is one who receives from others and offers himself to others." An African priest reflected, "He listened to my arguments, and reflected that what I was saying was not only Christian but something common between us. I have learned of Buddhism from classes, but I saw living Buddhism through him." Another African said, "I was initially skeptical, but won over by his friendship and kindness." Another remark: "I hope God will enable us to say as we go home from Birmingham, and continue our journey in life, 'This is what a Christian college can be like.'"

Sutadhara's response was characteristically generous. "This kind of Christian community," he said, "is a good place for children to grow up in." He gave an example of a college child who had gently reprimanded a friend from outside the college who was misbehaving, saying, "You should not do that kind of thing here." Sutadhara said, "I have enjoyed all the classes I have participated in, and attending chapel, where I have watched the faces of the congregation and noted the devotion expressed there. I came here with no preconditioning about Christianity. I have let what I have experienced here impact upon me. Such learning has been more important than what I have read in books. I am particularly impressed by the contribution Christianity makes to social justice. I will treasure this experience as one of the best times I have ever had in my life." A humbling contribution for us to hear, when so often we do ourselves down, or take what we have been given for granted.

I personally gained much from Sutadhara's time with us. I heard him expound Buddhism in a class I was convening on Christian Responses to Hinduism and Buddhism. Here we were responding to living Buddhism, not just to history or theory. He attended a class I was leading on Mission and St. Paul's Epistle to the Corinthians, and it was fascinating to hear him respond to this letter to a Christian community, with all its graces and divisions. He naturally focused on these issues of community so prominent there, and could see some of the experiences Paul was confronting mirrored in Buddhist communities.

I asked the class to prepare reactions to 1 Corinthians 11, the account of the institution of the Eucharist. It was he alone who highlighted the fact that if there are social and economic divisions coming to the fore, what is celebrated is not a true Eucharist at all. As a Buddhist he highlighted what the Christians had passed over, as they looked for theological niceties in the meaning of the words of Institution. He attended a class on the Psalms, and he loved seeing the way these enrich the devotion of Christians, as they expressed their religious feelings. He also attended my weekly Bible study group. Here students offered interpretations of biblical stories or parables that meant much to them; we heard from Sutadhara a beautiful story of the Buddha and how it could impact on daily life.

A further course he attended was on Development Issues. Here he was interested to see what is the distinctive religious contribution. He was clear that development should be harmonious with the environment in which we live. He was struck by the story of Noah and the place of the dove and the olive twig in the story. Human beings, animals, and plants all together can offer peace to the world if they are integrated one to another.

Not all, of course, found Sutadhara's presence easy to accept. In the ten years I was at the college, opinions about interfaith theology were the most polarized during the term he was with us. I am not sure if this was coincidence or if this was because someone in the community, though so self evidently a good soul, was not a Christian. This raised all the questions of such theology in practice and not just in abstract. How can we account for this goodness? Is it through the grace of God or should this not be presumed if he is not a Christian? Should this goodness therefore be accounted for as purely of nature and not of God? Can a man like Sutadhara be saved? If so, is it in spite of his religion or inclusive of his religion?

This discussion came to a head at an open evening, where I explained my kind of inclusivism and invited others to respond. Sutadhara said nothing, and just listened as some of the speakers excluded him from heaven, or even consigned him to worse, not of course by name, but because of the implications of their arguments. Afterwards, slightly anxiously, I asked him what he felt. He said with a twinkle, "I feel fine. It has been an exciting evening. I love hearing Christians disagree with one another! Some have very extreme views, but I enjoy seeing all these differences under one roof. And even if someone rejects the possibilities of interfaith dialogue, they are nearly always kind, or at least civil to me. If anyone appears unfriendly, I remember them in my meditation, spread kindness toward them, and they are then usually friendlier than before when I next meet them. One person found me difficult, but I found out that he had some major difficulties with people of other faiths in his earlier life. I then understood why he felt as he did."

Much sadder in one respect was the occasion when he was invited to lead a meditation in the weekly common prayer time, held between colleges. The staff of another Christian college made an announcement officially discouraging their students from attending. One of their staff members still attended, making a clear statement of her views, but none of their students attended. Sutadhara led the meditation in a characteristically inclusive way, encouraging participants to focus on Jesus if they wished, while he focused on the Buddha. It was a loving kindness meditation, Metta, which he likens to what Christians would know as God's love. We were asked to evoke our compassion first for ourselves, then for our families, friends, and neighbors, then for those to whom we are indifferent, then our enemies, and finally, for all living beings in the natural world. He ended by saying, "I know it is your custom to say the Grace as you leave; could someone please lead the Grace?" I rejoiced with those who had come to this special occasion, and felt sad for those whose views had prevented them being there. I thought also of a monastery in a forest in the hills near Kyoto in Japan, where, as a focus for meditation in the prayer hall, there is a sculpture of the Buddha engaged in dialogue with Jesus. This, of course, was impossible historically, but is a fascinating possibility in the imagination. It seemed to come near to the spirit of some of our discussions between this disciple of the Buddha and today's disciples of Jesus.

I relate one more incident of many. One Sunday afternoon, I was in the college when a destitute family knocked on the door, seeking help. I took them to the college kitchen to find them what food I could. Sutadhara saw us and asked if he could help. We gave them food and talked with them. As they were leaving, the father asked me for money; they had to get to Cornwall! I said I could not help them that far, but would give them a little. Sutadhara said, "Wait," and went to get his purse and gave from his modest allowance. After they had gone, I thanked him. He said, "Why are you thanking me? I want to thank you for giving me the opportunity to share with you in doing a deed of compassion. You remind me of my abbot who would have acted in the same way." What a lesson for those who expect acknowledgement as a right for the charitable works that they do.

After he had left, Sutadhara was interviewed about what he had learned. He said that he had learned things about his own faith and things useful for the practice of Buddhism. He had been impressed with the educational programs he had witnessed in the churches and felt there was a need to restructure their monastery programs, particularly to learn about other faiths, and also the different Christian denominations, which Buddhists all lump together. The aim should be to learn from each other, though being clear we have significant differences between us.

He had also learned from observing the lives of others. One example was an English Christian couple going to work in Belize, giving up their prison ministry in Britain. They showed to him the Christian way of life. It was not that everything in life was smooth for them, or their children were all doing well, but with all the difficulties, they enjoyed life and helped others as much as possible. He learned too from visiting three other Christian communities and reflecting with the monks there. He also used the opportunities of community life to engage in dialogue. These included the obvious places such as the dining room, but also the unexpected—the pool table, where he was a constant opponent to players of all cultures, faiths and ages, and the computer room. He was in the end provided with a computer in his room. But he felt that for an interfaith fellow, to go to the communal room was a real opportunity, maybe not to complete his work, but for engagement, and for helping others who were finding word processing quite a challenge.

My wife and I met Sutadhara again two months ago in Sri Lanka. It was one of the highlights of a short visit there, to be entertained to lunch in Colombo. He greeted me with a great embrace and we heard that he was recovering from a major car accident. As a passenger, he had suffered three breaks in his leg. He remarked that he had learned how to practice the right attitude to physical pain, and not just to teach it. He added with his usual humor, "It is great to be involved in interfaith. I was visited by the Anglican Bishop whom I met in Birmingham, and by Muslim, Hindu friends, as well as my Buddhist brothers. I have received so many blessings and prayers, and so I am recovering fast."

The meal we shared, he explained, had been given by Muslim neighbors, whom he had told of our coming. It was not only first-class food, but I felt a real sacrament of interfaith understanding and love, as six of us shared it together. Sutadhara asked me to sit next to him and serve him. A Buddhist monk is not supposed to serve himself, he explained!

As we left, he presented me with a book titled *Seeing Ceylon*, written by an inveterate traveller, who treks through forest, mountain, and remote village, in order to discover the true Sri Lanka. I will value this much. But I suspect it is Sutadhara who will always bring me closest to the heart of this fascinating, if tragic, island and to its profound but perplexing majority faith of Buddhism. He is also someone who for many has transformed "interfaith dialogue" from a slogan to a reality. Here we experienced true World Faiths Encounter.[3]

---

3. *World Faiths Encounter* is the title of the journal published by the World Congress of Faiths, in which this article first appeared. The journal title has since changed to *Interreligious Insight: a Journal of Dialogue and Engagement*.

13

Youth in Interfaith Dialogue

Intercultural Understanding and its Implications on Education in the Philippines[1]

Jayeel S. Cornelio and Timothy Andrew E. Salera

EDITOR'S NOTE

The following article was written by Philippine sociologists Jayeel S. Cornelio, Director of the Development Studies Program at the Ateneo de Manila University, and his senior student, Timothy Andrew E. Salera.

The Muslim-Christian Youth for Peace and Development program in the greater Manila area in the Philippines is an inspiring initiative indeed. Organized in 2011 as a forum for joint action and reflection by Christian and Muslim teenagers and young adults, ages twelve to twenty-four, in a neighborhood notoriously suffering from religious tensions and violence, the program is managed and run entirely by the youths themselves. In their weekly meetings they rarely discuss their religious differences, but rather focus on how to enhance the quality of the living togetherness in the community they share. It is by this concern for the common good that they bond across religious and cultural divides, forming personal relationships, and thereby arrive at a deeper understanding of and genuine respect for existing differences, no longer demonizing or fearing the religiously other. These same individuals then become critical agents for working toward sustainable peace in culturally and religiously diverse environments.

Continued

---

1. "Youth in Interfaith Dialogue: Intercultural Understanding and its Implications on Education in the Philippines," by Jayeel S. Cornelio and Timothy Andrew E. Salera. Reprinted in *Revista Innovación Educativa*, ISSN-e 1665-2673, Vol. 12, e 60, 2012, pages 41-62. Used by permission.

EDITOR'S NOTE *Continued*

The article, condensed for use in this book, reports about the results of interviews with twenty-two members of this Muslim-Christian program. The authors first screen some of the most current literature on interreligious/interfaith dialogue before introducing the project and sharing their findings. They identify, above all, the encounter between persons, the establishment of friendships, and the collective participation in local community affairs as the most important elements for cultivating intercultural and interreligious understanding—not discussion of questions of controversial doctrines—and call the project a "living dialogue" and a "dialogue of cooperation."

Abstract

In the wake of religious conflicts around the world, interfaith dialogues are being introduced to facilitate intercultural and religious understanding and tolerance. Although the participation of young people in interfaith dialogue and its impact on education is crucial to its sustainability, the literature on youth and interfaith has been very limited. This article addresses this gap by probing the significance or impact of interfaith on the views of our youth respondents on other religions. The views of our youth respondents show that interfaith dialogues do not have to begin and end in theological discussions. To them, the significance of interfaith revolves around the *person* (and not his or her religion), *friendships*, and *collective participation in the community*. . . . The article draws from interviews with the members of the Muslim-Christian Youth for Peace and Development (MCYPD), an interfaith community based in a neighborhood in Metro Manila.

Introduction

Many parts of the world have long been characterized by religious conflict, or at least by tensions that are justified religiously.[2] The 9/11 attacks on the United States simply globalized awareness of such a reality.[3] Historically rooted strife between Christians, Hindus, and Muslims is evident in societies around Asia and Africa, for example; and even in the West, the arrival of immigrants has engendered everyday forms of religious xenophobia. While Huntington[4] argues

---

2. M. Juergensmeyer, *Terror in the Mind of God: The Global Rise of Religious Violence. Comparative Studies in Religion and Society*, 3rd ed. (Berkeley: University of California Press, 2003).

3. D. Smock, "Introduction" in *Interfaith Dialogue and Peace-building*, ed. D. Smock (Washington, DC: United States Institute of Peace Press, 2002), 3–11.

4. S. P. Huntington, *The Clash of Civilizations and the Remaking of World Order* (New York: Simon and Schuster, 1996).

that contemporary conflicts are between geographic civilizations along religious lines, the reality is that tensions do exist within everyday local contexts as well.

The connection between religion and violence can be explained by how religious ideas are often employed to instill religious commitment, organize resistance, or even effect martyrdom.[5] Other observers argue though that religion, because of its inherent social boundaries, is predisposed to inflict violence especially on others who do not share it. In Wellman and Tokuno's view, conflict is necessary to create and nurture religious identity: "We believe it is folly to assert that true religion seeks peace; or that religion is somehow hijacked when it becomes implicated in conflict or even violence. Indeed religion does produce conflict and, less frequently, violence."[6]

Not many share Wellman and Tokuno's pessimism, however. Institutions around the world have responded to religious conflict by initiating interfaith dialogue as a way of fostering understanding between religions, building peace in the region, and even facilitating community development. In the Philippines, a predominantly Catholic country with significant religious minorities including Muslims, Protestants, and indigenous peoples, efforts to encourage dialogue have also been introduced. The Philippine Department of Education, for example, recently adopted the Face to Faith initiative of former British Prime Minister Tony Blair, a program that involves interfaith dialogue as part of the basic curriculum.[7] This, including the establishment of international and local interfaith organizations, is in response to the growing recognition of the need for interfaith dialogue among peoples of different religions to assuage the tensions that may be caused by discrimination among them. In particular, the goal is to establish peace and solidarity between Muslims and Christians in Mindanao.

Deemed central to these efforts is the involvement of young people for they do not only "share in the problems . . . but they also inherit the responsibility to sustain the peacebuilding effort in the region."[8] It is therefore not surprising that novel approaches in interfaith dialogue like Face to Faith now target young people. Yet despite this recognition, there has been a dearth of research on youth and their involvement in interfaith efforts. . . .

---

5. J. R. Hall, "Religion and Violence: Social Processes in Comparative Perspective" in *Handbook of the Sociology of Religion*, ed. M. Dillon (Cambridge, New York: Cambridge University Press, 2003), 359–381.

6. J.K. Wellman, Jr. and K. Tokuno, "Is Religious Violence Inevitable?" *Journal for the Scientific Study of Religion* 43, no. 3 (2004): 293.

7. T. Quismondo, "DepEd Adopts Tony Blair Religious Literacy Program," *Philippine Daily Inquirer,* August 24, 2011, *http://newsinfo.inquirer.net/46945/depedadopts-tony-blair-religious-literacy-program.*

8. Philippine Council for Islam and Democracy, "Interfaith Dialogue and Peacebuilding in Mindanao" (2004): p. 6, *www.muslimmindanao.ph/inter_faith_dialogue.html.*

Methods and Significance

This article addresses this gap by drawing from the experiences of young people involved in the Muslim-Christian Youth for Peace and Development (MCYPD). MCYPD is an interfaith organization based in a neighborhood in Caloocan, one of the cities of Metro Manila, the capital region of the Philippines. Ranging from twelve to twenty-four years old, twenty-two youth members and officers (out of thirty-five) agreed to be interviewed. Interviewees were invited according to gender and religious affiliation: Catholic, Evangelical Christian (or Born Again as colloquially known), and Muslim. Interestingly, one of our informants considers himself multifaith.

Drawing from these interviews, we probe the different ways by which our respondents have articulated the significance or impact of MCYPD on how they view interfaith and fellow members of different faiths. At one level, this article contributes to the journal's thematic focus on youth studies by looking at interfaith dialogue as a means of nonviolence. We do this by arguing that interfaith dialogues do not have to begin and end in theological discussions. In the case of our respondents, the significance of interfaith revolves around the *person* (and not his or her religion), *friendships*, and *collective participation in the community*. In view of these three aspects, we argue that interfaith is both a "living dialogue" and a "dialogue of cooperation."[9] One possible study that resonates with ours focuses on the meaning of participation in volunteer projects for English youth in Latin America.[10]

But at another level, this chapter is an important inquiry because it also assesses how interfaith dialogues can reshape pervading stereotypes about other religions in changing societies. Lessons drawn from our interfaith youth can then contribute to innovations in education.[11] The Philippines, of course, is predominantly Catholic with 81% of the population professing the faith. But the presence of Protestant and Muslim groups is also considerable at 7.3% and 5.1%, respectively, according to the census in 2007.[12] Metro Manila, although distant from the realities of conflict in Mindanao, is fast becoming home to migrating Muslims from the South. In Metro Manila, the Muslim population has

9. M. S. Haney, "Envisioning Islam: Imam Mohammed and Interfaith Dialogue," *The Muslim World* 99, no. 4 (2009): 608–634.

10. P. Hopkins, *et al.*, "Young Christians in Latin America: The Experiences of Young Christians Who Participate in Faith-based International Volunteering Projects in Latin America," *www.ncl. ac.uk/gps/assets/documents/YCLAEnglish_Report.pdf.*

11. J. Gundara, "Religion, Human Rights and Intercultural Education," *Intercultural Education* 11, no. 2 (2000): 127–136.

12. R. Pangalangan, "Religion and the Secular State: National Report for the Philippines," in *Religion and the Secular State: Interim National Reports,* eds. J. Martinez-Torron and W. C. Durham (Provo, Utah: The International Center for Law and Religion Studies, 2010), 557–568.

increased from 95 in 1903 to 58,859 in 2000.[13] Indeed, the mobility of Muslims in the capital is revealed by a recent survey showing that 66.5% of Muslim households have resided outside of Metro Manila for at least six months.[14] More recently, Watanabe[15] estimates that the Muslim population in Manila could in fact be around 120,000. In her fieldwork, she has also been able to count at least eighty mosques in the metropolitan area, although official data show only thirty-two. These demographic trends are certainly reflected in everyday life, notwithstanding the classroom. Drawing from his research and experience as educator, Baring points out that the classroom today has also become pluralistic as students come with different religious and ethnic backgrounds.[16] . . .

. . . The literature on interfaith dialogue has predominantly dealt with the experience of adult participants. From a sociological perspective, much of the problems of religious conflict could possibly be drawn from years of socialization during childhood. At that stage, ideas about one's religion—and [that of] the other—are shaped gradually.[17] These ideas, in the end, arguably inform the perceptions and treatment of other religions. In this light, interfaith activities for the young become part of their religious socialization process, and not simply an intervention that takes place during adulthood. We thus agree with the claim of Phua, Hui, and Yap[18] that interfaith youth engagement affords "gradual education" to advance beyond "mere tolerance" toward "true respect from understanding." By focusing on the significance of interfaith dialogue on youth, we add to the study conducted by World Vision[19] on young people's notions of peace and conflict in the Philippines.

13. A. Watanabe, "The Formation of Migrant Muslim Communities in Metro Manila," *Kasarinlan: Philippine Journal of Third World Studies* 22, no. 2 (2007): 68–96. Interestingly, Manila was a predominantly Muslim area with strong political and economic activities before the Spaniards arrived in the sixteenth century. C. Aguilar, "The Muslims in Manila Prior to Colonial Control," *SOJOURN: Journal of Social Issues in Southeast Asia* 2, no. 1 (1987): 150–158. As a result of Spanish rule, Muslims became marginal and have been mostly confined to other regions, including Mindanao.

14. N. Ogena, "Social Survey on Muslim Migrants in Metro Manila" (Institute for Asian Muslim Studies, Waseda University, 2012).

15. A. Watanabe, "Migration and Mosques: The Evolution and Transformation of Muslim Communities in Manila, the Philippines" (Afrasian Centre for Peace and Development Studies Working Paper Series 37, 2008).

16. R. V. Baring, "Plurality in Unity: Challenges Toward Religious Education in the Philippines," *Religious Education* 106, no. 5 (2011): 459–475.

17. J. Bartkowski, "Religious Socialization Among American Youth: How Faith Shapes Parents, Children, and Adolescents," in *The Sage Handbook of the Sociology of Religion*, eds. J. A. Beckford and N. J. Demerath (London and Thousand Oaks: Sage Publications, 2007), 511–525.

18. C. Phua, A. Hui, and C. W. Yap, "Interactions Among Youth Leaders of Different Faiths: Realities from the Ground and Lessons Learnt," in *Religious Diversity in Singapore*, ed. Lai Ah Eng (Singapore: Institute of Southeast Asian Studies and the Institute of Policy Studies, 2008), 642.

19. Inter-Agency Working Group on Children's Participation (IAWGCP), 2007.

MCYPD

The Muslim-Christian Youth for Peace and Development (MCYPD) is one of the several interfaith initiatives established by the Peacemakers' Circle, a local nongovernmental organization that facilitates dialogues, peace workshops, and self-awareness retreats.[20] Peacemakers' Circle began as a pioneering entity of the United Religions Initiative (URI) in the Philippines, which explains its emphasis on grassroots participation.[21] MCYPD is in the local district of Barangay[22] Tala in Caloocan, one of the cities of Metro Manila. Around Metro Manila are other interfaith communities under Peacemakers' Circle,[23] which, as described above, is a testament to the needs of the growing presence of Muslims and other faiths.

The original members of MCYPD are children of the adults active in the pioneer interfaith group in the community, the Muslim-Christian Peacemakers' Association (MCPA). As the population of immigrants from other provinces and with different religious background increased, these adults deemed it necessary to bring in the youth in their neighborhood. MCYPD began in early 2011 when children of the adults went house-to-house to invite their neighbors and "barkadas" (close friends) to a meeting and discuss the possibility of interfaith activities. They were then formally recognized as a cooperation circle by the Peacemakers' Circle in July 2011.[24] Indeed, the history of snobbery and discrimination between Muslims and Christians in Barangay Tala has been particularly hurtful for the Muslims. Quite telling is the story of Macklis Bala, an interfaith leader in the community who was interviewed for a documentary:

> My Christian brothers and sisters here were afraid of us because they heard that we were bad people. That was heavy for me to take because I really wanted to befriend them, most especially my neighbors. If they had the chance, they would have even petitioned our non-entry because they heard that Muslims were evil—like we were murderers.[25]

Today, success stories can be gleaned from both the youth and adults. As will be further elucidated, some of our Christian respondents, for example, have

---

20. See *www.thepeacemakerscircle.org/*.

21. C. Gibbs, "The United Religions Initiative at Work," in *Interfaith Dialogue and Peacebuilding*, ed. D. Smock (Washington, DC: United States Institute of Peace Press, 2002), 115–126.

22. Smallest administrative unit in the Philippines.

23. Culiat and Taguig are other areas of the Peacemakers' Circle.

24. A cooperation circle (in URI's language) is a group composed of at least three or more religions. Although autonomous, it should be noted that MCYPD constantly seeks assistance and guidance from its elders.

25. The Peacemakers' Circle (Producer), *In the Light of the Crescent Moon: A Peacemakers' Story* DVD (Philippines, Quezon City: The Peacemakers' Circle Foundation, 2006).

indicated in the interviews that they now know the personalities of their Muslim friends with whom they are living. Contrary to stereotypes, they are now considered "kind" and "friendly." As regards the adults, their own interfaith group is now involved in livelihood activities. In fact, they were recently granted another loan by the Department of Social and Welfare Development (DSWD) to help them in their business. The granting of this new loan is attributed to the fact that the organization has paid their previous dues on time.

In what follows, we draw from our interviews with the youth of MCYPD. The youth group is composed of at least thirty active Muslim and Christian (Catholic and Evangelical) youth leaders and members (twelve to twenty-four years old). Their usual meeting place is in the house of one of their elders, but they are planning (with assistance from the URI) to construct a small office of their own. Its leadership structure maintains a balance between Muslim and Christian youth leaders, although the number of members is subject to fluctuation since families in the community are mobile. Some, for example, have decided to leave to study elsewhere while others have returned to Mindanao. Interestingly, MCYPD is being moderated by an adult Muslim who is married to a Christian. The group gathers weekly for interfaith prayers. What is interesting, however, is that their meetings are not necessarily about theological differences. Most of the time, they are driven by efforts that can aid their community. These projects, for example, have included river cleanups, tree planting, and waste segregation.

The Significance of Interfaith for the Youth of MCYPD

In this section we directly address the main point of this paper, namely, what our youth respondents consider the significance of being part of an interfaith community. For this we align with Forward's fundamental understanding of interfaith dialogue.[26] To him, to dialogue is to go through a process in which individuals are willing to risk in order to learn from each other and, in so doing, be transformed accordingly. In this sense, interfaith is not just a conversation. Forward's understanding of such transformation, however, is primarily in relation to theological discourse. This emphasis on theology is also the tendency among other interfaith thinkers and practitioners. In the case of our respondents, it is not so much about theology as it is about the relationships they are able to form. Three areas are emergent from the interviews: the person (and not religion), friendship, and community engagement. Through these areas, we suggest that in the lives of our young people, interfaith has been a transformative relational experience.

---

26. See Martin Forward's paper on "Inter-religious Living in an Age of Globalization" in this anthology page 74.

Person, not Religion

The first salient theme in our interviews was, to us, a fascinating discovery. When asked what they have learned about the other religion through MCYPD, our respondents have constantly pointed to the character of the follower rather than the contents and doctrines of the religion. To be sure, some of them have described the differences in terms of food restriction or even the names of God, for example, but references to the character of a Muslim or Christian is more prevalent. Manilyn (17) explains that she realized that her Muslim peers are in fact "kind" and "friendly." She then admits that "my view of Muslims has drastically changed. I thought before that they were a bad people. But now it has changed. I see that they are very nice and sincere." A Muslim, Ali (21), recounts that when he was much younger, "I could not really go out of the house. So to me, it is important to really know my friends. Whenever they pass by our house, I would ask, 'Are they [Christian neighbors] nice or are they cranky?'"

Ali happily shares that he now knows his Christian peers very well. Further, Aslaine (17), a Muslim, shares how through joining the circle, she was able to befriend her enemies (who were also Christians) from before: "If not for the MCYPD, I would not have been able to get to know my enemies. Now we are really close friends. We learned to respect each other."

This is not to say they have not learned the substantive differences between their religions. Our respondents have been able to identify some differences in terms of feasts like Ramadan and Christmas, dietary restrictions, and even wedding rituals. But in explaining these differences, our informants are quick to suggest that learning made more sense as they can now associate these with specific friends of theirs. As Marilhyn (18), a Catholic, puts it, "It is more interesting to learn directly from my Muslim friends than from our books at school."

The experience of interfaith dialogue among our youth informants shows that it has helped them humanize the other religion. The narratives are consistent in recounting how they harbored negative impressions or stereotypes about the other religion. Through interfaith, discussions of religious differences have been surfaced but these are not, in the end, the most important realization for our informants. What has changed is that Islam or Christianity is no longer an abstract idea or religion dominated by pervading stereotypes. Instead, friends with whom they have established relationships have become the human face of Islam or Christianity. In this regard, while interfaith practitioners would see the value of theological engagement,[27] the experience of our youth informants reveals that it is not the most important consideration at all. Interfaith dialogue has definitely allowed them to recognize the different religious beliefs and practices, but these are secondary. To them the most significant impact lies in being

---

27. J. Cilliers, "Building Bridges for Interfaith Dialogue," in *Interfaith Dialogue and Peacebuilding,* ed. D. Smock (Washington, DC: United States Institute of Peace Press, 2002), 47–60.

able to see that Muslims or Christians can be their friends, thereby negating pervading stereotypes against each other.

Friendship

In our interviews, we also noticed that our informants see their participation in MCYPD as an opportunity to make new friends. There are two possible reasons for this. One, our informants are in their formative adolescent years wherein the need for socialization and belonging is heightened.[28] And two, many of our informants are relatively new as immigrants to the community. When we ask Asmin (18), a Muslim, what motivated her to participate in the organization, she admits, "I really want to have friends from around here." She has also shared with us that the most memorable occasion for her at MCYPD was when "we all participated in a fundraising activity. We prepared a dance number together and we were all there. These were my friends." Although she has only been with MCYPD for a year, Asmin has now taken the role of the organization's auditor. Asmin's narrative demonstrates that the interfaith community is able to bridge religious and cultural differences by tapping into the needs of young people for friendship. To us, this is in itself a fascinating finding because immigrants can have the tendency to isolate themselves from the mainstream.[29]

Several have pointed out, too, that the most meaningful memories they have of the circle involves interaction with their peers, including youth from other interfaith cooperation circles in other parts of Manila. For Aslaima (21), a Muslim, she considers performing an ethnic dance in Makati City for a URI-sponsored fund-raising activity as one of her most memorable experiences in the MCYPD. To her, its significance lies in having done it with her friends. As Faisal (19), a Muslim, puts it, "The reason why I constantly involve myself, why I do not want to quit, is because I have found true friends here—they will not leave you."

What the data reveal is that the youth view the organization as a community of friends. Although MCYPD began with the help of the elders' encouragement, most of the members joined because their friends were part of it. What the MCYPD's example demonstrates therefore is that interfaith dialogue has a sustainable foundation when members begin as friends. Indeed, the growth of their friendships is what motivates them. When asked how MCYPD can be improved, they did not refer to administrative or structural matters. They highlighted personal qualities that they need to change. They have cited, for example, arrogance, stubbornness, and misunderstanding as some of their typical

28. S. Miles, *Youth Lifestyles in a Changing World* (Buckingham: Open University Press, 2000).

29. J. Singh, "British Sikh Youth: Identity, Hair and the Turban," in *Religion and Youth*, eds. S. Collins-Mayo and P. Dandelion (Farnham and Burlington: Ashgate, 2010), 131–138.

issues. To them, these are negative attributes that can affect the friendships within the community.

And because friendship has become the main motivation for participating in MCYPD, it has also become the main reason for trying to understand the other. For our Christian informants, new realizations about Islam point to prohibitions such as that of eating pork and its protectiveness when it comes to women. Put differently, our informants constantly recall those aspects of religious difference that could help them avoid offending their peers and thereby maintaining healthy friendships. Relevant lessons mentioned by our informants like Rowell (16) and Kevin (18), both Catholic, include the importance of being nonjudgmental as the Golden Rule in keeping their friendships. Indeed, given that there has been a history of snobbery and discrimination in the area, there is a need to encourage friendships, and the young people are able to accomplish it. As Regie (19), a Christian, puts it, "Although there are those who are stubborn in our community, what is important is the friendship that has been formed. That's what is important—the friendship."

Participation in the Community

The suburban neighborhood where MCYPD is located is reputed to be dangerous. What feeds this stereotype is not just the lower-income status of its residents, but the fact that there are new Muslim immigrants. Faisal (19), a Muslim, recounts how he has tried to parry even the jokes hurled at him about his neighborhood:

> Some people have asked me if it [is] true that when an outsider enters our village he will no longer be able to come out alive. And then they ask me if I [am] a Muslim. I said to them that people have different temperaments [and we cannot blame religion]. Like there are Christian killers as there are good Christians as well. So for me, we are all equal.

It takes time to finally eradicate these stereotypes, and interfaith communities are formed to that end. But interfaith discussion is most of the time confined only to the members of the community. Building bridges with the wider community is therefore necessary to effect change at that level. Indeed, as Steele sees it, peacebuilding, which covers a wide array of community engagement, should "contribute toward the transformation of society into a just and harmonious order."[30] Our youth informants, interestingly, are engaged in their community in different capacities.

---

30. D. Steele, "Contributions of Interfaith Dialogue to Peacebuilding in the Former Yugoslavia," in *Interfaith Dialogue and Peacebuilding*, D. Smock, ed. (Washington, DC: United States Institute of Peace Press, 2002), 73–88.

Being the only registered youth organization in their village, MCYPD is often invited to help in cleanup drives, participate in the local government's projects, and even send a representative to the monthly meetings with the local youth council. The United Religions Initiative (URI) has also invited them to participate in rallies advocating for peace. Apart from these invitations, our youth informants have also initiated their own projects such as tree planting and waste segregation in the community.

But beyond these community activities, MCYPD has begun to see its potential in local youth politics. They have campaigned, for example, for Marilhyn, one of the members who is now an elected representative in the local youth council. She relates how it was through the MCYPD that she decided to run and that without her friends' support, her victory would not have been possible: "Aside from gaining awareness we were given opportunities to get involved in the community. The MCYPD actually became my driving force for running in the elections. Before, I used to loathe politics since I viewed it as dirty."

Collectively, these engagements project an image that Muslim and Christian youth can in fact work together for the community. As Marilhyn has articulated, the MCYPD has also been an avenue for opening new opportunities for the youth. Local participation (and by extension youth involvement as well) in development efforts has been criticized either as sheer rhetoric or tyrannical.[31] This, however, goes against the logic of interfaith involvement at the grassroots level where conflicts are taking place and must be addressed. Interfaith at the level of the religious and the clergy is welcome, but it cannot be the only form of dialogue. The experiences of our young people show the potential of dialogue and involvement among their peers.

Additionally, we argue that our youth informants find their participation in the community meaningful precisely because they themselves have experienced discrimination in one way or another. It is these everyday modes of discrimination that they are contesting. Indeed, young people can be aware of their social issues and be instrumental in effecting changes.[32]

Finally, our informants also see the spirituality of community engagement. Camille (15), a Christian, explains that "we are also able to help out in times of calamities whether here or elsewhere. We help others, especially those in the midst of conflict. If we are unable to do so, our conscience pushes us to help, even a little. . . ." Interestingly, this spirituality aligns with observations concerning the religiosity of young people around the world, which seems to be

---

31. H. Henkel and R. Stirrat, "Participation as Spiritual Duty, Empowerment as Secular Subjection," in *Participation: The New Tyranny?*, eds. B. Cooke and U. Kothari (London: Zed Books, 2001), 168–184.

32. G. Lansdown, "The Realisation of Children's Participation Rights: Critical Reflections," in *A Handbook of Children and Young People's Participation: Perspectives from Theory and Practice*, eds. B. Percy-Smith and N. Thomas (London and New York: Routledge, 2010), 11–23.

predominantly characterized by social engagement.[33] In the Philippines, Cornelio has identified this as a form of action-oriented reflexive spirituality among Catholic youth.[34]

Interfaith and Youth Participation

In discussing youth participation and interfaith dialogue, it may be instructive to recall that such dialogue comes in different forms. For this we draw from Haney's framework.[35] These forms include: 1) "living dialogue," or that which consists of building positive relationships with people from other faith traditions, as they are neighbors and fellow human beings; 2) the "dialogue of cooperation," an interfaith collaboration for a unifying cause, such as that of promoting peace and justice in the world; 3) the "dialogue of religious experience," which opens a person to respect what the other deems sacred—how one experiences God in one's life; and 4) "theological dialogue," discussions on the knowledge and interpretations of God. All these forms of interfaith dialogue stress that individuals should learn *from* rather than just *about* other religions. But as we argued in the review of literature above, much of the discussion concerning interfaith has revolved around theological considerations. In this section, we show how in fact the first two (living dialogue and dialogue of cooperation) are the most crucial in the experience of our informants.

The participation of youth in interfaith efforts shows that they have both the capacity to *learn* and to *contribute* to interreligious understanding and community building. Indeed, young people are in their formative years, which allows them to explore the other more readily and openly. The narratives above show their personal realizations that run counter to the stereotypes formed about the other. In other words, many of our informants have realized that their Muslim or Christian peers are, in the end, "nice people" to have as friends. In addition, our informants have longed to establish friendships with their peers in the neighborhood especially because many of them are immigrants from other regions. Here we highlight how friendships naturally facilitate the growth of MCYPD. Although other youth interfaith efforts are driven by the government, MCYPD demonstrates how dialogue can be run, managed, and facilitated by youth themselves, as in the case of Singapore.[36] Arguably, the potential of MCYPD lies in

---

33. R. Flory and D. E. Miller, "The Expressive Communalism of Post-Boomer Religion in the U.S.," in *Religion and Youth*, eds. S. Collins-Mayo and P. Dandelion (Aldershot: Ashgate, 2010), 9–15.

34. J. S. Cornelio, "Being Catholic as Reflexive Spirituality: The Case of Religiously Involved Filipino Students," in *Asia Research Institute Working Paper Series* (2010), *www.ari.nus.edu.sg/docs/wps/wps10_146.pdf*.

35. Haney, "Envisioning Islam," 608–634.

36. Phua, "Interactions Among Youth Leaders," 642–667.

the social support-seeking behavior of Filipino adolescents. According to a 2002 survey, 97.4% of Filipino youth (15–24) belong to a peer group.[37]

As a result, the interfaith community has certainly afforded them the space to be spontaneous as Muslims or Christians without the fear of discrimination. Put differently, relationships in the organization are deemed significant because of the equality and respect given to each one. As Aslaima (21), a Muslim, describes it, "We are free to express ourselves here. We respect each other regardless of class or religion." In this sense, MCYPD is a strong and positive case of how interfaith can rectify negative and discriminatory attitudes against people of other religions. The neighborhood in which MCYPD is located has a history of religious tension. Indeed, MCYPD has become an example of a peacebuilding and transformative organization.[38] That the goal has been to establish positive interpersonal relationships makes their community an example, too, of what Haney considers as "living dialogue."[39] . . .

Conclusion

This paper has drawn from the experience of young people involved in interfaith dialogue and intercultural understanding. These young people have become the key stakeholders of the Muslim-Christian Youth for Peace and Development (MCYPD), an interfaith circle located in suburban Metro Manila. We have argued at the onset that interfaith dialogues have become more important in light of increasing religious diversity in the capital region and the Philippines as a whole. We have also suggested that encouraging interfaith and intercultural dialogue among young people is more strategic in introducing the values of religious respect and cooperation that can impact educational understanding.

We have sought to understand in what sense being part of an interfaith community has had an impact on young people. Three themes proved to be emergent. First, MCYPD has helped them humanize the other. When they talk about Islam or Christianity, for example, they are now thinking about individuals they realized could also be their friends. Second, MCYPD has effectively become a peer group for our informants. In context, many of their members, especially the Muslim ones, are considerably new to the neighborhood. Establishing friendships is very important, and MCYPD has afforded them the space to do so. And because the other religion now has a human face, learning about religious differences is meant to help them show respect and avoid offending

37. UPPI, *The Filipino Youth: 2002 YAFS Datasheet* (Quezon City: University of the Philippines Population Institute and Demographic Research and Development Foundation, 2004).

38. R. Neufeldt, "Interfaith Dialogue: Assessing Theories of Change," *Peace and Change* 36, no. 3 (2011): 344–372.

39. Haney, "Envisioning Islam," 624.

each other's sensibilities. Finally, our informants see the value of making an impact on their community as an interfaith youth group. They have been invited to participate in various activities of the community, including environmental projects and other government initiatives. They have also fielded their own candidate for the local youth council, thus demonstrating their political leverage as a youth group.

Clearly, the interfaith experience of our informants has not dwelt largely on theological matters. To be sure, they did discuss religious differences in terms of rituals, beliefs, and clothing and dietary restrictions. But in our interviews with them, these matters did not dominate their understanding of MCYPD. If anything, discussing these religious differences has helped them identify those aspects of everyday life that could be offensive had they not known enough. To them, what matters most is that through interfaith, they were able to gain new friends from another religion, whether Catholicism, Protestantism, or Islam. The engagement has been powerful in contesting pervading stereotypes about the other religion. For this reason, MCYPD can be considered a "living dialogue." But our informants have gone beyond sheer dialoging. Their organization has become instrumental in showing the community that Muslim and Christian youth can cooperate for specific projects. In this sense, MCYPD can also be considered a "dialogue of cooperation."

Sacred Book Club

Reading Scripture Across Interfaith Lines[1]

Jeffrey W. Bailey

EDITOR'S NOTE

In the mid-1990s, Jewish and Christian theologians, religious philosophers, and textual scholars in Great Britain came together jointly to study each other's holy scriptures as a means for interfaith conversations, later also inviting Muslims to participate. This sacred book club began as an academic exercise among likeminded friends and colleagues interested in cultivating post-critical and post-liberal scriptural reasoning (over against modern reasoning), for the promotion of wisdom and deeper mutual understanding. It has become a worldwide movement, especially in the English-speaking world. The Archbishop of Canterbury has endorsed scriptural reasoning as a key practice to further Jewish-Christian-Muslim relationships in England, and Islamic authorities in London issued a fatwa (i.e., a scholarly opinion on matters of Islamic law) in 2007 advising Muslims to participate in this practice, too.

Jeffrey W. Bailey's account of scriptural reasoning gives some insight into how it came about, how it is being done, and why it is so important for an informed citizenship in a religiously diverse democratic culture. He stresses that "the participants share one important conviction: they believe that the resolution of religiously rooted political tensions will be attained not by avoiding religion in public, but by initiating more and better religious conversation in public." Scriptural reasoning exposes not only deeply rooted differences, but oftentimes surprising agreements, while developing mutual respect and, quite often, genuine friendships.

---

1. Jeffrey W. Bailey, "Sacred Book Club," *Christian Century* (September 5, 2006). Copyright © 2006 *Christian Century*. This article is reprinted with permission from *Christian Century*.

On a blustery Wednesday evening in central London, about a dozen people from different parts of the city made their way to St. Ethelburga's Centre for Reconciliation and Peace. They included an attorney from a large London law firm, a political lobbyist, a corporate consultant, a Muslim college chaplain, a university professor, a female rabbi, and a research scientist. After pouring cups of coffee, the group began a two-hour discussion marked by moments of intense debate as well as laughter. Conversation veered from economics, to the nature of citizenship, to London politics.

One might think this was a meeting of a neighborhood council or chamber of commerce, except for one thing: in front of each participant were selections from the Hebrew Bible, the New Testament, and the Qur'an.

After finishing its discussion of a passage from the Hebrew Bible, the group began focusing on a passage from Matthew's Gospel in which Jesus instructs his questioners to "render unto Caesar what is Caesar's."

"I thought most Christians read this as justification for supporting their government's policies," said a Muslim participant, looking up from his text.

"I was taught that in my church growing up, actually," said one woman, a bit sheepishly.

"I wonder if Jesus isn't saying something a bit more subversive than, 'be a good citizen,'" suggested a Jewish participant. "Perhaps Jesus is actually making a larger point about an alternative economic system."

This looks like a Bible study. But St. Ethelburga's is a public space, not a church or temple, and the participants are Jewish, Christian, and Muslim. Profound religious differences emerge over the course of conversation.

But the participants share one important conviction: they believe that the resolution of religiously rooted political tensions will be attained not by avoiding religion in public, but by initiating more and better religious conversations in public.

Participants in this practice, known as scriptural reasoning (SR), are part of a movement that wants to protect religiously plural societies while simultaneously encouraging religious people to enter more deeply into public discourse. Such aims might appear paradoxical to those who were taught that the emergence in the seventeenth century of secular liberalism, with its privatization of faith, rescued the West from "wars of religion." Voices on all sides of the religious and political spectrum have begun to recognize—not least because of the increased presence of Islam in Western societies—that a purely secular, liberal approach to public discourse is not sustainable in a world increasingly shaped by religions.

If we can no longer conduct public debates according to the "objective" language of "self-evident truths"—ways of reasoning that purport to cut across religious and cultural distinction—how will political debate move forward? How can laws be passed if representatives reason differently about the common good? A post-Enlightenment public square sounds positively tribal; it would mean

Muslims arguing for Shari'a law and Christians arguing from the Bible about sexual ethics. Can such a society flourish? Can such different groups find ways to talk to each other?

Scriptural reasoning is an attempt to navigate the diversity. The practice has been central to recent gatherings of political and religious leaders in Qatar, Karachi, Berlin, and Washington, DC. Archbishop of Canterbury Rowan Williams and Anglican bishop N. T. Wright of Durham (England) have promoted SR as a key to Muslim-Christian-Jewish relations in England. SR groups have been established at universities such as Duke, Virginia, Colgate, Cambridge (England), and Cape Town (South Africa). The American Academy of Religion has been devoting sessions to SR for several years. An introduction to SR was included in the inaugural festivities of Princeton Theological Seminary's new president last spring [in 2004].

At the local level, groups of clergy and laypeople are beginning to meet under the auspices of the Children of Abraham Institute. Peter Ochs, professor of Judaic studies at the University of Virginia and one of the founders of the Society for Scriptural Reasoning, encourages this trend.

"Often the best people with whom to do SR are not academics, but regular folks who have been raised reading and listening to the Bible, who have received some basic socialization into the world of scripture," says Ochs. All SR participants must represent a house of faith and usually a denomination. "The interfaith nature of SR simply cannot exist if its participants are not deeply rooted and trained within a particular house of Judaism, Christianity, or Islam."

Creating Mutual Hospitality

What is SR in practice? Jews, Christians, and Muslims (roughly equal numbers of each) gather to read passages from three scriptures that are usually thematically related. Sessions are not held in a synagogue, church, or mosque. Instead, SR, invoking the shared "tent of meeting" imagery of Genesis 28, seeks out a neutral space. When SR participants meet outside of a specific house of faith, studying all three scriptures together, they create "a three-way mutual hospitality," says Christian theologian David Ford, another cofounder of the Society. When it is not clear who is the host and who is the guest, "each is host to the others and guest to the others as each welcomes the other two to their 'home' scripture and traditions of interpretation."

In a typical gathering, a member of one faith will make a few introductory comments about a scripture passage, and then the entire group attempts to understand what the passage is teaching and how it ought to be applied today. Slow, patient work is done to unpack how a faith tradition has interpreted the passage. The same is then done with texts from the other two scriptures. At the end the three texts are brought into dialogue with each other. Many questions ensue, not only from representatives of other faiths, but also among members of one faith who may disagree over the interpretation of their scripture. A member of a different faith may bring the strongest insight into a scripture that is not his or her own. Adding to the richness of conversation is the fact that members of different faiths may, at the same time, share similar cultural or academic backgrounds—all of which means that no one can easily predict the lines of agreement in any SR session.

Putting scripture at the heart of interfaith dialogue has certain advantages. The Hebrew Bible, the Old and New Testaments, and the Qur'an are foundational to each faith's worship, community life, and ethics; major developments cannot happen without reference to these scriptures. But what is most striking about SR is that vexing gaps or lacunae in various texts are not considered problems to be quickly resolved by reference to, say, modern critical methods, but divine invitations to use human creativity and reason in making sense of the passage. (Although historical-critical questions are not avoided in the discussions, neither are they given priority.)

Advocates of SR claim that the richness of conversation is directly tied to the fact that the scriptures are at the center of the dialogue. Instead of neatly pushing readers to entrenched positions, scripture has a way of provoking new ways of thinking and unexpected insights. Scripture becomes a mode of instruction in how to have a "thick" way of knowing God. It tutors its students in a different mode of relating.

SR began more than twenty years ago when Ochs and a group of Jewish scholars, including Robert Gibbs, Laurie Zoloth, and Steve Kepnes, grew frustrated about the gap between scripture study and modern scholarship. As Ochs puts it, SR developed from the particular logic of scripture itself: "I think SR is a return to how the primary community has tended to read scripture throughout history. It's a Midrashic [i.e., an interpretative] way of reading scripture—a Talmudic form of reasoning [like reasoning done in the Talmud, the central text of Rabbinic Judaism]—that was dominant in rabbinic times, but interrupted by modernity."

Jeffrey Stout, president of the American Academy of Religion [in 2007], has helped pave the way for SR's work with his book *Democracy and Tradition.* Stout has tried to move discourse beyond an either-or approach to the question of what counts as rational. "If we want people who have been formed according to different rationalities and communities to be able to contribute to the common good, we need to really understand where they are coming from."

Ochs applies this approach to discourse between people of different faiths. "People assume that problems among religious groups arise out of religious differences. So, to bring such groups together, they try to avoid religion altogether and turn to some supposedly shared interest, like economic development," he says. "Our assumption is the opposite: that religious people like each other because they *are* religious. They are moved by piety, discipline, and love of God to pursue similar ends and find solutions."

SR participants are attentive to contemporary issues seen as they seek deeper levels of meaning in scriptural texts. "We start with the question, 'What does it mean to encounter God?'" says Ochs. "We presume that God is everywhere in our lives, and very accessible—God literally pours in on the world. And reading scripture is central to that encounter. But encountering God in scripture doesn't necessarily translate into clear propositional forms with single, static meanings. Individual words of scripture generate broad fields of meaning. That doesn't mean we eschew the plain sense of the words of scripture—not at all. But we assume that there are deeper, contingent meanings in scripture yet to be disclosed within the particular time and place of the seeker."

New and Surprising Insights

Scripture study, in other words, actually brings about new and surprising kinds of reasoning that would not occur apart from the engagement with scripture. And the insights generated may well have application beyond the boundaries of one's faith.

The interfaith study started after Christian theologians David Ford and Daniel Hardy attended the lively study sessions that Jewish scholars held at the American Academy of Religion in the early 1990s. "We saw ways of reading scripture that seemed enormously generative," says Ford. "We also saw an overlap between the way they were reading scripture and Christian, post-liberal approaches to scripture some of us had learned at Yale under Hans Frei."

In 1996, Ochs, Ford, and Hardy, concerned about Jewish-Christian relations in light of the Holocaust, formed the Society of Scriptural Reasoning. Muslim scholars soon joined. "We knew as soon as we began," says Hardy, "that we needed the Muslim voice to be part of this." The challenge was that "large parts of Islam have not encountered modernity in the same way that Judaism and Christianity have. So the Muslims who joined us early on were deeply committed to their faith, but also very aware of the multiple challenges of Islam's relation to Western modernity."

Members of the Society hope to include other religions. "We see that SR is beginning to work outside of Jewish, Christian, and Muslim faiths—with Hindus and Buddhists who are text-based, for example," says Ochs. "We also see that certain strands of secular rationality are more compatible with SR than others."

Whether SR is compatible with nonreligious reasoning remains an open question for some. Stout affirms the approach that SR takes. "I've made a habit of attending SR sessions at the American Academy of Religion, and have found those sessions impressive and rewarding." But as to whether his own nonreligious stance is compatible with SR, he says, "They try their best to make me feel welcome, but the ground rules aren't really designed to bring nontheists like me into the discussion. It's pretty clear that I'm an interloper." He adds, "I don't say that as a criticism. It would be foolish to expect this group to accomplish all of the bridge-building that needs to happen."

What about consensus among Christians, Jews, and Muslims—current participants in SR? Is there hope for a kind of broad, Abrahamic "third" way beyond the particularities of each faith?

Basit Koshul, a Sunni Muslim who teaches at Concordia College in Moorhead, Minnesota, says, "Past experience taught me that most interfaith forums were basically 'interfaith-less' forums where agnostic Muslims, Christians, and Jews met to confirm each other's agnosticism." After joining an SR group, however, he discovered that, "each of the three traditions confidently asserted its claims to uniqueness and universality—but didn't view these claims as being obstacles to genuine dialogue."

Trust, Friendship, not Concensus

The SR movement is a far cry from a search for lowest-common-denominator faith, for an all-roads-lead-to-the-same-place consensus. It insists that believers go deeper into their own tradition. At the same time, it insists that each participant engage with those of other faiths. This concern for both particularity and encounter means that SR avoids philosophical attempts to resolve the conflicting claims of each faith. The resolution of such important questions of truth is not unimportant; but for now, the anticipation of such resolution qualifies as an eschatological [i.e., final, ultimate] hope.

If SR does not lead to consensus, it does lead to trust and friendship. "The friendships we developed opened us not only to deeper lessons from our scriptures, but also to deeper friendship with God," said Ochs. Hardy concurs. One of the most important things to understand about SR, he says, is that "mutual hospitality is more than learning to argue in courtesy and truth, although that's part of it."

Talk of friendship serves to underscore the eschatological hope shared among the three faiths—that God has an ultimate purpose of peace among all. "It is this kind of hope which actually provides a deeper foundation for honest disagreements," Hardy says.

Ford is candid about the impact of his longstanding friendship with Ochs, a devout Jew. "I have been endlessly amazed at the generativity of our friendship," he declares. "He has changed me as only a real friend can. I find his passionate argumentativeness liberating. Some of the deepest moments have been when Peter, with his insistent yet disarming directness of questioning, has pressed at the differences between us, as Jew and Christian. I do not know how to articulate at all adequately what has happened at such times: it is a paradox of not reaching resolution yet becoming better friends, and knowing this has somehow to do with God."

Participants in SR claim that it is only in the development of interfaith friendships that some of the most important conversations can take place. One active participant recalls an SR session that he was part of several years ago:

> We were reading and discussing certain Hebrew Scriptures, and one of the Jewish participants in our group suddenly broke down and told us how painful it was to hear the way Christians were interpreting "his" texts. Some of the pain being expressed, I think, was the realization that these were texts which belonged not only to the Jews but to others as well—and that their readings could paradoxically exclude his identity as a Jew. It really helped us realize the real-world implications for how we read each other's texts, and how vulnerable we feel when others are interpreting our scriptures in certain ways.

It has been suggested that SR serves as a model not only for interfaith dialogue, but also for political discourse. It departs from modern political discussions in that, while it seeks agreement, it does not try to determine in advance what the grounds of agreement might be.

An Emphasis on Practice

According to Nicholas Adams, a lecturer at the University of Edinburgh in Scotland, "SR is a practice that can be theorized about, but it does not start as 'theory' that one then attempts to put into practice." Instead, the SR approach assumes that such understanding just happens, and proceeds on that basis. It is content to acknowledge that while there may be certain basic conditions for understanding or agreement, one does not need to be able to specify those conditions.

"I like SR's emphasis on practice," affirms Stout. "It's a mistake to think that communities are always bound together by shared beliefs and theories. Shared activities often matter more. Often the best way to establish a community is to get different sorts of people doing things with one another."

A primary concern of SR, therefore, is practical: to create space in which the "deep reasonings" of a community can be made more public than they are at present.

"Deep reasonings," notes Adams, "are not just the grammar or vocabulary of a tradition, but the way their use gets handed down from generation to generation." And while "deep reasonings" of the three Abrahamic traditions are hardly a secret (most mosques, synagogues, and churches admit guests, and most religion scholars publish their work in journals), Adams notes that "the quality of public debate between members of different traditions is dangerously low. Most public debate concerns ethical issues such as the beginning and the end of life, or the permissibility of certain sexual behaviors. But where are the public contexts for understanding why a tradition argues the way it does?"

Mass media outlets like television treat viewers to sound and vision bites, not deep reasonings; instead of enhancing understanding, Adams says, the medium encourages the over-dramatizing of rival claims. SR, in contrast, aims to carve out space and time for deeper discussions.

Ochs urges the following approach:

> We have to figure out ways of letting religion return to the public sphere. Secular pluralism says religion is bad for freedom or democracy or tolerance; SR says that's not the case at all, and that to have any hope of achieving peace, we can no longer push religion off to the side or into some private belief system. That is simply not an option for the world today, and certainly not for Islam. Let's go back to religion and have serious conversations about the heart of our belief systems.

Stout acknowledges religious people's reaction against an ideological secularism, but he sees a danger in overstating that case.

> One theme that I keep encountering in SR sessions is the idea that there's something called modern discourse, which operates according to rigid rules dictated by secular liberalism. I think this idea is inaccurate. American political discourse has always been a freewheeling, relatively chaotic affair, and religion has almost always influenced it significantly. There have been particular institutions that have been dominated for a while by secular liberalism, but it's a mistake to generalize on the basis of those examples.

"The fact is," Stout continues, "our religious traditions—like our secular traditions—combine benign and malignant impulses. That's one reason all of this needs to be talked through in a self-critical, democratic spirit. We need one another in part because we need interlocutors to help us own up to the malignant impulses in our own traditions." He views SR as an example of this kind of democratic accountability at work.

Stout offers the following example:

> Any interpretation of the Exodus story that authorizes a once-oppressed people to cleanse the landscape of its opponents or oppress them is bad for freedom and democracy. A good thing about an SR session on the Exodus story is that anybody who wanted to interpret it in that way would have to answer objections from the Muslims in the room.

Unexpected Agreement, Surprising Friendships

William Taylor oversees St. Ethelburga's implementation of SR in London. The British Home Office is funding development of SR across the city, and plans to train imams, rabbis, ministers, and other community leaders in SR practice.

"Once you have called at the local mosque a few times, expressed 'solidarity' with the imam and taken away a few flyers on the Five Pillars, what's next?" asks Taylor. "People of different faiths are aware that we need to get to know one another, but it's not always clear how to begin the conversation."

What is most exciting, Taylor adds, is that SR is a genuinely new approach to debate:

> Scriptural reasoning gives us a model for political disagreement that can be considered productive, even without reaching consensus. Politics often looks to overcome debate by looking for some "position" or statement people can assent to. But those kinds of agreements are usually pretty thin and generate little sense of loyalty. Here we observe a group of people with deep differences finding unexpected areas of agreement, and surprising friendships developing amid those remaining differences.

Behind St. Ethelburga's is a freestanding, Bedouin-style tent. It was donated to provide space for Jews, Christians, and Muslims to read their scriptures together, reason together, and become friends. It looks small and fragile against the solid buildings of London, but it is a powerful sign of hope.

Spanish artist Pablo Picasso (1881–1973) created "The Dance of the Youth" (1961) depicting people of different colors—red, yellow, brown, pale—twirling around the dove of peace to music of which only the opening bars are sketched. What a vision for what interreligious dialogue may achieve! Certainly it will not be Paradise, but life in peace despite diversities.

Epilogue

How to Get Moving?

Christoffer H. Grundmann

Reviewing the materials presented in this anthology one notices that all authors are convinced of the irrefutable need for interreligious dialogue. Interreligious dialogue, they hold, has become a pivotal question for maintaining peaceful convivence (i.e., respectful coexistence) in today's all-pervasive multi-religious environments. They also contend that such dialogue is not about trying to prove others right or wrong, to win them over to a particular faith, or to discredit them. Instead, the authors understand interreligious dialogue to be an ongoing process of human communication among individuals with different religious and cultural roots challenged by common existential questions. Consequently, they all encourage us to get involved in conversation with the religious others and to listen to them attentively. Doing so is the only way to build trust, which incidentally also may lead to personal bonding and genuine friendship.

Personal bonding and friendship across cultural and religious divides, however, are not the prime goals of interreligious dialogue; they are precious byproducts. Rather, the chief goal for getting involved in interreligious dialogue is establishing mutual trust and understanding. To do so implies respecting the cultural and religious "other" as an equal who is as seriously concerned about peaceful convivence as oneself. "Genuine dialogue . . . is possible only in an atmosphere of mutual respect, based upon a consensus that it is being conducted among equals" (Ratanasara). One of the patent ways to achieve this is by meeting face to face in a formal or casual way (Wingate) and getting involved on the local level in hands-on activities, ideally of a liberating character (Knitter, Rao). Trust does not emerge as the result of intellectual argument (Merton). Trust grows whenever persons rely and depend on one another in day-to-day collaboration, as so impressively demonstrated by the Muslim-Christian Youth for Peace and Development project in Manila, Philippines (Cornelio and Salera). Another way toward understanding the religious other and building mutual trust is by engaging in the study of one another's religious scriptures, as practiced by the Sacred Book Club (Bailey; see also Gispert-Sauch, Ratanasara). Once robust trust is established, conflicts and frictions within a multi-religious society no longer will give rise to suspicion, scapegoating, and fear; they will be dealt with in dialogue and pragmatically resolved.

To engage in interreligious dialogue for the common good does not mean to ignore existing religious differences or to regard religious teachings and doctrines as irrelevant. None of the authors advocates any such conviction. To the contrary, they all hold dear the religious teachings and doctrines of their own tradition, but argue against using doctrinal differences, conceptual disagreements, and conflicting hallowed traditions as an excuse for refusing dialogue, because the "only alternative to talk is the buildup of resentment and anger, which in time must inevitably become open hostility and conflict" (Ratanasara). Rather, some authors consider today's dialogical imperative to be a "*kairos* of 'liberation'" (Knitter), a unique opportunity to "enrich our own religious consciousness . . . to lead richer, more fulfilling religious lives" (Tyagananda), to appreciate the "precious gift of faith" (Braybrooke), to authentically re-own and re-shape the religious tradition in which one has been raised (Rao, Knitter, Forward), to discover that "we are already 'honorary members' of each other's religion" (Ratanasara), and also to realize that "God is greater than religion . . . and only partially comprehended by any one faith" (Sacks; see also Rao).

Finally, far from advocating interreligious dialogue as fashionable ideology (Ratanasara) or as a means to construct syncretistic entities (Gispert-Sauch), the authors represented here don't turn a blind eye to the fact that getting involved in interreligious dialogue involves risk. Genuine dialogue demands that everyone honestly opens up to those with whom one is in conversation. When engaging in dialogue one "chooses to disclose oneself, one's 'truth' . . . in the hope that what is shared will be received with welcome" (Knestout). Besides, one also has to be prepared to change attitudes and convictions when, in the course of dialoging, it becomes obvious that the opinions entertained are unjustified and unwarranted. "Having come to new insights, having identified the good where we did not expect it" one "must live those insights and do that good. . . . Dialogue without this possibility of conversion is like a sleek aircraft that can take us anywhere but is not allowed to land" (Knitter). This is to say that dialogue fails whenever and wherever people—against their better judgment—are not willing to revise long-held convictions and change attitudes.

Becoming aware of these perils might be unsettling for many—and understandably so—while for others, for the more daring and curious, it might be exciting to move beyond the well-known and familiar into *terra incognita* and try something different. Yet, neither fear of risks nor excitement over possible transformations is sufficient to the challenges posed by interreligious dialogue, where one's identity is at stake. In a multireligious, multicultural environment, the only best choice is to redefine one's religious identity over against the cultural-religious others in one's midst. The instructive reflections in this volume can enable one to approach this demanding task somewhat at ease, informed and motivated by the constructive attitudes modeled here to get moving. I would like to highlight only three such attitudinal directives here: (1) think outside the box of conventional wisdom, (2) dare to trust the religious other, and (3) stay authentic.

1. Think Outside the Box of Conventional Wisdom

Conventional wisdom and practice tend to make life clear and simple, reducing life's complexities to some basic insights with down-to-earth applicability by availing of mutually exclusive patterns of thinking. Thinking in simple alternatives like right or wrong, good or bad, true or false, black or white, and so on, provides handy categories for easy judgment and quick decision-making. That is their undeniable advantage. Yet, such thinking, while everywhere, fails in our globalized age; frankly, it has never worked in any age. Today's situation, however, has pushed all of us out of such emotional, mental, and religious comfort zones. The times demand heightened and critical differentiation in order to comprehend the broad diversity of complex issues and to do justice to their challenges. The authors in this volume, too, assert that we should not—because we cannot any longer—think in alternatives of particularistic identities or disembodied universalisms (Sacks, Knitter). "Instead of thinking in terms of right or wrong," we, rather, should begin to "think in terms of 'different'" (Tyagananda).

Surely, to overcome the habit of thinking in simple alternatives requires a bold and conscious effort. But to succeed in overcoming any deeply ingrained conventional attitude takes time. Dialoguing makes one not only get accustomed to listening attentively to the other with genuine openness, but also moves one to more and more think in terms of difference and diversity rather than mutually exclusive alternatives. Reminding that in dialogue "half of talking is listening" (Merton), the authors here admonish to cultivate the art of "listening well" whenever engaging in dialogue (Knestout; see also Tyagananda).

Listening, however, is only one element of dialogue. One must also respond and share by talking to counterparts. Participants must be willing honestly to open up to one another and to accept that in any genuine interreligious dialogue "nothing should be taken for granted and nothing should be considered non-negotiable" (Tyagananda). It is unavoidable that sooner or later in the course of any such dialogue the deepest, most cherished convictions of everyone participating will get exposed. People, therefore, have to be bold and courageous enough to leave behind any line of hiding or defense and to present themselves as vulnerable to one another (Knestout). Because of this, interreligious dialogical encounters are quite different from other disputes or intellectual discourses. They are interpersonal communications of a witnessing nature (Knitter, Braybrooke) about different approaches to resolving existential questions and challenges, approaches authenticated by lives actually lived, not by argument. That is why learned insiders speak of interreligious dialogue as a "dialogue of life" (Gispert-Sauch; see also Knestout, Ratanasara).

Interreligious dialogue is at its heart an exchange of differing ways of lived responses to existential challenges experienced by all humans, not in the same way, of course, but experienced by humans nonetheless. "*All* are bound to seek in honest perplexity" (Merton). As such, interreligious dialogue serves a much broader cause than just obtaining information about differences in explaining world and life, action and culture. Interreligious dialogue is also—and much more so—an indispensable eye-opener for realizing the truly amazing diversity of human existence and the broad variety of its interpretations. It leads beyond what one much too often uncritically holds for granted within the confines of a partic-ular worldview and its conceptual standards. Thus, interreligious dialogue makes the participant conscious of the contingent particularity of one's worldview, irre-spective of how universally applicable one might claim it to be. It is in precisely this way that one needs "to be witnessed to" by cultural and religious others and "learn from them" so as not to distort truth (Knitter; see also Forward).

2. Dare to Trust the Religious Other

Another important attitude the authors emphasize for successfully engaging in interreligious dialogue is daring to trust the religious other. That is easier said than lived, especially in post 9/11 times and in a culture of radical individual-ism with its systemic suspicion of the other-than-me as a potential competitor. Add to this the many cultural-religious differences in foods and clothing, in hal-lowing time and celebrating life, in rituals and languages (which by their very strangeness frequently give rise to misunderstandings, suspicion, and friction), and it becomes obvious that daring to trust those strangers is counterintuitive to the natural fight-or-flight reflex.

To overcome the chasm of culturally sanctioned, radically conflicting atti-tudes to life rooted in differing worldviews, as is the case for instance with monotheistic compared to nontheistic religions, one must first of all grant that "the other" holds these attitudes and worldviews for *good* reasons. To consciously concede this helps to stay focused on the one true common denominator, namely our shared human existence. Appealing to this commonness, monotheists call the faithful to engage in interreligious dialogue for the sake of finding "God's image in someone who is not in our image" (Sacks) or to "meet in God's love" (Nasr; see also Braybrooke, Knestout), while from within other faiths believers are encouraged to travel "the pathless path to the truth that is beyond all reli-gious labels" (Tayagananda), "to celebrate each other's way of Godrealization" (Rao), and to "end . . . suffering" (Ratanasara).

Whatever their particular frame of reference, almost every author in this anthology alludes to an overarching reality—God, God's love, God's image,

Transcendence, Truth, Dhamma—which serves them as the ultimate legitimation for pursuing interreligious dialogue at all. One author also reminds us that those "who are confident of their faith are not threatened . . . by the different faith of others" (Sacks; see also Ratanasara), while another bluntly declares that a "faith that is afraid of other people is not faith at all" (Merton). Those who truly believe overcome the natural fear of engaging with religious others by trusting that in the end, any such encounter will reveal the ultimate reality anew and in ways not known by them so far. Thus, the full potential of interreligious dialogue, which serves "the world in ways that professional diplomats cannot" (Knestout; see also Nasr), comes to fruition only if one has the stamina to leave behind all fears of potential threats posed by strangers and, instead, embrace "members of other faiths as fellow pilgrims" on the way (Braybrooke) or as "fellow servants" in the search for genuine understanding (Merton). "Within the heart of dialogue . . . there beats a deep act of faith and trust" (Knitter).

3. Stay Authentic

Last but not least several authors strongly maintain that the success—or failure—of interreligious dialogue critically depends upon the authenticity with which participants engage in it and articulate their convictions. Daring to be authentic, that is, to take "my own faith seriously" and say what is "in the deepest sense true to what I believe" (Merton), requires yet another bold move consciously to be taken, especially when considering the paranoia so prevalent in today's cyberspace world of identity theft, digital exposure, aliases, and fake virtual personalities. Shielding, hiding, and protecting our identity have become the rules of the game. Dialogue, however, does not work with proxies. Dialogue requires personal authenticity, and this implies to honestly open up to one another, to disclose who we really are and what we truly believe.

Staying authentic also obliges us to go beyond polite niceties and reassuring others about our good intentions. Playing down differences and sugarcoating worries cannot keep potential tensions at bay. Such an attitude only reflects naïve optimism that is ignorant of the real threats posed by intolerance, aggression, and fanaticism. Such an attitude also displays a grave misconception of what the task of interreligious dialogue is. Interreligious dialogue explicitly expects of people "to reveal where" they "agree and where . . . not" (Tyagananda; see also Ratanasara). This is important, indeed, because not only are "the religions of the world . . . more different than they are alike" (Knitter), but also because genuinely religious people cherish the "dignity of difference" (Sacks). Thus, participants cannot but be obliged to "speak frankly and openly . . . about where they differ" (Tyagananda; see also Knestout, Ratanasara).

Doing so implies that dialogue participants do not compromise their cultural-religious tradition and betray their identity. All are expected to stay "true to [their] own faith commitment" (Braybrooke) and "adhere firmly to it, while keeping an open mind regarding the Truth that may be available in other traditions" (Rao). This attitude is remarkably well demonstrated in the paper "We and You: Let us Meet in God's Love," in which fundamental differences between Muslims and Christians are named unabashedly, and also in the exposition by Havanpola Ratanasara on "The Importance of Interfaith Dialogue." Yet, despite noticing differences, both authors invite religious others to "join . . . in the battle against the desacralizing and antireligious forces of the modern world" (Nasr) and "to talk to each other" (Ratanasara). Interpreting these invitations as merely gestures of appeasing politeness of a concerned, antimodern conservative Muslim or a kind, generous Buddhist would certainly miss the point. These invitations, rather, nicely document what interreligious dialogue actually can achieve, namely not to break off or shun community with cultural-religious others despite well-acknowledged and apparently irreconcilable differences. Being authentically committed to interreligious dialogue means to remain committed "to mutual understanding, not as diplomats, but as sincere religious [people] standing before God and responsible to Him beyond all worldly authority" (Nasr). This genuinely religious attitude is what above all qualifies interreligious dialogue as such.

Appendix

Internet Resources[1]

Websites

A Common Word

www.acommonword.com/

This website is the official communication platform for discussion about the document "A Common Word between Us and You," published in October 2007 by The Royal Aal al-Bayt Institute for Islamic Thought, Jordan. Signed by 138 Islamic scholars, politicians, and clergy, the document was prompted by Pope Benedict XVI's ill-received lecture on interreligious dialogue at Regensburg, Germany, in September 2006. The document promotes interreligious dialogue between Islam and Christianity from a Muslim perspective. The powerful website updates regularly on news about related developments within the Muslim world, publications, audio-visual materials, "New Fruits," new endorsements by people of other faiths, and links to other Muslim sites. It is an important source for reliable information on Muslim-Christian dialogue.

Council for a Parliament of the World's Religions

www.parliamentofreligions.org/

The Council for a Parliament of the World's Religions (CPWR) is probably the best known of all initiatives dedicated to interfaith dialogue. Incorporated in 1988, the council was formed to commemorate the centenary of the World's Parliament of Religions, held in Chicago in conjunction with the Columbus World Fair 1893. The council's mission is to "cultivate harmony among the world's religious and spiritual communities and foster their engagement with the world and its guiding institutions in order to achieve a just, peaceful and sustainable world." The website serves as an information board for CPWR's conferences and ongoing programs, provides webinars on topics of relevance for interreligious dialogues, offers links to related sites, and is home to the Parliament's own social network, PeaceNext, a forum of lively exchanges via blogs and discussions.

---

1. Resources are listed in alphabetical order in each of three categories.

Focolare Movement

www.focolare.org/en/in-dialogo/grandi-religioni/

Founded in Trent, Italy, in 1943 during World War II, the Focolare Movement is an association of people inspired by the vision of human unity across denominations, religions, and cultures as a witness to God's unconditional love to all, with more than two million adherents in more than 180 countries. Originally a Roman Catholic initiative of single women and men living in separate communities (called *focolares:* Italian for *hearths*), the association was founded for the sake of keeping alive the motivational "fire." The movement, with its unique spirituality of unity and peace, has now spread far beyond its origins, not only to several hundred churches, but also to other religions. Cultivating dialogue on every level wherever divisions exist (intrachurch, intersocietal, interdenominational, interreligious, and intercultural), the movement practices dialogues as "dialogues of life" to witness to possibilities of living together peacefully in the global age—as Christians, with people of other faiths, and with people of no religious affiliation at all.

Fugees Family

www.fugeesfamily.org/

Even though the Fugees Family program is not a program dedicated to interreligious dialogue, their website provides information about a fascinating grassroots initiative receiving national attention due to its success in overcoming animosities and rejections based on cultural, religious, and gender prejudices. The program began with the formation of a soccer team for traumatized refugee children from all over the world residing in the eastern outskirts of Atlanta, in Clarkston, Georgia. Organized in 2006 by a female soccer coach from Jordan, the program has grown considerably and branched out into other areas of concern such as providing adequate schooling for about 280 refugee children (Fugee Academy) and offering support services for their parents, including those who do not speak English. It is by means of playing soccer together that healing occurs, language difficulties are addressed, and cultural and religious differences are overcome.

Interfaith Youth Core

www.ifyc.org/

The Interfaith Youth Core is a Chicago-based organization founded in 2002 by an American Muslim of Indian descent, Eboo Patel. Working in cooperation with the President's Interfaith Campus and Community Service Challenge, Interfaith Youth Core wants to create an interreligiously literate "critical mass" among college students on campuses around the United States with the aim to make interreligious cooperation a social norm of a religiously pluralistic society. Instead of accepting diverse religious-cultural traditions as causes of conflict and division, the Interfaith Youth Core movement turns diversities into "bridges of cooperation" with "Better Together" campus campaigns. Students of different religious backgrounds are invited to act together in a project for the common good and are coached in Interfaith Leadership Institutes to become facilitators of interreligious cooperation. The rationale behind the movement is: Doing things together generates mutual respect of diverse identities, enables bonding, and helps establish meaningful relationships despite acknowledged differences. This changes attitudes because, as appreciation for the other as a person of a distinct religion and culture grows in the course of time, so does the understanding of respective differences.

Scarboro Missions, Canada

www.scarboromissions.ca/Golden_rule/

Scarboro Missions is a Roman Catholic mission society founded in 1918 in Scarborough, Ontario, Canada, to train and send priests to China. Today the society's members serve as priests and lay missioners in ten Asian and African countries, the Caribbean, and Canada, emphasizing social justice and interfaith dialogue for peace on the grassroots level. As a conversation starter they share what has become a highly popular poster depicting symbols of thirteen major faith traditions, supplemented by "Golden Rule" quotations from each tradition's sacred writings (see also *World Congress of Faiths*). The poster is intended to show the common concern identifiable in all—that is, "Do to others as you would have them do to you." The comprehensive website lists valuable, easily available sources including texts, study guides, and audiovisual media for in-depth discourses.

Tony Blair Faith Foundation

http://tonyblairfaithfoundation.org/

Established in 2008 by former British Prime Minister Tony Blair, the foundation's mission is "to help prevent religious prejudice, conflict and extremism" by providing political and religious leaders as well as young people with "knowledge and analysis to understand the impact and complexity of religion in the world." To achieve its ambitious goal, the foundation, which is not a religious organization, invests funds and energy in educational programs and exposures, but gives some practical support, too. While the "Faith and Globalization Initiative" of the foundation focuses on the global conversation and exchange about faith among universities worldwide, its "Face to Faith" program aims at interfaith interaction of school children ages 12–17 via secure website video conferencing across the globe. The "Faiths Act" scheme of the foundation supports local programs to demonstrate that different faith traditions can in fact collaborate peacefully by working together for a common cause.

World Congress of Faiths

www.worldfaiths.org/

The World Congress of Faiths (The Inter-Faith Fellowship) is a British organization founded in London in 1936 as an individual membership body for people "of any variety of faith, belief or spirituality" for the sake of mutual enrichment through dialogue, thereby fostering mutual understanding and trust across religious divides. With its special emphasis on education for interreligious capacity building on all levels of society, the organization facilitates multifaith encounters through retreats, conferences, visits, and group travels to meet people of different religions. It publishes the journal *Interreligious Insight*, the member newsletter, *One Family*, and a "Golden Rule" poster as well (see also *Scarboro Missions*). The website informs about current events and news in the field of interreligious dialogue mainly in the UK, offers guides to valuable printed and audiovisual resources, maintains a blog, and links to several similar web-hubs.

Other Presentations, Interviews, Music

"Dialogue," by Sondre Bratland & Javed Bashir

www.youtube.com/
watch?v=tyu8FRsbtjA&list=PL5jyh0frZPxewLSa3nIlES9e96QquRxMl

> A visual presentation during a public performance of Norwegian folksinger Sondre Bratland, a Christian, and Javed Bashir from Pakistan, a Muslim singer, performing psalms and hymns from their different religious traditions (time: 0:05:00). See also their audio CD titled *Dialogue*.

The Faith Club

www.youtube.com/watch?v=wBguxfmqmL8

> NBC interview (*Today Show*, Oct. 2, 2006) with Ranya Idliby, Suzanne Oliver, and Priscilla Warner, the authors of *The Faith Club: A Muslim, A Christian, A Jew—Three Women Search for Understanding* (Atria Books, 2007) (time: 0:06:04). The book is highly recommended as well.

Getting to the Heart of Interfaith – The Three "Interfaith Amigos"

www.youtube.com/watch?v=soC_MSUo5Qo

> A presentation by UCC Pastor Don Mackenzie, Rabbi Ted Falcon, and Imam Jamal Rahman—now known as the Interfaith Amigos—about the importance of effective interfaith dialogue (time: 0:13:00).

The Golden Rule

www.youtube.com/watch?v=cqC6rbqghuw

A general explanation of the Golden Rule, which has been found in various forms throughout cultures and philosophies throughout history. Explanation given by Paul McKenna, interfaith activist and coordinator of the Scarboro Missions Interfaith Department in Toronto, Canada (time: 0:11:25).

Jonathan Sacks

www.youtube.com/watch?v=QrQ75meskWI

A lecture by the noted rabbi, philosopher, and scholar, formerly Chief Rabbi of the United Hebrew Congregations of the Commonwealth (1991-2013), on "The Dignity of Difference: How to Avoid the Clash of Civilizations" (time: 1:14:30).

Paul Knitter

www.youtube.com/watch?v=BVSv5y5RO288

A 2009 interview in Melbourne with the professor of theology, world religions, and culture and noted author, on the importance of interreligious dialogue (time: 0:05:34).

Sacred Book Club

www.youtube.com/watch?v=TsPjJ3gw-y8

A brief introduction to this interreligious discussion group at Mesa Community College (time: 0:02:44).

Seyyed Hossein Nasr

www.youtube.com/watch?v=6lNyiK-EkI0

Lecture by the Islamic scholar and author, "What it Means to be a Muslim in America Today" (time: 1:04:36).

Swami Tyagananda

www.youtube.com/watch?v=Cm3hT_Zt6CU

A brief introduction to the Ramakrishna Vedanta Society in Boston, MA. Ramakrishna was a nineteenth century Bengali Hindu sage and mystic (time: 0:04:06).

Thomas Merton

www.youtube.com/watch?v=O650TPCIXrI

A brief introduction to Thomas Merton, Trappist monk, writer, mystic, and social activist, noted for his promotion of East-West interreligious dialogue, from the TV series "Who Cares About The Saints?" with Fr. James Martin, SJ (time: 0:11:14).

Official Documents on Interreligious Dialogue

"A Common Word between Us and You," open letter, Oct. 13, 2007, from Muslim leaders to Christians, at URL: *www.acommonword.com/the-acw-document/*

Dabru Emet: A Jewish Statement on Christians and Christianity (Sept. 10, 2000), at URL: *www.firstthings.com/article/2000/11/dabru-emet-a-jewish-statement-on-christians-and-christianity*

"Declaration Toward a Global Ethic," Parliament of the World Religions, Sept. 4, 1993, at URL: *www.parliamentofreligions.org/_includes/FCKcontent/File/TowardsAGlobalEthic.pdf*. See also Bibliography of Publications on Global Ethic in English, compiled by Bettina Schmidt, Günther Gebhardt, Anette Stuber-Rousselle, June 2012, at URL: *www.weltethos.org/1-pdf/40-literatur/eng/bib-we-eng.pdf*

Guidelines on Dialogue with People of Living Faiths and Ideologies, World Council of Churches (WCC), Feb. 1, 2010, at URL: *www.oikoumene.org/en/resources/documents/wcc-programmes/interreligious-dialogue-and-cooperation/interreligious-trust-and-respect/guidelines-on-dialogue-with-people-of-living-faiths-and-ideologies*

Nostra Aetate: Vatican II Declaration on the Relation of the Church to non-Christian Religions, October 28, 1965, at URL: *www.vatican.va/archive/hist_councils/ii_vatican_council/documents/vat-ii_decl_19651028_nostra-aetate_en.html*

Index

Note: An *italicized* page number indicates a photograph or illustration.